# THE SPARK  IN

### Fred T. Corum

### and

### Hazel E. Bakewell

**as told to**

**James F. Corum and Kenneth L. Corum**

**Published By**

Corum & Associates, Inc.
Windsor, Ohio

E. N. Bell
June 27, 1866 - June 15, 1923

This little volume is gratefully dedicated to his memory.

"How I *cherish* the memory of that grand old man."

Reverend Harry E. Bowley
*Word and Work*, December, 1933

# TABLE OF CONTENTS

# Fred T. Corum

Fred T. Corum was born in Wasioto, Kentucky, on March 1, 1900. After living at Fort Sill, Oklahoma for several years, his family moved to Springfield, Missouri in 1905. As a young person, he was very active in the Pentecostal Church of Springfield - which subsequently became known as Central Assembly. He attended Drury College from 1918 to 1922, receiving an A.B. Degree in History and Economics. After teaching high school for one year at Lamar, Oklahoma (where, as the result of an accident, he was left totally blind - and in answer to prayer was completely healed by the Lord!), he entered the Harvard University Law School and graduated with an L.L.B. Degree in 1926. In 1926, he joined the Board of Directors of the Christian Workers Union in Framingham, Massachusetts, and subsequently became the editor of *WORD AND WORK* from 1931 to 1937. *WORD AND WORK* was the oldest international, full-gospel magazine and had been started by Samuel G. Otis in 1878. With Stanley Frodsham, S.A. Jamieson and others, Fred Corum was active in the formation of the Russian and Eastern European Mission in the late 1920's. He served on the faculty of the (Pentecostal) Boston Bible Institute in the late 1930's, teaching Bible Doctrine, Church History and Christian Evidence. Mr. Corum served as secretary of the Boston Christian Business Men's Committee, helped to organize the Greater Boston Youth For Christ, and was legal council for the famous Boston Billy Graham Crusade of December, 1949. In 1969, he was awarded the Juris Doctorus Degree from Harvard University. He and his wife, Lily, attended Calvary Temple Assembly of God in Lynnfield, Massachusetts. Brother Corum went to be with the Lord on June 5, 1982, after being a Member of The Massachusetts Bar Association, and maintaining a law practice in the Boston area for over fifty-five years. During this period of time, he incorporated over 37 churches in Massachusetts. He authored several legal text books during the prohibition era. In addition, he wrote numerous articles and compiled three books of interest to Christians: **Like As of Fire** (an original collection of Azusa Street papers, republished in 1981), **The Sparkling Fountain** (about Pentecost in Springfield, Missouri during the period from 1906 to 1925), and **An Inquiry Into the Legal Aspects of the Trial of Christ** (an expanded essay written while attending Harvard Law School and delivered at churches all over New England). The latter is soon to be released by his estate.

As with a number of the young people growing up in Springfield, Missouri at that time, his life was greatly influenced by many prominent early Pentecostal leaders. He was deeply stirred by these early experiences and often spoke of "Daddy Welch", Mother Barnes, the graceful and inspiring words of Sister Flower, and most of all - E.N. Bell. One of the last things he said, in his final hours, was the quote from Harry Bowley about Brother Bell, "How I cherish the memory of that grand old man."

## Hazel E. Bakewell

Hazel (Corum) Bakewell was born June 17, 1897, in Artemus, Kentucky. Except for a brief period of time, she has lived in Springfield, Missouri, since 1905. She attended Central Bible College when it first opened its doors, but had to miss one year, and graduated with the second graduating class in 1926. She attended Southern Missouri University, majoring in music, from 1928-1932. In 1932, she left Springfield to assist at Bethel Home for the aged with the Christian Workers Union in Framingham, Massachusetts. She was married to Lawrence W. Bakewell in 1937, and returned to Springfield in 1940. Brother Bakewell worked at the Gospel Publishing House for the next twenty-nine years. Over the years, Sister Bakewell has taught piano to hundreds of music pupils, many of whom are now preachers, evangelists, missionaries and Christian workers.

# PREFACE

"One generation shall praise Thy works to another, and shall declare Thy mighty acts." Psalms 145:4

Come, take our hands and walk with us down the corridors of the years, and listen as we describe the memorials which were raised up in former generations. This book is to give an account of the beginning of the greatest revival the world has seen since the early church period, and to prove beyond a doubt that God's time-piece has reached the dispensational hour in which He has promised to pour out His Spirit in Latter Rain significance. The stories which we are about to tell are true. The events may be looked up, and the facts corroborated with other witnesses. We are walking on Holy Ground. What we are telling is true to the very best of our recollections. Most of the events took place over seventy years ago, and almost all of the people that took part have gone on to their eternal rewards.

We are not holding these people up to be honored or glorified. The credit for anything of lasting value surely belongs to the Lord. And, it is for His glory that we attempt to retell these things from the past. This book is simply a documentation of some of our recollections. Wherever possible, we have tried to include the original words and testimonies of those involved, along with references so that those readers that desire to may go and compare other sources.

Although this is not a history book, it is a factual retelling of actual events. Those looking for an organized, historical development of the leaders and structure of the Pentecostal movement should consult the many good Pentecostal history books which are currently available.

As with any history, it is imperative that a writer take great pains to have his dates and the order of events perfect. In recording the dates of several of these occurrences, we wish to request the reader's indulgence. We are working from memory, notes, letters, scraps of paper, and articles which one of us (FTC) wrote many, many years ago. We also have a set of notes, prepared by our mother, Lillie Harper Corum, around 1920, which exists in several forms. However, our recollections of these saints is very clear, and we shall never forget how God mightily used them. Hazel and I were present at almost all of the events that we shall tell you about which occurred in Missouri.

As with any personal reminiscences, the reader should be on the alert for "sanctified exaggeration". In another history book, Timothy L. Smith has wisely admonished:

> ". . .Those who write the story of their own family, church, or nation must chasten both mind and emotion at every turn in the road, lest their history becomes . . . a tale spun out to influence the present by distorting the past. For this reason, history written by 'insiders' ought especially to be subjected to vigorous analysis."[1]

This is always true, and we invite you to carefully scrutinize what we have written. We may be off on some of the dates, but these events really occurred. Some of these people are still alive, and you may check the facts with them directly. If anything, we have probably understated the marvelous things which the arm of the Lord has done.

When dear Dr. Charles Price was telling the story of his life, he somewhat self-consciously wrote,

> "It is with a feeling of deep humiliation and eternal gratitude to God that I recount these events. There is a sense in which I dislike putting them down in this record, for fear that some should think that the ego is asserting itself too much. God forbid. I am only a sinner saved by grace; and it is for the glory of the Lord alone that I tell of the marvelous things that the Lord has done."[2]

The Sparkling Fountain

We wish to offer this little volume in the same spirit of
gratitude and humility. In the tapestry of charismatic history,
there are many threads which radiate outward from the old
Azusa Street Mission. This book is about but one of them.

We are sure that hundreds of others could be followed outward, and would lead to a great many of the readers of this
book. But we want to tell of the one that led into our lives,
and to the establishment of the first Pentecostal Church in
Springfield, Missouri. A sizable portion of the early chapters
of this book recount the story of the old Azusa Street Mission, and many of the people that were there. As children,
Rachel Sizelove told us many times of the Azusa Street
meetings and the camp meeting which they held. During the
1930's, she sent one of us most of the material for publishing
in *WORD AND WORK*, while he was the editor. The Azusa
Street Mission had published a little magazine called *THE
APOSTOLIC FAITH*. They published thirteen issues in Los
Angeles and all thirteen were republished in September of
1981 (the seventy-fifth anniversary of Volume I, Number 1),
as the book **LIKE AS OF FIRE**.

We believe that the power of God is still the same today.
This bit of our history should be made known afresh to people. God is still Baptizing hungry seekers with his Holy Spirit
as in New Testament times - for power to win souls before
the end day comes and it is too late. He has promised to pour
His Spirit upon our sons and our daughters.

There are several goals which we have in mind for
documenting the marvelous stories about the camp meeting,
and about the coming of the Holy Ghost to Springfield,
Missouri.

From a historical standpoint, it is important that future
generations know as much as possible about those gospel warriors that caught the vision, and fought the good fight of faith;
blazed the trails for righteousness, holiness, and full salvation, and how all of these marvelous events are woven

together. Many of these saints, whose stories will never be fully told, forsook all worldly ambitions, and sold out totally to the Lord; their only desire - just to walk with Him. For part of our lives, we were privileged to know some of these people intimately and to see the price which they paid, and to see the glorious ministry that they had in the Spirit. In the natural, they were mortal, but in the spiritual realm, they had wrestled with angels and prevailed. They were counted worthy to be servants of the Most High God. Truly, they were a chosen generation, and a royal priesthood. However, in no way do we wish to imply that all of these people were great leaders in the Pentecostal movement. If anything, quite the opposite was true. Many of them were the people that sat on the benches, danced up and down the aisles, and prayed through, not only around the altar, but also in the secret place. From the fiery evangelists and anointed messengers, they gladly received the news of the full gospel, and ran with it to their daily worlds. They were "living it straight and shouting it all the way"! They were Kohathites bearing the ark, and intercessors pressing the battle. So many times in the darkest hour, when in the natural all appeared to be lost, faith would rise in these saints, and the impossible was counted done and rejoiced over. And lo, we would soon see these things manifested in the physical world. Truly, we beheld "the evidence of things not seen."

But we have an even greater goal in mind as we desire to share these precious memories with you. These were simple folk in whose hearts burned "love's sweetest old story". From their lips and though their lives, we learned the wonderful message of the cross of Calvary.

We also wish to state in the clearest terms possible that we are only trying to tell what Pentecost was like to us and those we knew in the period from 1906-1925. These are personal reminiscences of how the Holy Spirit came into our family. We want to tell the background and the developments, which we witnessed from the pew-side of the pulpit. We want no credit, for we were only plain young people growing up in the Ozarks. All the glory belongs to our precious Redeemer. The great prayer warriors, that we shall tell about, would have preferred that the stories go untold, rather than have any attention called to themselves. But the time has come to "rehearse these things of the Lord in the ears of a new generation". This old time gospel message is as relevant to contemporary society as it was in the days that it happened. The hearts of Adam's fallen sons and daughters still reach out for reality.

Many years ago, a book about the Azusa Street meetings appeared. It was written by a man that was on the periphery of the revival. But to read his story, it would appear that virtually the entire revival centered around his ministry. We can now appreciate his dilemma. As eye witness observers, we can only testify about the events which we saw and experienced. We were certainly not the center of the revival, however, we hope that the threads of information which we offer will help others understand the broader tapestry of charismatic history. We believe that we have been faithful, in the smallest details, to those precious saints that appropriated the victory by faith. May these few pages reflect not only their deep devotion to the Master, and the continuing power of Pentecost in the Church, but also the glorious message that a fountain has been opened for sin and for uncleanness (Zech. 13:1), and that Calvary's stream is still flowing.

America is ripe for revival and a great ingathering of souls, precious in the sight of God. There is an air of expectancy. People are saying, "What is happening?" A great fear and confusion, in this nuclear and space age, is hovering over the nations. A great close of the century revival must sweep the continent and the world. Tears of surrender and repentance are beginning to flow.

Some have said, "There can never be another great revival. We will never again see the mighty Pentecostal manifestations. The Heavenly Choir has been lifted. The miraculous cannot penetrate our modern civilization."

But when our eyes have seen the response of the great throngs of people, and we have felt the moving of the Holy Spirit, we can say with Peter, "This is that which was spoken by the prophet Joel; and it shall come to pass in the last days, saith God, I will pour out of my Spirit upon all flesh." What a marvelous promise . . ."My Spirit - Upon all flesh."

And now, "Rejoice in the Lord your God, for He hath given you the former rain moderately, and He will cause to come down the rain, the former rain and the latter rain in the first month . . . And it shall come to pass that whosoever shall call upon the name of the Lord shall be delivered."

HEB
FTC

## REFERENCES

1. **Called Unto Holiness**, by Timothy L. Smith, Nazarene Publishing House, Kansas City, Mo., 1962, Pg. 351.

2. **And Signs Followed**, by Charles S. Price, Logos International, Plainfield, New Jersey, reprinted 1972, PP. 61-62.

3. **Like As Of Fire** (A photographic republication of the first 13 issues of *The Apostolic Faith* as published at Azusa Street in 1906-1907), collected and edited by Fred T. Corum, 1981, reprinted by Corum and Associates, Inc., 8551 State Route 534, Windsor, Ohio, 44099, in 1989.

# ACKNOWLEDGMENTS

The authors gratefully acknowledge the assistance of many people without whom this book would have been impossible.

The Argue Family
Lawrence W. Bakewell
Adele A. (Flower) Dalton
Joyce and Daniel Edwards
Virginia Erler
Alice Reynolds Flower
Vernon and Aileen Green
Billie Jean Huffman
Martha Childers Humbard
Blanch Sizelove McGee
Evelyn Stoll
Wayne Warner
The Assemblies of God Archives, Springfield, Mo.

There are dozens of others that have contributed material to this book and made it possible. We sincerely thank them all.

# Introduction

"There is no man at the head of this movement. God Himself is speaking in the earth. We are on the verge of the greatest miracle the world has ever seen, when the sons of God shall be manifested, the saints shall come singing from the dust (Isaiah 26:19) and the full overcomers shall be caught up to meet the Lord in the air. The political world realizes that some great crisis is at hand, the scientific world, the religious world all feel it. The coming of the Lord draweth nigh, it is near, even at the doors."

. . . The Apostolic Faith
September, 1906, Page 1

The interval of time between the mid-1890's to the early 1920's was a period of intellectual agitation, turmoil, enlightenment, productivity, and curiosity unparalleled in the chronicle of human endeavor. During this era, Planck advanced the Quantum Hypothesis, Einstein formulated the Theory of Relativity and curved space-time, Marconi's wireless linked continents, the Wright brothers launched mankind into a new dimension, Westinghouse and Tesla harnessed Niagara Falls bringing electrical power to the country's whirling wheels of industry, and Steinmetz untangled the mysteries of electrical currents. Each separate contribution was to make a break with previously held fundamental concepts and the flow of tradition in each individual discipline. Taken together, not only would man's comprehension of the physical universe radically change, but abstract scientific possibilities would soon become the applied technological realities of today.

This period would also reflect swirling changes and reform in social order. The Victorian Era with its well-ordered stability would pass. The world would be shocked as the un-sinkable White Star Liner, Titanic, would carry 1500 passengers to a watery grave below the icy North Atlantic (still the largest peacetime marine catastrophe in history). The League of Nations would soon appear. A political order would arise in Russia and soon spread its philosophy abroad.

Perry and Amundsen would reach the extremities of the globe. The world would see the fulfillment of the crusaders' dream to regain the Holy City of Jerusalem after centuries of Turkish occupation. The automobile and the telephone would revolutionize civilization's ability to communicate and travel. And, the struggle for women's suffrage would eventually modify western sociological traditions. The waters of the deep were troubled, and civilization was about to step into an era of drastic change from which there would be no retreat.

"The Twentieth Century looms before us big with the fate of many nations", spoke Teddy Roosevelt in 1899. That these things were about to happen was clearly perceived by the world's statesmen, poets and prophets. The stage was set, the scenery was in place, and the curtain was about to rise. Many violent storms were coming. Such winds as never blew on humanity were rising and many nations would wither before the blast.

But in His mercy, another wind was rising. The Spirit of God was moving upon the waters of the deep and, as though in preparation for this growing turmoil, the Heavenly Dove of Peace descended upon a humble band of prayer warriors at Azusa Street. They waited upon God, prayed through, and were covered with the Shekinah glory of the Lord. This marvelous revelation of God's goodness and holiness, like those of old, was intimately connected with new blessings for service and spread like a whirlwind to the far corners of the earth.

And now, this mighty flowing river of grace and glory has

rolled down through the Twentieth Century sweeping countless millions of broken and fallen humanity on through to victory. This precious river, issuing from the throne room itself, has bubbled forth into the Twentieth Century as a sparkling fountain and has flowed out through God's anointed servants to minister love's sweetest old story to the final generations of Adam's lost and fallen sons and daughters.

In a previous book, **Like As Of Fire**, we republished the old Azusa Street papers. In the next few chapters of this little book, we would like to return to the old Azusa Street Mission in Los Angeles, California, and retell the story of their first camp meeting, and pick up just one of the many threads radiating outward from Azusa Street. We will tell of the early days of Pentecost in Springfield, Missouri, in the years just before the General Council of the Assemblies of God was formed, and trace the events in Springfield which preceded its establishment. These are true stories of humble individuals who dared to obey the leading of the Holy Spirit, and how God honored their faithfulness.

The world system is again changing. International attention is again focused on Bible lands as the wealth of the earth flows in that direction. The Gentile Age is in its twilight hours and through the darkness, we see the rays of the Son of Righteousness blaze forth. In Israel, the fig tree is budding, and soon our Redeemer cometh, ". . . leaping upon the mountains and skipping upon the hills." (Song of Solomon 2:8)

It's harvest time and as we look upon the world scene, through the eyes of faith, we see fallen golden grain. Surely, we are living during the church's finest hour and we are beholding the final evangelization of the earth. There is a fresh wind blowing and the Holy Glow which rested upon old coals for all these years is leaping forth into flame. Generations of anointed servants looked forward and saw this very day, and we are now breathing the air and standing on the ground which they saw by faith. ''Surely, I come quickly, Amen. Even so, come, Lord Jesus.'' (Revelation 22:20)

## Chapter I

# PENTECOST COMES TO SPRINGFIELD

"...It's beginning to rain..."

I t was the latter part of May in the Spring of 1907. The rain was falling on the trees in front of our white, clapboarded farm house on Division Street, out beyond the city limits of Springfield, Missouri. My sister, Hazel (age 10), and I (age 7) were playing on the front porch when I heard the sound of wagon wheels coming up the road. We were expecting a visit from my Aunt Rachel Sizelove, who had been to the Azusa Street meetings in Los Angeles, California. Hazel and I ran through the front door into the farm house, "Mama, Mama, she's here! She's here!"

The taxi wagon pulled into our yard, and from behind Mother's apron, I saw my Aunt Rachel step through our doorway. Her face was aglow and her countenance was radiant. Her hands were uplifted, and she was speaking in a heavenly language. I don't remember all that she said, but I do remember that part of it was, "And the Dove of Peace shall hover over this home." With tears streaming down their faces, Mother and Grandma Harper, who was staying with us at the time, embraced Aunt Rachel. There was only one topic of conversation as they sat down in the parlor, "What was God doing in Los Angeles at Azusa Street?"

My folks had been good, Bible-believing Baptists. (The Indian Chief, Geronimo, had been led to the Lord by my Dad while he was a telegraph operator for the Frisco Railroad two years earlier at Fort Sill, Oklahoma.[1] Grandma Harper, who was born in 1836, had been a born-again Christian since she was a young girl. She had attended the old Presbyterian and Methodist frontier revival meetings which had been

1

started by such men as Lorenzo Dow and Peter Cartwright.)

Aunt Rachel and her husband, Josie Sizelove, were ordained Free Methodist Evangelists. Before going to Los Angeles, they had served the Lord in Kansas, the Oklahoma Territory, Arkansas, and Southern Missouri. Yet, somehow, they all felt the need of a deeper walk with the Lord. That He had granted Aunt Rachel some marvelous experience was evident, and Grandma Harper, Mother, and Dad were stirred by every word she spoke.

She told us of the marvelous scenes occurring at the Azusa Street Mission. She told about dear old Brother Worrell, who previously had written a translation of the New Testament. He was on his knees at the altar seeking the Baptism of the Holy Ghost. She told of many white and black faces mingled together, all seeking God, and receiving this precious gift to mankind. Her face was aglow, and we all sensed the glory of God upon her.

She had received the Baptism of the Holy Ghost, and when the Lord had laid upon her heart to travel back to Springfield, like the handmaid of the Lord in Bible days, she "...arose and went into the hill country with haste..." to tell her sister of the great things that God was doing. "He hath filled the hungry with good things; and the rich He hath sent away empty." (Luke 1:53)

Little did I realize that I was witnessing what I now believe to be a turning point in church history. I believe that an assembly of angels was rejoicing in the little cottage on Division Street on that rainy Spring afternoon. O, what joy! As the evening shadows began to fall, some of the neighbors dropped in, and Aunt Rachel gave the message of the wonderful Latter Rain outpouring and the soon-coming of Jesus. Late that night (actually the early morning hours of June 1, 1907), I remember hearing my mother singing and praising God in other tongues. The Fire had fallen here in Springfield, and she had received the Baptism of the Holy Ghost.

# REFERENCES

1.  "When Geronimo Smiled", by Fred T. Corum, *Pentecostal Evangel*, February 27,1977, PP. 6,7,8. Reprinted December 11,1988, PP. 6,7,22.

## Chapter II

# THE AZUSA STREET MISSION
"We are on our faces before God..."
(The Apostolic Faith, October, 1906)

Unspeakable joy... the glory, the beauty of Holiness... How can words express the divine manifestation of a wonderful God in the midst of His people? Have you ever seen it? Have you been there when God was moving by His Spirit? Have you experienced the joy of beholding souls swept into the Kingdom of God, or broken bodies made whole by the touch of the Master, or lives immersed into Holy Ghost rivers? Have you heard the Heavenly Choir while entire congregations move under the anointing of the Holy Spirit?

These were the scenes which Aunt Rachel described to us. As she told of these things occurring at the old Azusa Mission, not only did her very countenance glow, but Mother's and Father's hearts burned to experience these things of the Lord for themselves. Many times since then have we seen and experienced these precious things ourselves, but they have never become ordinary or common place to us. There is always a freshness and special anointing whenever the Lord ministers to His people. There is absolutely no human experience to be compared with the boundless joy radiating from people caught up in the profound experience of the presence of Christ Jesus the Lord.

### The Glowing Coals

Over the years, since the ascension of Christ, the hand of God has always moved upon His people. Wherever and whenever hungry hearts have reached out for the fullness of God, He has always satisfied the longing soul with Pentecostal fullness. There have been times in history when

4

the light of truth seemed as only a glowing ember, but the Holy Spirit has never ceased to move upon the earth.

The primitive Christians moved in Pentecostal power. Certainly, glossolalia (speaking in tongues) continued on into Medieval times. In the first history of the Pentecostal movement published by the Gospel Publishing House, *The Apostolic Faith Restored*, our Pastor, B.F. Lawrence, quoted the Encyclopedia Britannica, Vol. 27, pages 9-10 (11th edition), saying that glossolalia (tongues) "...recurs in Christian revivals of every age, e.g., among the mendicant friars of the Thirteenth Century; among the Jansenists and early Quakers; the converts of Wesley and Whitfield; the persecuted Protestants of the Cevennes; and the Irvingites."[1] Along with this phenomenon came reports of healing, miracles, and prophecy . . . Both the Encyclopedia Britannica and the *Life and Epistles of St. Paul* (by W.J. Conybeare and J.S. Howson) admit the presence of Glossolalia among the early Methodists. The latter work has the following in a footnote, "...If, however, the inarticulate utterances of ecstatic joy are followed (as they were in some of Wesley's converts) by a life of devoted holiness, we should hesitate to say that they might not bear some analogy to those of the Corinthian Christians."[2]

### The Welsh Revival of 1904-1905

There have been many, many instances where the Lord has moved upon hungry hearts, down through the years. But it would be negligent to try to discuss Azusa Street without first mentioning the great revival in Wales. Its story has probably never really been told either. A harbinger of the great Holy Spirit outpouring, which was to flow out from Azusa Street, was the unprecedented move of God in this great Welsh revival. Although the glossolalia had been restored and experienced in the U.S. by many people during the revivals of Charles F. Parham just after the turn of the century, it was the intense spirit of desire for more of Christ which so characterized the move of God in Wales, that was to fan the holy flames in Los Angeles.

Others have written accounts of this marvelous visitation. The reader should consult these books and also the original accounts by G. Campbell Morgan (a pamphlet entitled, "Revival in Wales") and S.B. Shaw (a book titled *The Great Revival in Wales*). Recently, Sherwood Wirt wrote a piece about the Welch revival.[33]

The Lord used a young coal miner named Evan Roberts (June 8, 1878-1951) from Loughor, Wales. Evan Roberts had experienced a glorious anointing of the Holy Spirit in the Spring of 1904.

> "I was lying in bed one day and felt vibrations; my body began to tremble. I got out of bed, and as I was kneeling down by the bedside, I was lifted up and my lips began to move in utterances which cannot be described. . . . I was taken up to a great expanse, without time or space. It was communion with God. Before this, I had a far-off God . . . There was a tremendous surging of joy that came over me."[3]

In September of 1904, Roberts, who was then 26, attended a religious service and was deeply moved as the evangelist cried, "Bend me, oh Lord!" Roberts' response was to, " . . . fall on my knees with my arms over the seat in front of me, and the tears flowed freely. I cried, 'Bend me, bend me, bend US!' . . . Tears streamed down my face. And a great burden came upon me for the salvation of lost souls."[4] It was only a matter of weeks before Wales would feel the impact of a heaven-sent visitation.

Evan Roberts said, "I had a vision of all Wales being lifted up to heaven. We are going to see the mightiest revival that Wales has ever known. The Holy Spirit is moving just now."[5]

Soon this move of God would spread abroad, not only throughout Wales, but wherever hungry hearts longed for reality. Describing these meetings, Evan Roberts wrote,

"The revival in South Wales is not of men, but of God. He has come very close to us. There is no question of creed or of dogma in this movement. We are teaching no sectarian doctrine, only the wonder and beauty of Christ's love. I have been asked concerning my methods. I have none. I never prepare what I shall speak, but leave that to Him. . . Wonderful things have happened in Wales in a few weeks, but these are only a beginning. The world will be swept by His Spirit as a rushing, mighty wind. Many who are now silent Christians will lead the movement. They will see a great light, and will reflect this light to thousands now in darkness. Thousands will do more than we have accomplished, as God gives them power."[6]

One of the most outstanding features of the Welsh revival was the song that swelled up in the hearts of the worshipping congregations.

"The singing - oh, the singing! The whole congregation has become a Spirit-led choir. . . . unless it is heard, it is unimaginable and when heard, it is indescribable . . . It is a mighty chorus rising like the thunder of the surge on a rockbound shore."[7]

Yet there would be times when such a burden for the lost would come upon them that Evan Roberts would exhort the congregation to prayer, "Don't sing, it's too terrible to sing."[8]

Frank Bartleman has written, "It was not the eloquence of Evan Roberts that broke men down, but his tears . . . Strong men would break down and cry like children."[9]

Donald Gee (who was himself saved under the ministry

of one of the ''children of the revival'', in London in October of 1905) made the following observations:

> "The profound impression which the Welsh revival made upon the entire Christian world can scarcely be realized by those who were not living at the time. Visitors came from far and near. Newspapers sent special reporters, and published lengthy reports. Some mocked; some were converted; all were impressed. It seemed, for a time, like an irresistible torrent.
>
> Perhaps the most formative result was the creation of a widespread spirit of expectation for still greater things. Men justly asked, 'Why Wales only? Why not other lands? Why not a world-wide revival?' . . . the spiritual soil was prepared in the providence of God for the rise of the Pentecostal Movement.''[10]

Even today, our hearts echo the same cry, ''Why Wales only? Why not other lands?'' And why not our generation too?

It was also Frank Bartleman's belief that, ''The present world-wide revival was rocked in the cradle of little Wales.''[11] Certainly, the Welsh revival would stir the hearts of those that were hungry for a move of God in Los Angeles in 1906.

### Azusa Street

There are several outstanding books that have been written recounting the marvelous events which transpired at Azusa Street, and we have listed some of them in the references for this chapter. We would encourage the reader to go to those books for more extensive accounts. Neither Hazel nor I ever attended Azusa Street and so our information is primarily from Aunt Rachel and Uncle Josie Sizelove. Let me tell the story as I told it through the pages of ''WORD

AND WORK'' years ago.

## Pentecost Has Come

"Rachel and Joseph (or Josie as we all called him) Sizelove were living in Los Angeles, California, when the Holy Spirit was poured out as on the day of Pentecost, and the great revival began. In the month of April, 1906, a few of God's children under the leadership of Brother William J. Seymour began to tarry before the Lord in a cottage prayer meeting for the Baptism as given in Acts 2:4, and Brother C.S. Lee, a black man, was the first to receive the Baptism of the Holy Ghost with the Bible evidence of speaking in other tongues as the Spirit gave utterance. The second was Sister Evans, and the power of God began to fall.''[12]

## Old Azusa Street Mission

"They sought a place to hold their meetings and the dear Lord was pleased to direct them down in the slum district of the city to a building on Azusa Street, where there were wholesale houses and stock yards on one side and a tombstone shop on the other. It was an old building that had been used for a store room below and for living quarters above. Yet the dear Lord saw fit to let the Shckinah Glory rest over that place until hundreds of people received the Baptism of the Holy Ghost.''[13]

Why is the Azusa Street Mission spoken of as so central to the Charismatic revival of the Twentieth Century? The Holy Spirit had already been moving in Pentecostal Fullness since about the turn of the century and perhaps it seems strange that old Azusa Mission should be singled out as a fountainhead. Of the Azusa Street meetings, Vinson Synan has written:

"The Azusa Street revival is commonly regarded

as the beginning of the modern Pentecostal movement. Although many persons had spoken in tongues in the United States in the years preceding 1906, this meeting brought this belief to the attention of the world and served as the catalyst for the formation of scores of Pentecostal denominations. Directly, or indirectly, practically all the Pentecostal groups in existence can trace their lineage to the Azusa Mission."[14]

Before we trace the lineage of the Pentecostal Church in Springfield, Missouri, we would like to give the reader a brief historical account of the revival at Azusa Street. The Old Azusa Street Mission published a little newspaper called "THE APOSTOLIC FAITH". Thirteen issues were published at Azusa Street and we have recently reissued all thirteen in one volume entitled "LIKE AS OF FIRE". We know of no way to recount the story of the Azusa Street revival better than to let those old prayer warriors tell it in their own words, as they did through the pages of "THE APOSTOLIC FAITH".

Pentecost Has Come

Los Angeles Being Visited by a Revival of Bible Salvation and Pentecost as Recorded in the Book of Acts

"The power of God now has this city agitated as never before. Pentecost has surely come and with it the Bible evidences are following, many being converted and sanctified and filled with the Holy Ghost, speaking in tongues as they did on the day of Pentecost. The scenes that are daily enacted in the building on Azusa Street and at Missions and churches in other parts of the city are beyond description, and the real revival is only started, as God has been working with His children mostly, getting them through to Pentecost, and laying the foundation for a mighty wave of salvation among the unconverted.

The meetings are held in an old Methodist church that had been converted in part into a tenement house, leaving a large, unplastered, barn-like room on the ground floor. Here about a dozen congregated each day, holding meetings on Bonnie Brae in the evening. The writer attended a few of these meetings and being so different from anything he had seen and not hearing any speaking in tongues, he branded the teaching as third-blessing heresy and thought that settled it. It is needless to say the writer was compelled to do a great deal of apologizing and humbling himself to get right with God.

In a short time, God began to manifest His power and soon the building could not contain the people. Now the meetings continued all day and far into the night and the fire is kindling all over the city and surrounding towns. Proud, well-dressed preachers come in to 'investigate'. Soon their high looks are replaced with wonder, then conviction comes, and very often you will find them in a short time wallowing on the dirty floor, asking God to forgive them and make them as little children. It would be impossible to state how many have been converted, sanctified and filled with the Holy Ghost. They have been and are daily going out to all points of the compass to spread this wonderful gospel.

### The Old-Time Pentecost

This work began about five years ago last January, when a company of people under the leadership of Chas. Parham, who were studying

11

God's word, tarried for Pentecost in Topeka, Kansas. After searching through the country everywhere, they had been unable to find any Christians that had the true Pentecostal power. So they laid aside all commentaries and notes and waited on the Lord, studying His word, and what they did not understand, they got down before the bench and asked God to have wrought out in their hearts by the Holy Ghost. They had a prayer tower from which prayers were ascending night and day to God. After three months, a sister who had been teaching sanctification for the Baptism with the Holy Ghost, one who had a sweet, loving experience and all the carnality taken out of her heart, felt the Lord lead her to have hands laid on her to receive the Pentecost. So when they prayed, the Holy Ghost came in great power and she continued speaking in an unknown tongue. This made all the Bible school hungry,and three nights afterwards, twelve students received the Holy Ghost, and prophesied, and cloven tongues could be seen upon their heads. They had an experience that measured up with the second chapter of Acts, and could understand the first chapter of Ephesians.

Now after five years, something like thirteen thousand people have received this gospel. It is spreading everywhere, until churches who do not believe backslide and lose the experience they have. Those who are older in this movement are stronger, and greater signs and wonders follow them.

The meetings in Los Angeles started in a cottage meeting, and the Pentecost fell there three nights. The people had nothing to do but wait on the Lord and praise Him,and they commenced speaking in tongues, as they did at Pentecost, and the Spirit sang songs through them.

The meeting was then transferred to Azusa Street, and since then multitudes have been coming. The meetings begin about ten o'clock in the morning and can hardly stop before ten or twelve at night, and sometimes two or three in the morning, because so many are seeking, and some are slain under the power of God. People are seeking three times a day at the altar and row after row of seats have to be emptied and filled with seekers. We cannot tell how many people have been saved, and sanctified, and baptized with the Holy Ghost, and healed of all manner of sicknesses. Many are speaking in new tongues, and some are on their way to the foreign fields, with the gift of the language. We are going on to get more of the power of God.

Many have received the gift of singing as well as speaking in the inspiration of the Spirit. The Lord is giving new voices, he translates old songs into new tongues, He gives the music, no instruments are needed in the meetings.''[15]

The story continues:

The Pentecostal Baptism Restored
The Promised Latter Rain Now Being Poured Out
on God's Humble People

"All along the ages, men have been preaching a partial Gospel. A part of the Gospel remained when the world went into the dark ages. God has from time to time raised up men to bring back to the world the doctrine of justification by faith. He raised up another reformer in John Wesley to establish Bible holiness in the church. Then he raised up Dr. Cullis who brought back to the world the wonderful doctrine of divine healing. Now He

13

is bringing back the Pentecostal Baptism to the Church.

God laid His hand on a little crippled boy seven years of age and healed him of disease and made him whole except his ankles. He walked on the sides of his ankles. Then, when he was fourteen years of age, he had been sent to college and God had called him to preach. One day as he was sitting reading his Bible, a man came for him to go and hold a meeting. He began to say to the Lord: 'Father, if I go to that place, it will be necessary for me to walk here and yonder. Just put strength into these ankle joints of mine.' And immediately, he was made whole and leaped and praised God, like the man at the beautiful gate. He has since been in evangelistic work over the United States, seeing multitudes saved, sanctified, and healed.

Five years ago, God put it into this man's heart (Bro. Charles Parham) to go over to Topeka, Kansas, to educate missionaries to carry the Gospel. It was a faith school and the Bible was the only text book. The students had gathered there without tuition or board, God sending in the means to carry on the work. Most of the students had been religious workers and said they had received the Baptism with the Holy Ghost a number of years ago. Bro. Parham became convinced that there was no religious school that tallied up with the second chapter of Acts. Just before the first of January, 1901, the Bible school began to study the Word on the Baptism with the Holy Ghost to discover the Bible evidence of this Baptism that they might obtain it.

The students kept up continual prayer in the praying tower. A company would go up and stay three hours, and then another company would go up and wait on God, praying that all the promises of the Word might be wrought out in their lives.

On New Year's Eve night, Miss Agnes N. Ozman, one who had for years 'the anointing that abideth', which she mistook for the Baptism, was convinced of the need of a personal Pentecost. A few minutes before midnight, she desired hands laid on her that she might receive the gift of the Holy Ghost. During prayer and invocation of hands, she was filled with the Holy Ghost and spake with other tongues as the Spirit gave utterance.

This made all hungry. Scarcely eating or sleeping, the school, with one accord, waited on God. On the third of January, 1901, Bro. Parham being absent holding a meeting at the time, while they all waited on God to send the Baptism of the Spirit, suddenly twelve students were filled with the Holy Ghost and began to speak with other tongues, and when Bro. Parham returned and opened the door of the room where they were gathered, a wonderful sight met his eyes. The whole room was filled with a white sheen of light that could not be described, and twelve of the students were on their feet talking in different languages.

He said they seemed to pay no attention at all to him, and he knelt in one corner and said, 'O God, what does this mean?' The Lord said: 'Are you able to stand for the experience in the face of persecution and howling mobs?' He said: 'Yes, Lord, if you will give me the experience, for the laborer must first be partaker of the fruits.' Instantly the Lord took his vocal organ and he was preaching the Word in another language.

15

This man has preached in different languages over the United States, and men and women of that nationality have come to the altar and sought God. He was surely raised up of God to be an apostle of the doctrine of Pentecost.

The Pentecostal Gospel has been spreading ever since, but on the Pacific coast it has burst out in great power and is being carried from here over the world. We are expecting Bro. Parham to visit Los Angeles in a few days and for a mightier tide of salvation to break out.

### Fire Still Falling

The waves of Pentecostal salvation are still rolling in Azusa Street Mission. From morning till late at night the meetings continue with about three altar services a day. We have made no record of souls saved, sanctified, and baptized with the Holy Ghost, but a brother said last week he counted about fifty in all that had been baptized with the Holy Ghost during the week. Then at Eighth Street and Maple Avenue, the People's Church, Monrovia, Whittier, Hermon, Sawtelle, Pasadena, Elysian Heights and other places, the work is going on and souls are coming through amid great rejoicing.

Four of the Holiness preachers have received the Baptism with the Holy Ghost. One of them, Bro. Wm. Pendleton, with his congregation, being turned out of the church, are holding meetings at Eighth Street and Maple Avenue. There is a heavenly atmosphere there. The altar is filled with seekers, people are slain under the power of God, and rising in a life baptized with the Holy Ghost.

The fire is spreading. People are writing from

different points to know about this Pentecost, and are beginning to wait on God for their Pentecost. He is no respector of persons and places. We expect to see a wave of salvation go over this world. While this work has been going on for five years, it has burst out in great power on this coast. There is power in the full Gospel. Nothing can quench it.

Missionaries for the foreign fields, equipped with several languages, are now on their way and others are only waiting for the way to open and for the Lord to say: 'Go.' We are on our faces before God. Let a volume of prayer go up from all the Lord's people. Awake! Awake! There is but time to dress and be ready, for the cry will soon go forth. 'The Bridegroom cometh.'''[16]

By now, the news was really beginning to spread:

### Bible Pentecost

### Gracious Pentecostal Showers Continue to Fall

''The news has spread far and wide that Los Angeles is being visited with a 'rushing mighty wind from heaven'. The how and why of it is to be found in the very opposite of those conditions that are usually thought necessary for a big revival. No instruments of music are used, none are needed. No choir - but bands of angels have been heard by some in the spirit and there is a heavenly singing that is inspired by the Holy Ghost. No collections are taken. No bills have been posted to advertise the meetings. No church or organization is back of it. All who are in touch with God realize as soon as they enter the meetings that the Holy Ghost is the leader. One brother stated that even before his train entered the city, he felt the power of the revival.

Travelers from afar wend their way to the headquarters at Azusa Street. As they enquire their way to the Apostolic Faith Mission, perhaps they are asked, 'O, you mean the

17

Holy Rollers', or 'It is the Colored Church you mean.' In the vicinity of a tombstone shop, stables and lumber yard (a fortunate vicinity because no one complains of all night meetings) you find a two-story, white-washed, old building. You would hardly expect heavenly visitations there, unless you remember the stable at Bethlehem.

But here you find a mighty pentecostal revival going on from ten o'clock in the morning till about twelve at night. Yes, Pentecost has come to hundreds of hearts and many homes are made into a sweet paradise below. We remember years ago, when a bright young missionary was dying in Bombay, India. In his last hours, unconscious with the fever, he kept crying, 'Pentecost is coming! Pentecost is coming!' It seemed prophetical. Pentecost has come and is coming to India, and thank God to many other places.

A leading Methodist layman of Los Angeles says, 'Scenes transpiring here are what Los Angeles churches have been praying for years. I have been a Methodist twenty-five years. I was a leader of the praying band of the First Methodist Church. We prayed that the Pentecost might come to the city of Los Angeles. We wanted it to start in the First Methodist Church, but God did not start it there. I bless God that it did not start in any church in this city, but in a barn, so that we might all come and take part in it. If it had started in a fine church, poor colored people and Spanish people would not have got it, but praise God it started here. God Almighty says He will pour out of His Spirit upon all flesh. This is just what is happening here. Tell the people wherever you go that Pentecost has come to Los Angeles.'

As soon as it is announced that the altar is open for seekers for pardon, sanctification, the Baptism with the Holy Ghost, and healing of the body, the people rise and flock to the altar. There is no urging. What kind of preaching is it that brings them? Why, the simple declaring of the Word of God. There is such power in the preaching of the Word in the Spirit that people are shaken on the benches. Coming to the altar, many fall prostrate under the power of God, and often come out speaking in tongues. Sometimes the power falls on people and they are wrought upon by the Spirit during testimony or preaching and receive Bible experiences.

The testimony meetings which precede the preaching often continue for two hours or more and people are standing, waiting to testify all the time. Those who have received the Baptism with the Holy Ghost testify that they had a clear evidence of sanctification first. Hundreds testify that they received the Bible evidence of speaking in a new tongue that they never knew before. Some have received the 'gift of tongues' or 'divers tongues' and the interpretation.

The demonstrations are not the shouting, clapping or jumping so often seen in campmeetings. There is a shaking such as the early Quakers had and which the old Methodists called the 'jerks'. It is while under the power of the Spirit you see the hands raised and hear speaking in tongues. While one sings a song learned from heaven with a shining face, the tears will be trickling down other faces. Many receive the Spirit through the laying on of hands, as they did through Paul at Ephesus.

Little children from eight years to twelve stand

19

up on the altar bench and testify to the Baptism with the Holy Ghost and speak in tongues. In the children's meetings, little tots get down and seek the Lord.

The singing is characterized by freedom. 'The Comforter has come' is sung every day, also 'Heavenly Sunlight' and 'Under the Blood'. Often one will rise and sing a familiar song in a new tongue.

Seekers for healing are usually taken upstairs and prayed for in the prayer room and many have been healed there. There is a larger room upstairs that is used for Bible Study. A brother fittingly describes it in this way, 'Upstairs is a long room, furnished with chairs and three California redwood planks, laid end to end on backless chairs. This is the Pentecostal upper room where sanctified souls seek Pentecostal fullness and go out speaking in new tongues.'

The sweetest thing of all is the loving harmony. Every church where this has gone is like a part of the family. This description is given for the benefit of the many friends who write in and who would like to be present. So many letters are received in the Apostolic Faith office which is in the same building as the mission. We cannot but weep as we read these letters and pray for those who are seeking.''[17]

### Pentecost With Signs Following

Seven Months of Pentecostal Showers, Jesus, Our Protector and Great Shepherd

''Many are asking how the work in Azusa Mission started and who was the founder. The Lord was the founder and He is the Projector of this movement. A band of humble people in Los

Angeles had been praying for one year or more for more power with God for the salvation of the lost and suffering humanity. They did not know just what they needed, but one thing they knew, people were not getting saved and healed as they desired to see. They continued to hold cottage prayer meetings for several months.

Then they felt led of the Lord to call Bro. Seymour from Houston, Texas, to Los Angeles, the saints in Los Angeles sending his fare. It was as truly a call from God as when He sent His holy angel to tell Cornelius to send for Peter. He came and told them about the Baptism with the Spirit, and that very afternoon at three o'clock they would pray for the endument of power. He told them he did not have the Pentecost, but was seeking it and wanted all the saints to pray with him till all received their Pentecost. Some believed they had it, and others believed they did not have it because the signs were not following. Hardly anyone was getting saved.

There was a great deal of opposition, but they continued to fast and pray for the Baptism with the Holy Spirit, till on April 9th, the fire of God fell in a cottage on Bonnie Brae. Pentecost was poured out upon workers and saints. Three days after that, Bro. Seymour received his Pentecost. Two who had been working with him in Houston came to Los Angeles just before Pentecost fell. They came filled with the Holy Ghost and power. One of them had received her personal Pentecost, Sister Lucy Farrow, and said the Lord had sent her to join us in holding up this precious truth. She came with love and power, holding up the blood of Jesus Christ in all His fullness.

21

And the fire has been falling ever since. Hundreds of souls have received salvation and healing. We can truly say the revival is still going on. The Lord God is in Los Angeles in different missions and churches in mighty power. In spite of opposition. This revival has spread through the towns about Los Angeles and through different places across the ocean. The blood of Jesus Christ prevails against every force and power of the enemy. Glory to God.

Some are asking if Dr. Chas. F. Parham is the leader of this movement. We can answer, 'no', he is not the leader of this movement of Azusa Mission. We thought of having him to be our leader and so stated in our paper, before waiting on the Lord. We can be rather hasty, especially when we are very young in the power of the Holy Spirit. We are just like a baby - full of love - and were willing to accept anyone that had the Baptism in the Holy Spirit as our leader. But the Lord commenced settling us down, and we saw that the Lord should be our leader. So we honor Jesus as the great Shepherd of the sheep. He is our model.

The Lord adds here daily such as should be saved, and plants them in the body to suit Himself, and all work together in harmony under the power of the Holy Spirit. There is no pope, Dowieism, or Sanfordism, but we are all little children knowing only Jesus and Him crucified. This work is carried on by the people of Los Angeles that God has united by the precious blood of our Lord Jesus Christ and the power of the Holy Spirit.

Bro. Seymour is simply a humble pastor of the flock over which the Holy Ghost has made him overseer, according to Acts 20:28, 'Take heed therefore, unto yourself and to the flock over which the Holy Ghost hath made you overseer, to feed the church of God which He hath purchased with His own blood.' And as missionary workers and teachers go out from this place, they have the same privilege of being pastors over the people the Lord puts them over by the Holy Spirit, and of feeding them with the pure Word of God. Each mission will be united in harmony having it's own pastor-simply that the Holy Ghost shall appoint.

We believe in old-time repentance, old-time conversion, old-time sanctification, healing of our bodies, and the Baptism of the Holy Ghost. We believe that God made Adam in His own image, according to Gen. 5:1; Ps. 8:4, and Matt. 19:4. We do not believe in any eighth day creation, as some have taught, and we do not believe in the annihilation of the wicked.

We stand on Bible truth without compromise. We recognize every man that honors the blood of Jesus Christ to be our brother, regardless of denomination, creed, or doctrine. But we are not willing to accept any errors. It matters not how charming and sweet they may seem to be. If they do not tally with the Word of God, we reject them.

This is the year of jubilee when God is sending the latter rain, and the refreshing times have come. He has raised up a nation in seven months time that will preach in spite of what it costs.

*'The long, long night is past,The morning breaks at last.'*

It seems that God is sweeping things. He is running right over the devil here - not paying any attention to Him - saving, sanctifying, and baptizing souls, bringing them out of darkness into the marvelous light of the Son of God. Hallelujah! Glory to God!''[18]

Concerning the marvelous meetings at Azusa Street and the great move of God in Los Angeles in 1906, Frank Bartleman wrote, ''I often said that I would rather live six months at this time than fifty years of ordinary life.''[19] The old Azusa Mission was just a simple barn-like structure, but something profound was occurring within its walls - something which would reach back through the years to the days of the New Testament Church and bubble forth into the Twentieth Century with a restoration and renewal of the Apostolic ministries.

### APPENDIX - AZUSA STREET TESTIMONIES

The group photograph which we have enclosed shows the original Azusa Street leaders before the Mission was purchased. Who were these people? Frank Bartleman has observed:

> ''One reason for the depth of the work at Azusa was the fact that the workers were not novices. They were largely called and prepared for years from the Holiness ranks and from the mission field. They had been burnt out, tried and proven. They were largely seasoned veterans. They had walked with God and learned deeply of His Spirit.''[20]

The testimonies of several of the early Azusa Street veterans have been published in *The Apostolic Faith*. Although we do not have the words of Brother Hiram W. Smith (an old Holiness Methodist preacher), or of Sister Prince, we do have the testimonies of most of the others included in the Azusa Street photograph.

First, let us listen to Glenn A. Cook, who had been a printer in Indianapolis, Indiana. After receiving the Baptism at Azusa Street, he briefly returned to Indianapolis to make right some old wrongs. It was on a Sunday afternoon in January of 1907, when Alice Reynolds (who later married J. Roswell Flower) first heard of Pentecost from the lips of Glen Cook. ''Pretty Sister Alice'', as the Indianapolis Star would call her in the April 18,1907 issue, received the Baptism of the Holy Spirit on March 31, 1907. Here is the testimony of Brother Cook:

### Receiving The Holy Ghost

''God has told His children to be witnesses, and the most convincing evidence is testimony of personal knowledge. To endeavor to help those who are sending in letters of inquiry to the Apostolic Faith office, asking how they may receive the Holy Ghost, the writer will state a little of his personal experience in obtaining this pearl of great price, the Baptism with the Holy Ghost.

I dropped into the meetings on Azusa Street some time in April, having heard that some people were speaking in tongues, as they did on the Day of Pentecost. Although I had been trying to preach Pentecost for five years, the speaking in tongues was as strange to me as though it had never been mentioned in God's Word. At first the meeting seemed a very tame affair to me, as I had been along the line of much fleshly demonstration and noise. As I was indoctrinated in the second blessing being the Baptism with the Holy Ghost, I had branded the teaching as heretical, not going to the meetings for some time.

In the meantime, Pentecost came to the place, and many began to speak in tongues. I now began to attend regularly. In fact,I could not stay away. My heart began to break up, and soon I was going from one person to another, asking them to forgive me for harsh words and criticism. God so melted my heart that I would cry at my work or riding on a street car. How the dear Lord began to teach me that what I needed was His loving, tender Spirit, and that power with God meant deep humility in our dealings with our fellow creatures. I now began to go to the altar and earnestly seek for the Lord to have His way with me. The Holy Ghost showed me that I must be clay in the potters hands, an empty vessel before the Lord. I laid aside all doctrine, all preconceived ideas and teachings and became absolutely empty. The Holy Ghost now settled down on me, and I could feel the power going through me like electric needles. The Spirit taught me that I must not resist the power but give way and become limp as a piece of cloth. When I did this, I fell under the power, and God began to mold me and teach me what it meant to be really surrendered to Him. I was laid out under the power five times before Pentecost really came. Each time I would come out from under the power, I would feel so sweet and clean, as though I had been run through a washing machine.

I now had come to the place where I was completely submitted to the whole of God. I had been seeking about five weeks, and on Saturday morning, awoke and stretched my arms toward heaven and asked God to fill me with the Holy Ghost. My arms began to tremble, and soon I was shaken violently by a great power, and it seemed as though a large pipe was fitted over my neck, my head apparently being off, I was now filled with the Holy Ghost. Words can not describe the power I felt. The nearest description that could be given would be the action of a pump under terrific pressure, filling me with oil. I could feel the filling in my toes and all parts of my body which seemed to me to swell until I thought I would burst. I do not know how long this continued but it seemed to me a long time. The pressure was now removed and my soul and spirit seemed to leave the body and float in the air just above. My body seemed hard and metallic like iron. This was undoubtedly the Baptism into the death of Christ.

It was now time for me to arise and go to work, so I got up without speaking in tongues. I believe I would have spoken in tongues then, if I had remained in the hands of the Lord long enough. About thirty hours afterwards, while sitting in the meeting on Azusa Street, I felt my throat and tongue begin to move, without any effort on my part. Soon I began to stutter and then out came a distinct language which I could hardly restrain. I talked and laughed with joy far into the night. Praise his name for such a wonderful experience of power and love and joy.''[21]

Next let us listen to dear sister Clara E. Lum. Sister Lum knew shorthand (in the picture she is holding a pencil) and she recorded many of the testimonies at Azusa Street in shorthand. She was a dear friend to Aunt Rachel. I believe that she later went to Portland, Oregon to assist Florence Crawford with the Apostolic Faith Movement - a Trinitarian outreach centered in the Northwest.

''Thank God for deliverance from all sin, through the precious Blood. I had been sanctified and anointed with the Holy Ghost years ago. Have been ten years in his work. When I came to Azusa Mission, I went on in for the Baptism with the Holy Ghost immediately. Had some digging to do, but the Lord met me. I was filled with the Holy Ghost many times and was shaken many times by the power of God. But when I became a little child, clay in His hands, He baptized me with the Holy

Ghost. At first He spoke just a few words through me. But recently He spoke different languages and sang songs in unknown tongues. Just lately the Lord healed me of quite a severe sickness. He has given me better health than ever, for which I thank' Him. O, it was so sweet to have Him talk and sing through me when I was sick, during the night seasons. Sometimes I sang for hours and a new voice and it did not tire me. He also interpreted. He said, 'Jesus is coming.' It rejoiced me so much, and then He sang a song right from heaven about His coming. O, praise God for the privilege of being in His work here.''[22]

By the way, G.B. Cashwell, who took the Pentecostal message to the Southeast, wrote that he received the Baptism ''. . . while Sister Lum was reading how the Holy Ghost was falling in other places.''[23]

Sister Florence L. Crawford wrote a great deal of the material which appeared in *The Apostolic Faith* and took the magazine to Portland, Oregon, with her when she ventured out to start the work there. She started in Portland with Volume II, No. 14 in Summer of 1908 and the magazine has continued to be published from Portland. Listen as she speaks:

''I can't forget how, kneeling at the dear old board in Azusa Street, I promised God I would go where He wanted me to go and stay where He wanted me to stay, and be what He wanted me to be. I meant every word of it and God has taken me at my word. How His glory is flooding my soul. O how I worship His precious name! I have to stop and wonder how God can bless the Word through me. To think He has saved me when all my family were infidels and everything that would drive me from God. No one can ever know how I feel

28

for the way God has dealt with me. O how I love Jesus. It thrills my very being to think of the Blood. It has done so much for me. I am filled with wonder, love, and praise that God would permit me to see the workings of His mighty power in these last days. O to think we have lived to see the gifts restored back to the church. I find we cannot compromise with anything or anybody. O we must stand for all the light we have received, and having done all to stand."[24]

The little girl in Brother Smith's arms is Mildred Crawford (Sister Crawford's daughter). She was ten years old when the fire first fell in Los Angeles.[25]

Next we hear from Brother and Sister Evans. It has been reported that Sister Evans was ". . . the first white woman to receive the Pentecost and gift of tongues in Los Angeles."[26] Here is her testimony of healing:

### Testimony of Healing

"Thirteen years ago, I was brought into the light of Divine healing through the Word of God. I had never heard any teaching from man. But I had been for a long time very greatly afflicted in body. I had taken physicians and medicine until I became discouraged and continued to grow worse till I decided to drop every remedy and take the Lord for my healer.

To this my people would not give consent. They thought I was losing my mind. One morning, through a nurse, I was chloroformed; and taken out of my home to the hospital where they performed an operation. After the physicians had cut and slashed and found that the seat of the trouble was deeper than they anticipated, they lost courage and said it was impossible for me to recover. It was

29

only a question of a few hours that I could possibly live. My husband was away in God's work at the time, and my people became alarmed, and realized what they had done, and decided to take me back to my home to die. But, praise God, He had another plan in store for me.

I did not regain consciousness for many hours, I opened my eyes in my own room and heard them praying around my bed. Then I realized my dreadful situation and in the most excruciating agony, I lifted my eyes to heaven and saw a light streaming down upon me. And in a moment, I heard the voice of Jesus telling me to trust Him, that He was my healer. I said, 'Yes Lord, I do trust Thee and will trust Thee, for Thou hast healed me and healed me now.' Then there was a wonderful joy that came into my very being, and I felt the Spirit and the healing power of Christ permeating my whole being, praise God. In three days time, I was up and around my room, and in less than a week, I was able to walk a mile. Never from that time have I doubted the healing power of Jesus. Since then, for thirteen years, I have been in the Lord's work.

Now I wish to relate another instance of His healing power. While in Oakland, California, during last August, through an accident, God permitted the old trouble to come back, and from Saturday evening until Tuesday noon, I suffered intensely. At noon time, we always held our workers' class there, and it was during the saints' meeting, I had a wonderful spirit of prayer, and I tried to say, 'Jesus is here', and found I had no utterance, but He was present in my soul. The spirit of prayer continued on me until 2:30. When the Lord permitted me to raise my eyes, I saw a vision of

30

beautiful rolling clouds, and Jesus suspended in the midst, and just then I realized that He was there for my healing. Sister Crawford and Sister Junk, who were with me also saw Jesus, and God revealed to them He had come to heal me. I felt the healing work of Jesus. Many of you loved ones have seen the mason lift up his trowel of mortar and throw it upon the wall that he was building, and just so it seemed to me that the Great Physician was rebuilding the temple of my body. O Hallelujah! Praise His Name. O, I know that He is the only physician that can heal all our diseases. All that afternoon and evening, no matter which way I turned, the form of my Savior was suspended in front of me, and I wish ever to hold the smile of His countenance as I saw Him that day. My healing was instantaneous, and today I rejoice in a perfect body.''[27]

Brother and Sister Evans and Sister Crawford held meetings in Oakland, California. In these meetings, Brother Evans had a marvelous vision while he was exhorting the people to come to Christ. ''. . . While he was speaking, the whole rear end of the hall became filled with faces of angelic beings from floor to ceiling and from wall to wall. A literal bank of beautiful faces, with Jesus in the center, and all faces turned toward Him.''[28]

Jennie Moore was in the meeting at 215 Bonnie Brae Street (near where Angeles Temple now stands) when the fire first fell on the night of April 9, 1906. This was just before the little band moved to 312 Azusa Street. When she received the Baptism, she spoke in tongues, prophesied, and ''. . . went to the piano, and for the first time in her life began playing beautiful music and singing a beautiful language with a beautiful voice. These gifts she never lost, and the piano is still in the cottage at 216 Bonnie Brae, where Willella

31

Asberry still lives.''[29] Here is Jennie Moore's testimony:

"For years before this wonderful experience came to us, we as a family, were seeking to know the fulness of God, and He was filling us with His presence until we could hardly contain the power. I had never seen a vision in my life, but one day as we prayed, there passed before me three white cards, each with two names thereon, and but for fear, I could have given them, as I saw every letter distinctly. On April 9,1906, I was praising the Lord from the depths of my heart at home,and when the evening came and we attended the meeting, the power of God fell and I was baptized in the Holy Ghost and fire, with the evidence of speaking in tongues. During the day, I had told the Father that although I wanted to sing under the power, I was willing to do whatever He willed, and at the meeting when the power came on me, I was reminded of the three cards which had passed me in the vision months ago. As I thought thereon and looked to God, it seemed as if a vessel broke within me and water surged up through my being, which when it reached my mouth came out in a torrent of speech in the languages which God had given me. I remembered the names on the cards: French, Spanish, Latin, Greek, Hebrew, Hindustani, and as the message came with power, so quick that but few words would have been recognized, interpretation of each message followed in English, the name of the language would come to me. I sang under the power of the Spirit in many languages, the interpretation both words and music which I never before heard, and in the home where the meeting was being held, the Spirit led me to the piano, where I played and sang under inspiration, although I had not learned to play. In these ways, God is continuing to use me to His glory ever since that wonderful day, and I praise Him for the privilege of being a witness for Him under the Holy Ghost's power.''[30]

Here is brief testimony given by Brother Seymour:

### Testimony and Praise to God

''O, I feel the coming of our Lord and Savior Jesus Christ drawing nigh. Hallelujah! Glory to His name! I am so glad that the Lord is holding the winds until the angel has sealed all of the saints of the living God in their foreheads, the Baptism of the Holy Ghost. The midnight cry will soon be made, when the morning and the night shall come. It will be morning in our souls, to those that are waiting for His coming: but the awful black night of tribulation as the black night of Egypt will come upon all the world. May God help all of His precious waiting Bride to be watching, waiting until our Lord shall come.

Oh, I am so thankful that I can work for my Christ and my God. The time is short when our blessed Jesus shall return to this earth, and snatch away His waiting Bride. After six thousand years of toil and labor, we are going to have one thousand years of rest with our Lord and Savior, Jesus Christ. Glory to His Holy Name!''[31]

We would also like to include the comments of dear old Brother A.S. Worrell, the author of *Worrell's Translation of the New Testament*:

### Work Increasing

''. . . The Almighty doth not pull down with one hand, what He buildeth up with the other. Satan

33

is not in the rescue work; nor does He lead his
followers to magnify the atoning blood of Christ,
nor fill people with a desire and a passion for saving souls. We have never known Christ more
magnified than in Azusa Mission."[32]

## REFERENCES

1. **The Apostolic Faith Restored**, by Bennett F.
   Lawrence, The Gospel Publishing House, St. Louis,
   Missouri, 1916, PP. 33,36.
2. **The Life and Epistles Of St. Paul**, by W.J. Conybeare and J.S. Howson, Eerdmans Publishing Co.,
   reprinted, 1968, Pg. 409.
3. **They saw It Happen**, by Gordon Lindsay, Christ for
   the Nations, Dallas, Texas, Pg. 16.
4. Reference 3, PP. 16-17.
5. Reference 4, Pg. 17.
6. **How Pentecost Came To Los Angeles, by Frank
   Bartleman, 3rd edition, 1925, Pg. 36. Reprinted
   as Another Wave Rolls In**, Voice Publications, Northridge, Ca., 1962, Pg.41, reprinted as **Another
   Wave of Revival**, Whitaker House, Springdale, Pa.,
   1982, Pg. 33.
7. Reference 3, Pg. 21
8. Reference 3, Pg. 21.
9. Reference 6b, Pg. 41.
10. **The Pentecostal Movement**, by Donald Gee, Vic-
    tory Press, London, 1941, Pg.6.
11. Reference 6b, Pg. 31.
12. "A Sparkling Fountain for the Whole Earth", by
    Rachel A. Sizelove, *Word and Work*, Vol. 56, No.6,
    June, 1934, PP. 1, 11, 12.
13. Reference 12, Pg. 1.

14. **The Holiness-Pentecostal Movement**, by Vinson Synan, Eerdmans, Grand Rapids, Mich., 1971, Pg. 114.
15. *The Apostolic Faith*, Vol. 1, No. 1, September, 1906, Pg.1. Reprinted in **Like As of Fire.**
16. Reference 15, Vol. 1, No. 2, October, 1906, Pg. 1.
17. Reference 15, Vol. 1, No. 3, November, 1906, Pg.1
18. Reference 15, Vol. 1, No. 4, December, 1906, Pg.1
19. Reference 6b, PP. 60-61.
20. Reference 6b, Pg. 82.
21. Reference 15, Vol. 1, No. 3, November, 1906, Pg. 2.
22. Reference 15, Vol. 1, No. 6, February-March, 1907, Pg.8.
23. Reference 15, Vol. 1, No. 4, December, 1906, Pg. 3.
24. Reference 15, Vol. 1, No. 9, September, 1907, Pg. 4.
25. Reference 15, Vol. 1, No. 4, December, 1906, Pg. 4, and Vol. 1, No. 5, January, 1907,PP. 1,4.
26. Reference 15, Vol. 1, No. 1, September, 1906, Pg.3.
27. Reference 15, Vol. 1, No. 3, November, 1906, Pg. 3.
28. Reference 15, Vol. 1, No. 3, November, 1906, Pg. 4.
29. **In Those Days**, by Thomas R. Nickel, Great Commission International, Box 538, Montery Park, Ca., 2nd edition, 1962, Pg.4.
30. Reference 15, Vol. 1, No. 8, May, 1907, Pg. 3.
31. Reference 15, Vol. 1, No. 9, June-September, 1907, Pg.4
32. Reference 15, Vol. 1, No. 6, February-March, 1907, Pg.6.
33. ''Revival in Wales'', by Sherwood E. Wirt, *Decision Magazine*, Part 1 - February, 1964; Part 2 - March, 1964, Pg. 11; Part 3 - April, 1964, Pg. 6; Part 4 - May, 1964.

# CHAPTER III

## WILLIAM J. SEYMOUR
"Above all, let us honor the blood of Jesus
Christ every moment of our lives."
(W.J.S., 1906)

onsidering the impact that the ministry of this singular
individual has had upon the Twentieth Century church,
and the amount of writing which he left behind, surprisingly little has actually been written about Brother Seymour.
Vinson Synan has indicated that W. J. Seymour was born
in Louisiana and had moved to Houston, Texas, where he
had become a Baptist preacher with a strong interest in the
Holiness Movement.[1] In 1905, Charles Parham started a
short-term faith Bible school in Houston, and Brother
Seymour began to attend. According to Bennett Lawrence,

"W.J. Seymour, an African preacher of Houston, became
interested in the new Movement and its doctrines, and allied
himself with it. Brother W. F. Carothers and C. F. Parham
instructed him in the doctrines held by the Movement at that
time. (They are substantially the same today.)"[2]

Howard Goss (who was converted in the Fall of 1903 when
Charles Parham held a revival in Galena, Kansas) was one
of a number of workers attending the Houston Bible School.
Concerning the Bible school at Houston and Brother
Seymour, Brother Goss has written:

"The Bible School at Houston was a great blessing to all
of us, as Mr. Parham was a very interesting teacher. Also
a revival was carried on in the city in connection with the
school and a great work was done on the streets. Many more
were saved and filled with the Spirit and spake in tongues.
Mr. Parham taught that all would speak in tongues when filled
with the Spirit.

36

This school is the place where Mr.
Seymour, later of Azusa Street, Los Angeles,
received the light about the Baptism in the
Spirit. I remember very clearly his coming
to the classes at 9 A.M. and he and Mr.
Parham preached to the colored people of the
city, and some of them received the light. Mr.
Seymour was already a minister, but was
seeking the Baptism.

He soon wanted to go to Los Angeles, but
was urged not to do so until he received the
Baptism. However, he did go before receiving, and later opened the Azusa Street work.
Later, Mrs. Lucy Farrow, a colored baptized saint that had cooked for the company of
workers while holding meetings at Bryan Hall
in Houston, and who had been in Mr.
Parham's family for several months, went to
Los Angeles to assist Seymour in his work
there."[3]

Sister Farrow would later return to preach at Brunner
Tabernacle on her way as a missionary to Liberia, West
Africa. And Brother Goss would later be one of the five
ministers signing the call for a conference, which led to the
formation of the Assemblies of God.

What was Brother Seymour like? Let's call several
observers to the witness stand that sat under his ministry at
Azusa Street.

W.H.DURHAM:  "He is the meekest man I ever met. He
walks and talks with God. His power is
in his weakness. He seems to maintain
a helpless dependency on God and is as
simple-hearted as a little child, and at the
same time so filled with God that you feel

the love and power every time you get near him.''[4]

A.W. ORWIG:  ''. . . I heard him counsel against all unbecoming or fleshly demonstrations, and everything not truly of the Holy Spirit. Brother Seymour constantly exalted the atoning work of Christ and the Word of God, and very earnestly insisted on thorough conversion, holiness of heart and life, and the fullness of the Holy Spirit. . . ''[5]

A.S.WORRELL:  ''I have. . . not a single doubt but that Brother Seymour has more power with God, and more power from God, than all his critics in and out of the city. His strength is in his conscious weakness, and lowliness before God. . .''[6]

FRANK
  BARTLEMAN:  ''Brother Seymour generally sat behind two empty shoe boxes, one on top of the other. He usually kept his head inside the top one during the meeting, in prayer. There was no pride there. The services ran almost continuously. Seeking souls could be found under the power almost any hour of the night or day. The place was never closed nor empty. The people came to meet God.''[7]

ANSEL M.
  POST:  ''As Brother Seymour preached, God's power seemed to be increasing in me. Just about the close of the sermon, as suddenly as on the Day of Pentecost, while I was sitting in front of the preacher, the Holy Spirit fell upon me

and filled me literally.''[8]

ARTHER G.
OSTERBERG:
''He was meek and plain-spoken and no orator. He spoke the common language of the uneducated class. He might preach for three-quarters of an hour with no more emotionalism than that post. He was no arm-waving thunderer, by any stretch of the imagination.''[9]

RACHEL
SIZELOVE:
''He . . . stayed behind the box on his knees before the Lord, hidden away from the eyes of the world . . . Oh, how the Lord used that old black Brother and gave him wisdom like Moses, to lead and teach the people.''[10]

SNOWDIE
(SIZELOVE)McGEE:
''My sister, Maud, was passing a kidney stone and had been in terrible pain for almost twenty-four hours. Mother, (Rachel Sizelove ) said to my brother, Matt, you go and get Brother Seymour. When Brother Seymour came, Maud was just writhing in agony. He went to the side of the bed and opened a little bottle of oil with which to anoint Maud's head. He spoke very calmly and said, 'Little girl, do you believe that God can heal you?' and then he prayed for God to heal my little sister - he didn't get all excited - but very calmly prayed, and anointed her with oil. Well, it was almost as though she had been given a hypodermic needle. She immediately rolled over and fell into a peaceful sleep and slept the

night through.''[11]

In addition to being used by the Lord as a leader at Azusa Street, Brother Seymour made several trips around the country to help spread the full-gospel message. He held meetings at Zion City, Illinois, at Chicago and also at Indianapolis, where Alice Reynolds (Flower) heard him speak. I believe that he passed away in the mid- 1920's, that he never accepted the Jesus Only teaching, and that he continued to remain independent from the various Pentecostal denominations. I'm sure that there are others more qualified than I to write about Brother Seymour. However, I would like to include a few of the statements made by him and concerning him which were published in the Azusa Street Papers. I think that his own words will tell far more about him than any biographical sketch that I could write.

### BRO. SEYMOUR'S CALL

"Bro. W.J. Seymour has the following to say in regard to his call to this city: 'It was the divine call that brought me from Houston, Texas, to Los Angeles. The Lord put it in the heart of one of the saints in Los Angeles to write to me that she felt the Lord would have me come over here and do a work, and I came, for I felt it was the leading of the Lord. The Lord sent the means, and I came to take charge of a mission on Santa Fe Street, and one night, they locked the door against me, and afterwards got Bro. Roberts, the President of the Holiness Association, to come down and settle the doctrine of the Baptism with the Holy Ghost, that it was simply sanctification. He came down and a good many Holiness preachers with him, and they stated that sanctification was the Baptism with the

Holy Ghost. But yet they did not have the evidence of the second chapter of Acts, for when the disciples were all filled with the Holy Ghost, they spoke in tongues as the Spirit gave utterance. After the President heard me speak of what the true Baptism of the Holy Ghost was, he said he wanted it too, and told me when I had received it, to let him know. So I received it and let him know. The beginning of the Pentecost started in a cottage prayer meeting at 214 Bonnie Brae.'''[12]

Brother Seymour wrote a considerable amount of material placed in the Azusa Street Papers. His doctrinal positions are stated quite clearly and, except for his traditional Holiness Movement position concerning sanctification, they are almost universally accepted among Trinitarian Pentecostals today.

Concerning the work of the Holy Spirit in the Church, he wrote:

" . . . The Holy Ghost is to infuse with divine power, and to invest with heavenly authority. No religious assembly is legal without His presence and His transaction. We should recognize Him as the Teacher of teachers.

The reason why there are so many of God's people without divine power today, without experimental salvation wrought out in their hearts by the Blood, by the power of the blessed Holy Spirit, is because they have not accepted Him as their Teacher, as their Comforter. Jesus said in His precious Word that if He went away He would send us another Comforter. The need of men and women today in their lives, is a Comforter. Praise our God! We have received this blessed

41

Comforter, and it is heaven in our souls. We can sing with all our hearts: 'What matter where on earth we dwell, On mountain top, or in the dell, In cottage or mansion fair, Where Jesus is, 'tis heaven there.'

Bless His Holy Name! May God help everyone of His Blood-bought children to receive this blessed Comforter. Glory to His Name! Hallelujah! Hosanna to His omnipotent name! Oh, He is reigning in my soul! Hallelujah!

Oh, thank God for this holy way. I am so glad that sham battles are over. Men and women must live straight, holy, pure lives, free from sin, or else they have no part with Christ Jesus. When men and women are filled with the Holy Ghost, wherever they go, living waters will flow. The Lord promised that out of our innermost being living rivers of water should flow. This is the Holy Ghost. Amen! The mighty Pison, the Gihon, the Hiddekel, the Euphrates of our soul will flow, representing the rivers of salvation. Amen!''[13]

These words are amplified in a later article entitled, ''Christ's Message to the Church''.

### The Vision of Jesus in His Church

''The most striking passage of Scripture in the first chapter (of Revelation) is where John was permitted to see Jesus walking among the golden candlesticks, which represent the church. Christ is in His church today to fill men and women, to heal their bodies, save and sanctify their souls, and to put His finger upon every wrong and mean thing in the church. His rebuke is against it, for He hates sin as much today as He ever did when He walked by the Sea of Galilee. Glory to His name. Jesus hates impure doctrine just as much as when He rebuked the Pharisees for their impure doctrine.

John beheld Jesus in His glorified body. What a holy scene it was: the Son of God clothed with a garment down to the foot and girt about the paps with a golden girdle.'His head and His hairs were white like wool, as white as snow.' Hallelujah. There is nothing but purity and holiness in our Saviour. And 'His eyes were as a flame of fire.' Glory to Jesus...

Repentance . . . . Dear beloved, if there is anything wrong in your life and Jesus has His finger upon it, O may you give it up, for Jesus is truly in His church today. This is the Holy Ghost dispensation and He does convince men of sin, righteousness, and the judgment, and if we will be honest, God will bless us.

### To The Church Today

When a church or mission finds that the power of God begins to leave, they should come as a whole and confess, and let all get down before God and repent and pray to God until the old-time fire and power and love come back again. . . . He expects to find the church, when He comes back to earth again, just fire and power and the signs following as it was when He organized it on the day of Pentecost. Bless His Holy Name. May God

help all His precious, praying children to get
back to the old Pentecostal power and fire and
love. The church at that time was as terrible
as an army with banners. She conquered every
power of evil. . . . I thank God for this
wonderful message to the church, a message
from heaven, given by Jesus to show that He
is in the church, that He does walk among the
golden candlesticks. He is in heaven, but
through the power of the Holy Spirit, He
walks in the church today. Nothing can be hidden from His pure eyes. He wants people to
live the highest and deepest consecration to
Him.''[14]

Concerning the Baptism of the Holy Ghost Brother
Seymour wrote:

### The Baptism of the Holy Ghost

. . . . . ''And when the day of Pentecost
was fully come, they were all with one accord in one place. ' O beloved, there is where
the secret is: one accord, one place, one heart,
one soul, one mind, one prayer. If God can
get a people anywhere in one accord and in
one place, of one heart, mind and soul, believ-
ing for this great power, it will fall and
Pentecostal results will follow. Glory to God!

Apostolic Faith doctrine means one accord,
one soul, one heart. May God help every child
of His to live in Jesus' prayer: 'That they all
may be one, as Thou, Father, art in Me and
I in Thee; that they all may be one in us: that
the world may believe that Thou hast sent
Me.' Praise God! O how my heart cries out
to God in these days that He would make

every child of His see the necessity of living
in the 17th chapter of John, that we may be
one in the body of Christ, as Jesus has prayed.

. . . . The Baptism of the Holy Ghost brings
the glory of God to our hearts.'

### The Holy Ghost is Power

There is a great difference between a sanctified person and one that is baptized with the
Holy Ghost and fire. A sanctified person is
cleansed and filled with divine love, but the
one that is baptized with the Holy Ghost has
the power of God on his soul and has power
with God and men, power over all the
kingdoms of Satan and over all his emissaries.
God can take a worm and thresh a mountain.
Glory to God. Hallelujah!

In all Jesus' great revivals and miracles, the
work was wrought by the power of the Holy
Ghost flowing through His sanctified humanity. When the Holy Ghost comes and takes us
as His instruments, this is the power that con-
victs men and women and causes them to see
that there is a reality in serving Jesus Christ.

### Tarry In One Accord

...O beloved, if you wait on God for this
Baptism of the Holy Ghost just now, and can
get two or three people together that are sanctified through the Blood of Christ, and all get
into one accord, God will send the Baptism
of the Holy Ghost upon your souls as the rain
falls from heaven. You may not have a
preacher to come to you and preach the doctrine of the Holy Ghost and fire, but you can

obey Jesus' saying in the passage, 'Where two or three are gathered together in My name, there am I in the midst of them.' This is Jesus' Baptism: and if two or three are gathered together in His name and pray for the baptism of the Holy Ghost, they can have it this day or this night, because it is the promise of the Father. Glory to God! . . .

### The Baptism Falls on a Clean Heart

. . . O that men and women would tarry for the Baptism with the Holy Ghost and fire upon their souls, that the glory may be seen upon them just as it was upon the disciples on the day of Pentecost in the fiery emblem of tongues. The tongues of fire represented the great Shekinah glory. So today the Shekinah glory rests day and night upon those who are baptized with the Holy Ghost, while He abides in their souls. For His presence is with us. Glory to His name. I thank Him for this wonderful salvation. Let us sing His praises through all the world that all men may know that the Comforter has come. Bless His dear name!

### The Holy Ghost Flows Through Pure Channels

If men and women today will consecrate themselves to God, and get their hands and feet and eyes and affections, body and soul, all sanctified, how the Holy Ghost will use such people. He will find pure channels to flow through, sanctified avenues for His power. People will be saved, sanctified, healed, and baptized with the Holy Ghost and fire

. . . . O how I bless God to see His mighty power manifested in these last days. God wants His people to receive the Baptism with the Holy Ghost and Fire.''[15]

Concerning the Holy Ghost and the Bride, he wrote:

### The Holy Ghost and The Bride

". . .The bride of Christ is calling the thirsty to come to Jesus, because this is the work of the Holy Ghost in the believer. He intercedes for the lost; He groans for them. The Spirit also calls the believer to come to Jesus and get sanctified. He points the sanctified to Jesus for his baptism with the Holy Ghost. When you are baptized with the Holy Ghost, you will have power to call sinners to Jesus, and they will be saved, and sanctified, and baptized with the Holy Ghost and fire. Amen!

Christ's Bride is pure and spotless. 'Thou art all fair, my love, there is no spoil in thee.' (Sol. Song, 4:7) Christ's Bride is clean, free from sin and all impurity. He gave Himself for her, that He might sanctify and cleanse the church with the washing of water by the word. That He might present it to Himself a glorious church, not having spot or wrinkle or any such thing, but that it should be holy and without blemish, (Eph. 5:25,27). . . .''[16]

Brother Seymour wrote several articles entitled, "Letters to One Seeking the Holy Ghost". In these, he clearly states the early Apostolic Faith teaching of Charles Parham concerning sanctification as a prerequisite to the Baptism of the Holy Spirit.

47

William J. Seymour

"Dear Beloved in Christ Jesus:

The Lord Jesus has said in His precious Word, 'Blessed are they which do hunger and thirst after righteousness, for they shall be filled.' (Matt. 5:6) God's promises are true and sure. We can rest upon His Promises. He says, 'Blessed are the pure in heart, for they shall see God.' (Matt. 5:8) 'Blessed are the poor in spirit, for theirs is the kingdom of heaven.' ( Matt. 5:3).

The Lord Jesus is always ready to fill the hungry, thirsty soul,. . . .

The first thing in order to receive this precious and wonderful Baptism with the Holy Spirit, we want to have a clear knowledge of justification by faith according to the Bible. (Romans 5:l). . . .

And then the second step is to have a real knowledge of sanctification, which frees us from original sin - the sin that we were born with, which we inherited from our father Adam. . . . 'This is the will of God, even your sanctification.' (I Thess. 4:3)...

Then after we were clearly sanctified, we prayed to God for the baptism with the Holy Spirit. So He sent the Holy Spirit to our hearts and filled us with His blessed Spirit, and He gave us the Bible evidence, according to the second chapter of Acts, verses l to 4, speaking with other tongues as the Spirit gives utterance.

Praise our God, He is the same yesterday, today, and forever. Receive Him just now and He will fill you. Amen. Don't get discouraged

48

but pray until you are filled. . ."[17]

No one can doubt the strength of the Holiness conviction which Brother Seymour espoused. He continues:

### Sanctified On The Cross

". . . 'Sanctify them through Thy truth, Thy Word is truth.' Jesus is still praying this prayer today for every believer to come and be sanctified. Glory to God! Sanctification makes us holy as Jesus is. Sanctification makes us one with the Lord Jesus. (Heb. 2:ll) Then the prayer of Jesus is answered, and we become one with Him, even as He is one with the Father. Bless His holy name.

...God is calling His people to true holiness in these days. We thank God for the blessed light that He is giving us. He says in II Timothy 2:2l: 'If a man therefore purge himself from these, he shall be a vessel unto honor, sanctified and meet for the Master's use.' He means for us to be purged from uncleanness and all kinds of sin. Then we shall be a vessel unto honor, sanctified, and meet for the Master's use, and prepared unto every good work. . . .

The Lord Jesus says, 'Blessed are the pure in heart'. Sanctification makes us pure in heart. Any man that is saved and sanctified can feel the fire burning in his heart when he calls on the Name of Jesus. O, may God help men and women everywhere to lead a holy life, free from sin, for the Holy Spirit seeks to lead you out of sin into the marvelous light of the Son of God. . . . .

Brother Paul says in order to become holy

and live a holy life, we should abstain from all appearance of evil. Then the apostle adds, 'And the very God of peace sanctify you wholly, and I pray God your whole spirit and soul and body be preserved blameless unto the coming of our Lord Jesus Christ.' ( I Thess. 5:22,23) 'To the end He may establish your hearts unblamable in holiness before God, even our Father, at the coming of our Lord Jesus Christ with all His saints.' (I Thess. 3:l3) Bless His holy name. O beloved, after you have received the light, it is holiness or hell. God is calling for men and women in these days that will live a holy life free from sin. We should remain before God until His all-cleansing Blood makes us holy; body, soul and spirit.''[18]

And so the full gospel message preached at Azusa Street- could be compactly stated:

### River Of Living Water

". . .In Jesus Christ we get forgiveness of sin, and we get sanctification of our spirit, soul, and body, and upon that we get the gift of the Holy Ghost that Jesus promised to His disciples, the promise of the Father. All this we get through the atonement. Hallelujah!

The Prophet said that he had borne our griefs and carried our sorrows. He was wounded for our transgressions, bruised for our iniquities, the chastisement of our peace was upon Him and with His stripes we are healed. So we get healing, health, salvation, joy, life - everything in Jesus. Glory to God!

. . . . Above all, let us honor the blood of

Jesus Christ every moment of our lives. . .''[19]

These statements are only partial reproductions of much lengthier articles by Brother Seymour. They not only provide a window into the very workings of this man's soul, but they also give a clear picture of the Holiness atmosphere that gave birth to the Azusa Street revival.

Concerning the strong Wesleyan doctrinal position, it should be said that within a few years, other qualified teachers would arise with contrasting positions concerning the concept of sanctification.

Whether it be instantaneous or progressive, the position of the New Testament concerning sanctification is quite clear - it is the will of God for all believers. Holiness is commanded by our Lord. However, the historical division arose among the various Pentecostal groups over how and when sanctification is appropriated in the Christian's life. Needless to say, there is not universal agreement in Pentecost as to what Sanctification actually is. How this issue was resolved historically is treated in several fine books [20] [21] and there also exist many well-written theological treatments of the various doctrinal interpretations. However, I do remember that Dad used to say that when the preachers began to say that you couldn't be sanctified or that you were already sanctified - that was when the Jesus Only issue swept through Pentecost. Whatever may be doctrinally correct, the Lord found ready recipients for the Holy Spirit in these dear old Holiness people for their hearts were prepared to receive the promises of God.

Although I never had the privilege to meet or hear Brother Seymour, I can only say that Aunt Rachel, like many others, thought that he was surely God's man for that hour and all the saints recognized it. She told us of his profound humility and how the Lord gave him great wisdom to lead the people at a time when Apostolic ministries were being restored to the Church. May God grant us such leaders today, and may we have the discernment to recognize both the leading of the Holy Spirit and the human instruments which He employs. For, under grace, as under the Levitical Law, they are worthy of double honor.

## REFERENCES

1. **The Holiness-Pentecostal Movement**, by Vinson Synan, Eerdmans, Grand Rapids, Mich., 1971, Pg. 103.

2. **The Apostolic Faith Restored**, by Bennett F. Lawrence, The Gospel Publishing House, Springfield, Missouri, 1916, PP. 55. 3.Reference 2, Pg. 64.

4. **The Apostolic Faith**, Vol. 1, No. 6, February-March, 1907, Pg. 4. Reprinted in **Like As of Fire**.

5. **With Signs Following**, by Stanley H. Frodsham, The Gospel Publishing House, 1926, PP. 31-32.

6. Reference 4, Vol. 1, No. 6, February-March, 1907, Pg.5.

7. **How Pentecost Came To Los Angeles**, by Frank Bartleman, 3rd edition, 1925, Pg. 58. Reprinted as **Another Wave Rolls In**, Voice Publications, Northridge, Ca., 1962, Pg. 59, reprinted as **Another Wave of Revival**, Whitaker House, Springdale, Pa., 1982, Pg. 58.

8. Reference 5, Pg. 30, and Reference 4, Vol. 1, No.5, January, 1907, Pg. 4.

9. Los Angeles Times, September 9, 1956. Reprinted in **Suddenly From Heaven**, by Carl Brumback, The Gospel Publishing House, Springfield, Mo., Pg. 38. (Reprinted as **A Sound From Heaven**, GPH, 1977, Pg. 36.)

10. ''A Sparkling Fountain for the Whole Earth'', by Rachel Sizelove, *Word and Work*, Vol. 56, No. 6, June, 1934, PP. 1, 11, 12.

11. Tape recorded interview, June 14, 1981.

12.   Reference 4, Vol. 1, No. 1, September, 1906, Pg. 1.
13.   Reference 4, Vol. 1, No. 9, September, 1907, Pg. 3.
14.   Reference 4, Vol. 1, No. 11, January, 1908, Pg. 3.
15.   Reference 4, Vol. 2, No. 13, May, 1908, Pg. 3.
16.   Reference 4, Vol. 2, No. 13, May, 1908, Pg. 4.
17.   Reference 4, Vol. 1, No. 9, September, 1907, Pg. 3.
18.   Reference 4, Vol. 2, No. 13, May, 1908, Pg. 2.
19.   Reference 4, Vol. 1, No. 3, November, 1906, Pg. 2.
20.   Reference 1, PP. 147-151.
21.   **Suddenly From Heaven**, by Carl Brumback, The Gospel Publishing House, Springfield, Mo., 1961, Chapter 9. (Reprinted as **A Sound From Heaven**, GPH, 1977, Chapter 9.)

# Chapter IV

## RACHEL AND JOSEPH SIZELOVE

"It was like Angels singing."
J.S.

n this chapter, we would like to provide a short account of how Rachel and Joseph Sizelove were led by the Lord to the old Azusa Street Mission, and how Rachel received the Baptism of the Holy Spirit in July of 1906. The following Spring, she would bring the Pentecostal message to Springfield, Missouri.

Rachel was born on September 3, 1864, in Maringo, Indiana. She was saved while attending Professor Johnson's Christian Girls' Academy in Indiana in the late 1870's. Here is part of her testimony:

> ". . . down upon my knees, I fell by a chair with my hands and face lifted toward heaven.
> I called mightily upon God to save my soul before it was too late . . . The dark clouds that seemed all about me began to disappear and as by faith I looked away to calvary's cross and saw Jesus hanging there for me, and as my faith took hold of God, the light of heaven poured into my soul. I said, 'O Glory!'
> And the Glory flooded my soul. I thought that when I got saved I'd shout like my mother, but I was so calm. I had found peace- it was calm as a river. The world was changed. I got the witness that I was born again. (Romans 8:16)."[1]

After finishing at the academy, she took a job teaching school at Hutchinson, Kansas, in September of 1883. It was

54

there that she met and fell in love with Joseph Sizelove (whom we all called Uncle Josie). They were married in 1885 and filed on a 160 acre claim and became settlers on the newly opened prairie. It wasn't long before Josie and Rachel felt the call of God to start holding meetings and reach out to help others on those lonely prairies. Sister Sizelove writes,

". . . We learned of a protracted meeting being held by the Free Methodists. We began to attend. I soon learned they had an experience in God that I did not have and at once I began to hunger for more of God in my life. We began to attend their meetings and their teachings were just what we were hungering for in our souls.

They taught that we could live in this present world without sin, and that there was a separation from the world. . . Well, several weeks passed on and I couldn't stay away from their cottage prayer meetings. Oh, they had such power with God. It made my poor soul cry out for more of God in my life."[2]

It was after this that she and Josie consecrated their lives to serving the Lord. They joined the Free Methodist Conference and became circuit riders and preached throughout Kansas, the Oklahoma Territory, Southern Missouri and Northern Arkansas. During the 1890's, they held revivals in Joplin, West Plains, and Thayer, Missouri, and Mammoth Springs, Arkansas - places which would receive an unusual visitation of the Holy Spirit a dozen years later.

In 1903, Josie took his family to the Free Methodist Colony in Los Angeles, California, to send his children to the Methodist School for an education. It was at this time in their lives that something remarkable happened which would eventually lead to a Pentecostal Church in Springfield, Missouri - a church which is today called Central Assembly of God.

Let me return to an article which I published in 'Word and Work' back in June of 1934.

"We were attending a Free Methodist camp-meeting in early June, 1906, and I heard there was a company of people in an old building, speaking in tongues as on the day of Pentecost. My husband told me he had just passed by and heard such wonderful singing in the Spirit. When he came home, he said to me, 'Rachel, I just now passed by the Azusa Street Mission and heard such singing as I never heard in my life before. It was like angels singing'. Josie did not understand it then, but when he read in the Bible where Paul said in the 14th chapter of First Corinthians and the fifteenth verse where he said, 'I will sing with the spirit and I will sing with the understanding also.'

They were singing in the spirit, which Josie had never heard before. He said to me, 'Do you want to go to the mission and see and hear them' Of course, I was soon dressed to go with him. Oh, such an out of the way place - way down in the slum part of the city. A tombstone yard on one side where they were making tombstones. On the other side there was a barnyard where there were a lot of mules and horses kept. We entered the old building and somehow I was touched by the presence of God. It was such an humble place with its ceilings and rough floor. Cob webs were hanging in the windows and joists. As I looked around, I thought of Jesus when He came to earth and was born in a manger. There was no place for Him in the inn. I thought of the fine church houses in the city of Los Angeles, but the Lord had chosen this humble spot to gather all nationalities, to baptize them with the Holy Ghost. The building was soon cleaned out and the ceilings were whitewashed. A large box served as the pulpit stand. Brother Seymour stayed behind that box on his knees before the Lord, hid away from the eyes of the world so much of the time. O! how God used that old black brother and gave him wisdom as he did to Moses to lead and teach the people.

It was in the afternoon when I first went there. There were about twelve of God's children, white and black, there tarrying before the Lord, some sitting and some kneeling. My attention was especially drawn to two young men, Brother Clifford and Brother Johnson. The latter soon after went to Sweden and later to Palestine as a missionary. These two young men were sitting with eyes closed, with faces uplifted toward heaven, a heavenly glow upon their faces, speaking in tongues to themselves and to God. 'Howbeit, in the Spirit they were speaking mysteries.'"[3]

### Wooing of the Holy Spirit

"My very soul cried out, 'O! Lord, the people have something I do not have.' Brother Seymour gave out the Word and made an altar call and said anyone wanting to seek the Lord for pardon or sanctification or the Baptism of the Holy Ghost and fire, to come and bow at the altar. I thought, well praise God, he is not doing away with any of my experience or

57

belief, but just adding to my experience that of the Baptism of the Holy Ghost, which he said could only come to a clean heart.

I knew I had received the born again experience (John 3:1-6) and I had received the experience of sanctification, but had never heard of receiving the Holy Ghost according to Acts 2:4. Brother Seymour said if our hearts were clean, washed in the precious blood of Jesus, we were the right recipients for the Baptism of the Holy Ghost.''[4]

### The Holy Spirit Descends

''I went home and began to search the Word of God. I saw it was in the Bible. I was again in the mission in July, 1906. By that time, crowds were beginning to gather. When Brother Seymour gave the altar call, I with many others went to the altar. Raising my hands toward heaven, I said,' Lord, I want my inheritance, the Baptism of the Holy Ghost and fire.' Instantly in the spirit, I saw as it were a bright star away in the distance and my very soul crying out to God, 'As the hart panteth after the water brook, so panteth my soul after Thee.' O! I knew it was He.

. . . it seemed my very heart cried out, 'Oh, this is He whom my soul desires.' How I reached my hands heavenward. I was afraid I would lose sight of Him. But I held on, my very soul crying out for the living water. As He came nearer, He was in the form of a beautiful white dove. As He came closer, . . . a dear black sister, Lucy Farrow, came over to me and placed her hands upon my

head and said to me, 'Receive ye the Holy
Ghost.' I went back under the mighty power
of God, . . . I was slain upon the floor. Then
the Lord began to work in me. I had died out
to everything of which I knew and believed.
I had a clean heart in the sight of God, but
He asked me if I cared what my church said.
. . . He said to me, 'Will you care for what
your church will say if I Baptize you with the
Holy Ghost?' I said, 'O Lord, my church will
receive anything that is from you.' Then O
how I was shaken by the power of God, and
my head on the floor. My whole body seemed to be made over by the mighty power of
God, and He shook me until I said, 'Lord,
I won't care what my church will say.'

A stillness as death came over me and the
Lord whispered, 'Clay in the potter's hands.'
I had read that many times in the Scripture,
but never until now did I really know the
meaning. I thought, ' O! I know I can receive
Him now.' In the spirit, I looked up to where
He had stopped between me and the ceiling.
To my surprise, He was not up there, but had
descended to me. There was a great open
space in my heart and He just came in and
took up His abode. There was such a holy
hush that it seemed that the whole world was
put to silence. Someone whispered to my husband sitting near that Sister Sizelove was not
breathing. I thought, ' I dare not breathe the
breath of life in the holy presence of the
Father.' So bless God, I cannot tell. I do know
that I was in the most holy place. How can
I ever praise Him for what He had done for

me?

He knew that my church would not receive it. I did not know for it was in the beginning and I did not know the churches would fight it. So He had me die out to the opinion of my church before He could baptize me with the Baptism of the Holy Ghost."[5]

Rachel Sizelove wrote in her book:

"Oh, Hallelujah, can I ever praise Him enough for what He did for me at the old Azusa Street Mission in 1906.

Now Papa and I went to those meetings about every night. Crowds began to come. About this time, we lived on Wall Street near Third, in Los Angeles."[6]

By the way, Aunt Rachel mentioned Lucy Farrow above. Much could be said about this dear woman of God. Back before the Civil War, she had been sold into slavery as a young girl in Norfolk, Virginia. In 1905, she was a cook for the workers at Brother Parham's school in Houston, Texas. According to the first issue of *The Apostolic Faith*, "Sister Farrow, Brother W.J. Seymour, and Brother J.A. Warren were the three that the Lord sent from Houston as messengers of the Full Gospel." In the same place, it is said of Lucy Farrow, ". . . whom God had greatly used as she laid her hands on many who have received the Pentecost and the gift of tongues . . . "[7] Rachel Sizelove was one of those.

Sister Farrow felt the call of God to go as a missionary to Johnsonville near Monrovia, Liberia (West Africa). Along the way East, she ministered at Brunner Tabernacle near Houston, Texas, in July 1906. Howard Goss has written about this meeting,

". . . We all gathered there again and the power fell mightily. Here Mrs. Farrow came and gave us a detailed account of what was happening in Los Angeles. She was endued with an unusual power to lay hands on people for the reception of the Holy Spirit. At one time, I saw a row of about twenty-five lined up before her, she laid hands upon them and many began to speak in tongues at once.

Hundreds and thousands of Houston people came to hear the Gospel. From the camp-meeting, the preachers scattered again with this great message, some of them going to other states."[8]

Brother Goss has also spoken of this meeting:

"She was received as a messenger of the Lord to us ... I went forward that she might place her hands upon me. When she did, the Spirit of God again struck me like a bolt of lightning; the power of God surged through my body and I began speaking in tongues... I thank God for Sister Farrow."[9]

This remarkable meeting is also described in *The Apostolic Faith*:

### Pentecostal Scenes

"At Brunner, Texas, in August, a wonderful meeting was held by the Apostolic Faith people. Fifty, seventy five, and one hundred seekers at a service crowded the altars for two whole weeks. The sixty foot altar was doubled half way back, then trebled, until the whole front half of the Tabernacle was occupied with the great altar service. Think of one hundred seekers and twice as many faithful Christians assisting, all praying before God. Glory to His great name! Then see them rise with shining faces and Pentecostal power."[10]

From Houston, this remarkable woman continued on and

held meetings in New Orleans, La. and Portsmouth, Virginia.

### Pentecost in Portsmouth

"God has done a wonderful work in Portsmouth, Virginia. It is reported that about one hundred fifty have received the Pentecost. The whole country about there is stirred by the power of God. The Lord sent Sister Lucy Farrow there from Los Angeles and has been using her to preach this Gospel. She feels a call from God to go to Monrovia, Liberia, Africa, and wants someone to come and help carry on the work. She says, 'Give all the saints love from me. Tell them I have many children here too. They do not want me to leave, but you all know when the Lord says go, I must go. I move as the Lord says move. No time to visit, only for the Lord. I go night and day in rain and sunshine. There is no time to stop. Jesus is coming soon. Pray for me and the work here.' "[11]

And so it was with all the Azusa band. They just surrendered themselves to the Lord to be used of God wherever He led. Rachel Sizelove wrote:

"It is wonderful the things God will do for us if we just surrender ourselves to Him. I can still look back and see the wonderful things God did for us in the great outpouring of the Holy Spirit in the old Azusa Street Mission in Los Angeles, California. But God's hand is not shortened that He cannot do the same thing for us today if we will only consecrate ourselves to go through. These experiences make me feel how closely we should walk before our God."[12]

Although the old Azusa Mission was little more than a stable, truly the Glory of the Lord rested upon the people that met there to seek the face of God. Today, the Spirit of God abides, not in the grandeur of temples like Solomon's, but in temples of clay.

## REFERENCES

1.  Unpublished Autobiography, by Rachel Sizelove, n.d., (200 pages), PP. 38-39.
2.  Reference 1, PP.
3.  "A Sparkling Fountain for the Whole Earth", by Rachel A. Sizelove, *Word and Work*, Vol. 56, No. 6, June, 1934, PP. 1,11, 12.
4.  Reference 3, PP.
5.  Reference 3, PP.
6.  Reference 1, PP.
7.  *The Apostolic Faith*, Vol. 1, No. 1, September, 1906, Pg.1. Reprinted in **Like As of Fire**.
8.  **The Apostolic Faith Restored**, by Bennett F. Lawrence, The Gospel Publishing House, St. Louis, Missouri, 1916, Pg. 66.
9.  **The Winds of God**, by Ethel E. Goss Word Aflame Press, Hazelwood, Mo, 1977, pg. 98.
10. Reference 7, Vol. 1, No. 2, October, Pg.3.
11. Reference 7, Vol. 1, No. 4, December, 1906, Pg. 1.
12. "A Sparkling Fountain", by Rachel Harper Sizelove, *Word and Work*, Vol. 57, No. 3, March, 1935, PP. 1, 2, 12.

# Chapter V

## AN EVENING AT AZUSA MISSION

"I looked on, not knowing what to think. My heart was
hungry for God."
Earnest S. Williams

**T**he magnificent temple which Solomon built stood as
a jeweled diadem crowning old Jerusalem. There on
Mt. Moriah, surrounded by luxurious courts, porches, col-
onnades, galleries, and palaces, it stood as a splendid and
glorious centerpiece - the most graceful and elegant sanctuary ever erected by human hands.

What was it that gave this structure its grandeur and glory?
Was it the wonderful sacrifice given every morning and in
the evening? Was it the glorious rituals and sweet temple
music that accompanied the sacrificial worship? Was it the
great day of atonement when the High Priest put on those
wonderful garments of glory and beauty to minister on behalf
of God's chosen people? Was it the temple ornaments - their
workmanship being everywhere exceedingly curious, and
their overlayings rich and costly? Was it the construction
materials - great large stones hewn out in the most curious
and artful manner? The ancient Rabbis have mentioned *five
things* which were present at Solomon's Temple, but were
*absent* at the reconstructed temples of Zerubbable and
Herod.[1,2] They speak explicitly of the *ark of the covenant*,
in which were put the tables of the Law and the mercy seat
which was upon it, from whence the divine oracles were
given out by an audible voice as often as God was consulted
in behalf of His people. They mention the *Urim and Thum-
mim*, or as the Septuagint says . . Revelation and Truth, by
which the High Priest could consult God in difficult and

momentous cases relating to the nation's public interest. They tell of the *Spirit of Prophecy*, accompanying Temple worship, by which the people of God spoke as they were moved by His Spirit. And they speak of the *Holy Fire* which came down from heaven and ". . . rushed with violence upon the altar . . .and caught hold of and consumed the sacrifices. . ." at the consecration of the Temple.[3] But what was it that gave this Temple its glory?

The splendor of this great structure was not in its architectural beauty - no,nor any of the equally marvelous human and divine adornments mentioned so far. The beauty, grandeur and excellency, which even yet stirs the deepest emotions of Jacob's children, consisted in that Jehovah Himself crowned this marvelous sanctuary with His own divine presence and visibly manifested Glory. In the fifth chapter of II Chronicles, we read how *the Shekinah Glory* was manifested as a cloud which came down and visibly "filled the House of God".

Concerning the dedication of the great Temple at Jerusalem, described in II Chronicles 5:ll-l4, Rachel Sizelove has written,

> . . ."What a beautiful comparison is the dedication of Solomon's Temple with Acts 2:4, when on the Day of Pentecost, one hundred and twenty were all with one accord, praising God, when there came a sound from Heaven as of a rushing mighty wind, and it filled all the house where they were sitting, and there appeared unto them cloven tongues like as of fire, and they were all filled with the Holy Ghost. We notice in II Chronicles 5:l3, that the house was filled with a cloud, even the House of the Lord: so that the priests could not stand to minister by reason of the cloud for the Glory of the Lord had filled the

House of God.

But the contrast on the Day of Pentecost is that the Holy Ghost came to dwell in TEMPLES OF CLAY. The church triumphant now a temple for the habitation of God through the Spirit. I Cor. 3:16, 'Know ye not that ye are the temple of God, and that the Spirit of God dwelleth in you.' And as Solomon's Temple was built on new stones, hewn out in the most curious and artful manner, so the church is spoken of as lively stones, built up as a spiritual house, I Peter 2:5, and how we find the church comforted with gracious promises. 'O thou afflicted, tossed with tempest, and not comforted, behold, I will lay thy stones with fair colors, and lay thy foundations with sapphires.' (Isaiah 54:11). O! Hallelujah! what a wonderful Rock we have to build upon, Jesus Christ being the chief corner stone.

The prophet Haggai calls the old men who remembered Solomon's Temple to witness to the new generation how greatly that structure exceeded the present in magnificence. Haggai 2:3, 'Who is left among you that saw this house in her first glory? And how do ye see it now? Is it not in your eyes in comparison of it as nothing?' Yes, the prophets today, many of them, like the prophet Haggai, ask me the same question, when they find I was at the old Azusa Street Mission in Los Angeles in 1906 when the Pentecostal power first fell which has spread all over the world, and I have to answer, like Haggai. They ask me, 'Is it not in your eyes in comparison of it as nothing?' (Haggai 2:3) and I have to answer, 'Yes, in my eyes, as nothing to compare to it,' and I find so many places I go, the assemblies ask me to tell them how it was at the Azusa Street Mission, and so many times I am led to say 'No flesh could glory' in His presence. As the saints would gather at the Azusa Street Mission, they felt they were treading upon holy ground. Our conversation would be yea, yea, nay, nay; so sacred was the very air we breathed, we did not stop to salute any man by the way, that is when we met there, we did not meet and shake hands with each other, we were so shut in with God, expecting to receive fresh manna right from Heaven. We felt all flesh should keep silent before the Lord, and upon entering the building, we would kneel at our seats or the altar, with tears dripping on the seats, as the Sun of Righteousness was melting our hearts, and when someone would begin to pound the seat, with their hand or fist while they were praying, Brother Seymour would go to them gently and tap them on the shoulder and say, 'Brother, that is the flesh.' And a holy hush and quietness would settle down upon those tarrying for the Baptism of the Holy Ghost. At times, some saint filled with the Spirit would be led to go and lay their hands upon them and they would be filled with the Holy Ghost, 'and the slain of the Lord were many.' In the testimony meetings when someone, or some preacher would get up in the audience to read some scripture and try to preach a sermon or give a long testimony, Brother

Seymour would get up and say, 'Dear loved ones, these meetings are different from any you ever saw in all your born days. These are Holy Ghost meetings and no flesh can glory in the presence of our God.'

My dear husband, Josie, used to say the Lord gave Brother Seymour wisdom to lead the people as he did to Moses. No one dared to get up and sing a song or testify except under the anointing of the Spirit. They feared lest the Holy Ghost would cut them off in their song or testimony. We would wait upon God expecting Him to use whom He would. Sometimes the Lord would have a small black girl arise in the audience with eyes closed, tears running down her cheeks and sing a song under the anointing of the Spirit. . ."[4]

What were these songs like, when "the Lord dropped down sweet anthems from the Paradise of God, electrifying every heart. . ."?[5] We have a brief description published in January of 1907:

### The Heavenly Anthem

"One of the most remarkable features of this Apostolic Faith Movement is what is rightly termed the heavenly anthem. No one but those who are baptized with the Holy Ghost are able to join in - or better, the Holy Ghost only sings through such in that manner. Hallelujah!

'I have heard and understand both in the Gujerathi and Hindustan languages, the singing of different Psalms and other portions of the Holy Scriptures. The singing is done in various foreign languages.' Geo. E. Berg,

Hermon, California, former missionary to India.

On Sunday night, December 9, a sister sang in the Gujerathi language of India, the first four verses of the eighth chapter of Solomon's Song. It was a song such as a bride might sing of the bridegroom. 'Awake not my beloved.' It was most blessed and beautiful to notice as the Holy Spirit sang through the dear sister, it brought a great wave of heavenly fire and blessings to those present.

Again a beautiful song was sung in tongues: 'Hosanna to the Son of David; Blessed is He that cometh in the Name of the Lord; Hosanna in the highest.' (Matt. 21:9). This was the greeting given our Savior at His triumphal entry into Jerusalem. The brother who understood the language said in the foreign tongue it was the sublimest poetry. At the same time, the room was filled with the glory of God.

We afterward learned of a remarkable coincidence. The same song was being sung at the Pentecostal Mission at 327 South Spring Street (where E.K. Fisher was the leader - Ed.) and was interpreted there the same. The saints worshipping in these two places were in perfect harmony of spirit, and the Holy Ghost witnessed to it.

At the all day meeting on Christmas, a day never to be forgotten, we had a Christmas in tongues. It began with one voice, just as on Bethlehem plains, and a chorus of voices joined in. It was interpreted by one who knew the language: 'Glory to God in the highest and on earth, peace, good will to men.' This was very sweet and heavenly. It followed the reading of the Scripture.

People are melted to tears in hearing this singing. It is the harmony of heaven and the Holy Ghost puts music in the voices that are untrained.''[6]

Concerning the Heavenly Anthem, Brother Bartleman has also written,

''The spirit of song given from God in the beginning was like the Aeolian harp in its spontaneity and sweetness. In fact, it was the very breath of God, playing on human vocal cords. The notes were wonderful in sweetness, volume and duration. In fact, they were ofttimes humanly impossible. It was indeed 'singing in the spirit'.''[7]

### Heavenly Music

This sweet heavenly music began to be manifested in Pentecostal worship across the country. In 1913, Sister Maria Woodworth-Etter held a convention at Long Hill, near Bridgeport, Connecticut. It was sandwiched in between the Worldwide Pentecostal Campmeeting at Arroyo Seco, California and the great Latter Rain convention at The Stone Church, in Chicago. Was the day of miracles over? Oh no - God was among His people with great power and Glory! And in response to the Rose of Sharon, the Altogether Lovely One, a great Song of Songs welled up from an enraptured Bride. The lovely Shulamite ''. . . found Him whom my soul loveth, held Him and would not let Him go''. Like the spikenard, very precious, that Mary anointed the feet of Christ with, the fragrance of this sweet heavenly music filled all the house:

''    Let me try to describe it for the benefit of

those that have never heard this glorious music. The meeting was in progress and the power of the Holy Ghost was resting upon us in a wonderful way. There was flowing from the hearts of the precious saints a stream of worship and praise of the most intense description - something which I never saw anywhere else, or in any meeting which I ever attended. I have seen love and worship flowing out to the Lord in many meetings in the past, but never before have I witnessed, and experienced, such intense worship and praise as I witnessed and experienced not only in our assembly at Ottawa, Canada, but also at the convention at Long Hill.

Suddenly there fell upon my ear - for the sound, strange to say, all seemed to pour into my right ear - a song of the most wonderful description. It did not at all appear like human voices, but seemed much more like the tones of some wonderful instrument of music, such as human ears never before heard. It began on the right side of the audience, and rolled from there over the entire company of baptized saints in a volume of sounds resembling in its rising and falling, its rolling and sinking, its swelling and receding character, the rolling waves of the ocean when being acted upon by the wonderful force which produces the tides. The nearest thing to which I can compare it is a complete band of skillful Italian violinists playing the most sacred music that could be imagined, combined with the mellow tones of a pipe-organ, and this is but a very poor description of what my ears heard.

71

Sometimes the sounds would rise to the highest possible pitch for human voices to utter, on the one hand, while at the same time in the company that went down to the lowest notes which could be sounded on a good organ. It was not simply the singing of four parts of music such as we do when we sing hymns, for, according to the notes we listen to, there is no telling how many parts is being sung, and it seemed to me there must have been scores of them. Such blending of tones, such perfect harmony of sounds, such musical strains, my ears never before heard, and I never expect to hear it again in this world under any other circumstances, not even from the most perfect band of music which human ingenuity can provide, and yet all these sounds were produced by a company of people which had that day gathered from all over the continent of North America, very few of whom had ever seen each other.

It would be just as impossible for men to train that company of people to sing the heavenly anthem as 'twould be to pull the sun down out of the sky, and yet there they were, singing it in the most perfect harmony that mortal ears ever listened to. It filled me with such holy awe, worship and praise to the Lord, that before I was able to realize the fact fully, the Holy Ghost lead me to join in that heavenly song of praise with the rest. Glory, and honor, and worship be rendered to Him forever.

My ears have been permitted to hear, and my own voice has been allowed to join them, the heavenly anthem which none but the redeemed and baptized saints can sing, and it has so ravished my heart with His beauty, and the glory that awaits all who suffer persecution for His dear name's sake, that all reproaches now seem as only a passing breath which can scarcely move a feather.''[8]

Indeed, it is as though Temple Worship has been restored again! God is ever unchanging. He manifests Himself today as at the Temple of Solomon. True Pentecostal worship still has the precious blood sprinkled *mercy seat*, the *Holy Fire* consuming the sacrifice, *Revelation and Truth*, the testimony of Jesus which is *the Spirit of Prophecy*, and the glorious bright, infolding, overflowing, fiery, covering *Shekinah*. Open the gates of the Temple!

Enter into His gates with thanksgiving, and into His courts with praise. Come before His presence with singing. Lift up your heads, O ye gates; and be ye lift up, ye everlasting doors. Lift up your heads, O ye gates; even lift them up, ye everlasting doors; and the King of glory shall come in.

### A Meeting At Old Azusa Mission

Many wonderful people have left accounts of their visits to the old Azusa Mission. In September of 1906, Ernest Williams, who was later to become one of the most diplomatic of Pentecostal statesmen, felt the leading of God to go down to Azusa Street.

"There I saw what I had never seen before. Although there was considerable inspiration in the meeting, it was the altar service at the conclusion that fascinated me. The front of the mission was packed with seekers and persons trying to assist them. Christians and unsaved spectators crowded around to see what was going on. Some at the altar were seeking

73

to be filled with the Holy Spirit; others were
worshipping God in unknown tongues. I looked on, not knowing what to think. My heart
was hungry for God.''[9]

Surely, such hunger would not go unsatisfied. Would you
like to go back to an evening at Old Azusa Mission and attend a meeting where the Shekinah was present in temples
of clay? One night, a visitor recorded the meeting in shorthand and it was published in *The Apostolic Faith* in April
of 1907. Here is the Report as published.

"The power of God came down in a marked manner on Monday, April 29, at Azusa
Mission, beginning especially in the
ministerial meeting held during the day and
culminating in the evening service, while
testimonies were being given by baptized
witnesses. To a returned missionary from
China upon whom the Pentecostal power is
now residing, the message was given in
tongues by one brother and interpreted by
another, 'Open thy mouth wide and I will fill
it, wait not for the words to be formed in your
mind, but give out just what the Spirit puts
within and let Him control.'

A sister who had been attending the
meetings some time, testified to having received liberty only recently, and said that on
visiting a sick woman during the day, the Lord
had convinced an unbelieving girl. Upon this,
the husband of this witness arose and spoke
in tongues very forcibly, but the interpretation was not given until the brother in charge
of the meeting, had told how this sister had
received liberty by going and for the first time
seeking to help the unsaved in a meeting, after

which the message in tongues was translated with even more power as: 'Oh, how we praise the Lord for the way He works; when we go to do a work for Him, He will work another by His Spirit through us. He wants to teach us that His ways are not our ways, nor His thoughts our thoughts, but as the heaven is high above the earth, so are His ways higher than our ways and His thoughts than our thoughts.'

A little later in the evening, as a young colored brother was testifying, he began to sing in another language: 'O Jesus, Thou wonderful savior.' After a few more words of praise to God in his own language, he sang in another beautifully: 'Oh, see how the King comes in triumph,' upon which the power was so great that many baptized believers arose one after another and joined in a mighty chorus in the Spirit, while the young brother went on with his testimony and then sang: 'Oh, pour out your hearts before Him and bend yourselves in obedience.' Whereat the leader of the meeting arose and, although he had not heard the interpretation of these messages, cried out: 'Come to the altar! Come to the altar!' And the young messenger continued in a tongue: 'Oh, seek the Lord while He may be found, call upon Him while He is near to you', and another brother spoke forcefully in another language to the hearts of the people: 'Oh, turn to Him while He is calling today and seek Him while He may be found.'

The interpretation of these messages was

not given out at the time, but recorded in shorthand. The effect of the manifestation of the Spirit's power was, however, immediate and very marked, for the people came forward to the altar and fell all around under the power of the Holy Spirit, demons being cast out in the name of Jesus, saints being quickened, and four receiving the Baptism with the Holy Ghost with the evidence of speaking in tongues.

To those who ask why we should speak in tongues and what use it is unless understood by those to whom the message is given, this report is sufficient evidence that it is not by the understanding of mind or by great intellect that God would speak to the children of men, but in the mighty power and demonstration of the Holy Ghost.[10]

Azusa Mission, Thursday Evening, May 1

After some hearty singing and earnest prayer, a converted Jewish brother testified. Then a little boy mounted the altar and said plainly: 'I thank the Lord for saving me, and now I am seeking the Baptism. I want you to pray for me, that I may get it. Tonight, I had a toothache and I prayed for the Lord to take it away, and He took it away.'

A sister said: 'Rejoice in the Lord. Rejoice always, and again I say rejoice. I am rejoicing in His life, I am rejoicing in His presence with me, I am rejoicing in His unchangeableness, I am rejoicing in His faithfulness, I am resting on His promises, and looking and expecting Him moment by

76

moment. Hallelujah! Hallelujah! Praise our God forever.'

A black brother arose and sang the verse of a hymn, the people joined in the chorus: 'The Blood, the Blood, is all my plea; Hallelujah, it cleanseth me.' He then said: 'Hallelujah! I am so glad I can testify that the Blood cleanseth me. Oh, the sweetness! My heart is full of love for Jesus. I am so glad I can take up the cross and work with Him now and follow Him. Oh, I know I am leaning on the Almighty arm.'

An old gentleman who has recently received the Baptism said: 'Just take the blessings that God sends down to us. Oh, I thank God that He has found an old man, a sinner like me. I was not worthy of anything, but He gave Himself to me. O glory, O glory!' (Then he spoke in another language, the interpretation being): 'Glory to Thee, my Great Redeemer, for Thy great love towards me. O, how I praise Thee.' (He continued in English) 'Oh, glory to God for the gift He has given me. Now if there is any sinner here tonight, seek Him. Now we all may have it without money.'

Another testified as follows: 'I praise God tonight that I am under the Blood; Jesus' Blood covers me and cleanses me from all sin.'

Someone else said: 'I know that the Blood of Jesus saves me and sanctifies me and keeps me from day to day. He is my Healer, I praise Him and thank Him for the way He is increasing my faith and instructing me today. The Lord gave me a verse since I have been standing here: 'Wait on the Lord, be of good courage, and He shall strengthen thine heart.' I am just standing on His promises. With His stripes I am healed. I praise Him and thank Him with all my heart. He saves me and sanctifies me and baptizes me with the Holy Ghost.'

A new song of much power was then sung through in the Spirit by all.

'Jesus Christ is made to me
All I need, all I need
He alone is all my plea,
He is all I need.

Chorus -  Wisdom, Righteousness and Power,
Holiness, forever more
My Redemption full and sure,
He is all I need.'

A brother testifies: 'There is power in my soul tonight because God put it in there: it is the power of the Spirit that came down from the throne of God, from the Everlasting Father, before whom we must one day stand and give an account of the deeds done in the body. Oh, how careful we as professing Christians ought to walk before this ungodly generation. The Lord showed me a few years ago that out of California would come a movement that would startle the world, and here is this prophecy fulfilled. Praise God for this personal Pentecost.' He then said in another tongue: 'Jesus died that you might be saved. Oh, be saved tonight and seek Him with all the heart, and let Him have His way.'

A young black sister then said: 'I want to praise God tonight. He is all in all to me. Glory to Jesus. Dear ones, you do not know how sweet it is to trust Jesus. Do not sit back laughing and scoffing - Oh, you are laughing at Jesus, not us.' (In tongues) 'He that sitteth in the heavens shall laugh, the Lord shall have them in derision, Oh, why do you not come unto Me that ye might have life? Oh, why do you resist My pleadings with you at this time? Oh why do you not come to Me and turn to Me with thy heart?'' Dear ones, accept this blessed salvation, I do praise my blessed Redeemer for saving me from sin, for giving me a clean heart. When I was a sinner, I would go to church and look around laughing, but then I did not know I was laughing at Jesus, but praise God, He is all in all to me now. He has taken all the laugh out of me, all criticism. He has given me a perfect heart and filled me with love. Dear ones, oh it is precious to have a clean heart. He saved my soul and He has baptized me with the Holy Ghost.' (In tongues) 'O, why do you resist the strivings of the Spirit? Why do you not turn to Him in repentance?' 'Dear ones, it is so sweet to walk with Jesus. I take Him as my Healer. He heals all my diseases. O, glory to God.' (in tongues:) 'Why do you not look to Him and live at this time?'

Bro. W. J. Seymour then started the congregation singing:

'Jesus, Jesus, how I trust Thee,
How I've proved Thee o'er and o'er,

Jesus, Jesus, blessed Jesus,
Oh, for grace to trust Thee more.'

He then said: 'Beloved, I want to say good night to you all for a short while. It has now been over a year ago since I left Texas and came up in this portion of the country to labor and work for the Lord, and I am going back there through that old state where the Lord called me from a year ago. I am going to pass through there and see those precious children that prayed with me for Pentecost, and while I am gone, I want you all to pray that God may use me to His own honor and glory.

I want to read some of God's own precious Word in the first chapter of the book of Isaiah.' (He read to verse nine and then said) 'I am so glad the Lord God has raised up a people right in Los Angeles, and San Francisco, they seem like Sodom and Gomorrah, but out of these cities, the Lord God has raised up a people for His holy name. He has cleansed them from sin, He has sanctified them, and has baptized them with the Holy Ghost, and sealed them unto the day of Redemption. Glory to His holy name! I can go and rejoice with the people in Texas, telling them of the wonderful things that God has done in Los Angeles. They said I should be back in a month's time, and now this is the first chance I have had to get back.'

(He then read to the end of verse 20.) 'But if ye refuse and rebel, ye shall be devoured with the sword: for the mouth of the Lord hath spoken it.' 'Every man, every church, every home, that rejects the full Gospel of the Lord and Savior, Jesus Christ, shall be devoured. We are living in a time when the Holy Ghost is working -O, bless God - convincing men and women of sin and righteousness and judgment, and every man and every woman that hardens their heart against the Word of God shall fail. If the men and women of this city will repent and turn from their sin and accept our Lord and Savior, Jesus Christ, 'Ye shall eat the good of the land.' Glory to His holy name! God has fat things to feed all His hungry people. Oh, He will fill you tonight. Oh, the music will be singing in your soul and, oh, the love of Christ that passes all understanding will be dwelling in your heart. Just read what He says: 'If ye be willing and obedient, ye shall eat the good of the land.' Jesus says: 'Abide in me, as the branch cannot bear fruit of itself except it abide in the vine, no more can ye except ye abide in Me.' Oh, beloved, if we abide in the words of the Lord Jesus Christ and feed off of Christ, I'll tell you, we shall live off the good of the land, - bless His holy name. We will have the fat - bless God - we will have everything to cheer our heart, we shall have healing and health and salvation in our souls. Oh, glory to His holy name. Oh, do not refuse the Word of God. Oh, accept it, accept all the doctrine of our Lord and Savior, Jesus Christ, and oh, beloved, it will fill your hearts with good things.

But just listen to what He says: 'If ye refuse and rebel, ye shall be devoured with the sword: for the mouth of the Lord hath spoken it.' Beloved, if you reject Christ, if you reject

His precious Blood, if you reject the Holy
Ghost, ye shall be devoured with the sword:
but if you accept Jesus Christ, He will prepare
a table before you and the Lord God Himself
will spread it and He will feed you Himself.
When Jesus had gotten through feeding His
disciples, He told His disciples to feed his
lambs and sheep. What are we going to feed
them with? We are going to feed them with
the precious Word of God. We are going to
teach them to accept Jesus Christ as their
Savior and as their Sanctifier to destroy the
root of sin, and then we are going to teach
them to accept the Holy Ghost. He shall baptize them with the Holy Ghost and fire, and
when He comes in, He is going to speak
through them, and He says 'In the last days,
I will pour out of My Spirit on all flesh.' Glory
to His holy name. I want to say 'Good night'
to you.

'God be with you till we meet again' was
then sung as Brother Seymour shook hands
with as many as possible and left for the train.
Brother Anderson spoke a few words of encouragement to the saints on the necessity of
our continuing faithful in the pastor's
absence.''[11]

How like the true temple worship this must have been, for
the Spirit of Prophecy, the Holy Fire and the Shekinah were
all present, not to mention the temple music. Only a barn
- but Heaven touched Earth, and Christ Himself was there.

How could it ever come to an end? Aimee Semple McPherson mentioned in a note in 1936 that:

"The tiny Mission has long since crumbl-
ed. Its dusky portals no longer ring with the

shout of Hosannas. Eager feet of hungering
saints no longer tread its dusky cobblestones.
The passerby has long since ceased to pause
and look in wonder at the strange sight of
black faces intermingled with those of white;
lifted in raptured blessing, 'neath the Latter
Rain.''[12]

I believe that the old mission was, in fact, torn down in
the late 1920's. Why did it cease? I'm sure there are many
answers. Pentecost is in no need of an earthly shrine. The
topic can be discussed by others more knowledgeable than
I. However, Frank Bartleman wrote,

"If ever men shall seek to control, corner
or own this work of God, either for their own
glory or for that of an organization, we shall
find the Spirit refusing to work. The Glory
will depart.''[13]

By the close of 1909, things were already changing at Azusa
Street and Bartleman laments, ''But at this time old Azusa
Mission became more and more in bondage. The meetings
had to run in appointed order.''[14]

When the power was there and the Glory was falling,
Rachel Sizelove said,

''. . . No one dared to say, 'We will now
have a song by brother or sister so and so,'
and then as they would come to the front to
sing, for the congregation to clap their hands
and laud them for their singing. O, no! O, how
the Holy Ghost did detect strange fire that
would try to creep in, and how the burden
would come upon the saints while they would
be sitting in their seats.

The one that would try to bring in strange
fire would have to sit down or they would be
rebuked by the Holy Ghost. The sin of Nadab

and Abihu was in acting in the things of God without seeking the mind of God. (read Lev. 10:1). It was will worship (Col. 2:23) which often has a show of 'wisdom' and humility. It typifies any use of carnal means to kindle the fire of devotion and praise.

A few years ago, Josie and I were on our way through the East, and hearing of a camp meeting where hundreds of people were gathering, we drove past and stopped and were given a place where we could park our car and put our tent. I was tired and went to bed, when it was time to begin the meeting, and O, such crowds of people gathered. I heard drums beating and different kinds of instruments, it was so worldly, nothing sacred about it. I thought, O these dear people, some coming for miles to a supposedly Pentecostal campmeeting and to hear such worldly music, next to nothing to compare with the heavenly music we had at the old Azusa Street Mission in its first glory, for they had no earthly instruments, but the heavenly choir, and no mortal tongue can describe the glory that filled the place while all the saints stood with hands raised to heaven, eyes closed and all singing in the Spirit.

No, we do not hear such singing now, I Cor. 14:15. The next day as we went out to the meeting, the pastor or superintendent of the campmeeting heard there was a sister in the audience that was in the Azusa Street Mission in Los Angeles when the power first fell and called on me to tell my experience of the first outpouring of the Pentecostal revival. I told how they had no piano, drums, or any musical instruments of any kind and no visiting or talking among the saints, but a continual waiting upon God, they had no strange fire, which typifies any use of carnal means to kindle the fire of devotion and praise. Brother Seymour would never say, 'All stand to your feet and reach up your hands and praise the Lord.' But O, how wonderful when the Holy Ghost would raise them to their feet and they would sing in the Spirit. O, how could the Holy Ghost have right of way if they had carnal instruments to depend on. I told how the Holy Ghost would come upon people and shake them off their seats, especially when the Lord began to deal with a soul and they began to draw back, the Lord would shake them until they would surrender and say yes to God. While I was telling this assembly of how they acted at Azusa Street Mission, the power of God began to take hold of people. They were so hungry for the old time power. They began to come running down to the altar and the power of God began to shake them in their seats all over the audience. Many were slain under the mighty power of God.

O, how hungry they were to get back to the old time power. The altar was full, -some calling on God. I sat down when I saw the Lord had the reins of the meeting in His own hands. As soon as I sat down, the pastor or superintendent of the meeting, who had asked me to speak, arose and said, 'Let all at the altar take their seats.' Most of them raised up and went back to their seats, some remained at the altar, but O, the Holy Dove took its flight. God could not work. Josie and I went to our tent. Many followed us crying and saying, 'O, we want the old time power you told us about;' and many left the campmeeting because they felt the brother would not let the Holy Ghost have His way.

While the Holy Ghost was having His right of way at the Azusa Street Mission, money was not spoken of. They had a small mail box nailed to a post that was in the center of the mission with the words printed above it, 'Free Will Offerings'. Many times when it was opened, it would be full of gold and silver. It was never mentioned to the assembly to raise money for the missionaries going out from there to all parts of the world. As long as the Holy Ghost had right of way, their needs were all supplied. When the Lord would speak to some one in the audience many times about giving to the Lord, and they would draw back, the Lord would shake them off their seats until they would say yes to God.

I saw a brother who owned a large orange grove, and the Lord spoke to him to give some certain one going to the foreign fields to take the message, quite a sum of money. As he sat in the Mission, the Lord speaking to him about it, he began to draw back, and how well I remember we had to move the chairs out of his way when the Lord shook him off of his seat and shook him around upon the floor. We did not know at the time what it all meant, but the brother told the saints how God was dealing with him and made him say, 'yes,

Lord.'

But alas, how well I remember the first time the flesh began to get in the way of the Holy Ghost, and how the burden came upon the saints that morning when Brother Seymour stood before the audience and spoke of raising money to buy the Azusa Street Mission. The Holy Ghost was grieved. You could feel it all over the audience, when they began to ask for money, and the Holy Ghost power began to leave, and instead of the Holy Ghost heavenly choir, they brought in a piano. They had never had any kind of a carnal instrument before. It reminded me of the scripture where Peter said to Jesus. 'Lord, it is good for us to be here.' (Matt. 17:4)''[15]

Brother Bartleman has described these agonizing changes in similar terms. For the disciples on the mountain top, it was good to have been there. The experience would stay with the Apostle Peter to the end of his life. As an old man, he would write, concerning the transfiguration of Christ, we ''. . . were eyewitnesses of His majesty.'' (II Peter 1:18). But there was work to be done. In contrast to the mountain top scene of the transfiguration, at the foot of the mount there was a demoniac child to be healed. The glory which was beheld upon the mountain top was to prepare those disciples to pass victoriously through the valley and conflict which was before them.

And similarly, it is so with the Pentecostal blessing. Not only does the glory put the ''go'' in your feet, but it empowers one to minister in what would otherwise be hopeless and impossible situations. As with the Levitical feasts, after Pentecost comes a time of busy months, during which a harvest is to be gathered in.

## REFERENCES

1. **Talmud** (Yoma, f. 21, C. 2)
2. **The Temple**, by Alfred Eidersheim, Eerdmans Publishing Co., Grand rapids, Mich., 1978, Pg. 62.
3. **Antiquities of the Jews**, Josephus, translated by William Whiston, 1737. Reprinted by Kregel Publications, Grand Rapids, Michigan, 1960. Book VIII, Chapter IV, paragraphs 2,4, PP. 176-178.
4. "The Temple", by Rachel Sizelove, *Word and Work*, Vol. 58, No. 5, May, 1936, PP. 1,2,12.
5. *The Apostolic Faith*, Vol. 1, No. 4, December,1906, Pg. 2. Reprinted in **Like As of Fire**.
6. Reference 5, Vol. 1, No. 5, January, 1907, Pg. 3.
7. **How Pentecost Came To Los Angeles**, by Frank Bartleman, 3rd edition, 1925. Reprinted as **Another Wave Rolls In**, Voice Publications, Northridge, Ca., 1962,Pg. 58. (Reprinted as **Another Wave of Revival**, WhitakerHouse, Springdale, Pa.,1982).
8. **Signs And Wonders**, by Marie Woodworth-Etter, 1916. Reprinted by Harrison House, Tulsa, Oklahoma, PP. 261-263.
9. "My Personal Experience at the Azusa Mission", by Earnest S. Williams, printed as Chapter 13 in **Touched By The Fire**, Edited by Wayne Warner, Logos International, Plainfield, New Jersey, 1978, PP. 45-46.
10. *The Apostolic Faith*, Vol. 1, No. 7, April,1907, Pg. 2. Reprinted in **Like As of Fire**.
11. *The Apostolic Faith*, Vol. 1, No. 7, April,1907, Pg. 2. Reprinted in **Like As of Fire**.
12. From a note by Aimee Semple McPherson, sent to *Word and Work* on April 30, 1936.
13. **How Pentecost Came To Los Angeles**, by Frank Bartleman, 3rd edition, 1925. Reprinted as **Another**

**Wave Rolls In**, Voice Publications, Northridge, Ca., 1962, Pg. 90. (Reprinted as **Another Wave of Revival**, Whitaker House, Springdale, Pa.,1982).

14.     Reference 13, Pg. 104.

15.     ''The Temple'', by Rachel Sizelove, *Word and Work*, Vol. 58, No. 5, May, 1936, PP. 1,2,12.

# Chapter VI

## AZUSA'S FIRST CAMPMEETING

"God is breathing down on that site. Every time I go out to it, Heaven seems to open."

R.J. Scott

**A**lthough not an American creation, campmeetings and the historical development of the "Campmeeting" phenomenon in North America is a wonderful story. Its great impact upon society has been woven throughout the tapestry of our pioneering history. Describing these frontier gatherings, one of the campmeeting evangelists from the early 1800's, Peter Cartwright, has written:

"Somewhere between 1800 and 1801, in the upper part of Kentucky, at a memorable place called 'Cane Ridge', there was appointed a sacramental meeting by some of the Presbyterian ministers; at which meeting, seemingly unexpected by ministers or people, the power of God was displayed in a very extraordinary manner; many were moved to tears and cried aloud for mercy. . . The meeting was protracted for weeks. . . Ministers of almost all denominations flocked in from far and near. The meeting was kept up by night and day. Thousands heard of the mighty work, and came on foot, on horseback, in carriages and wagons. It is supposed that there were in attendance at times during the meeting from twelve to twenty-five thousand people. Hundreds fell prostrate under the mighty power of God, as men slain in battle.

From this campmeeting, for so it ought to

be called, the news spread through all the churches, and through all the land, and it excited great wonder and surprise; but it kindled a religious flame that spread over Kentucky, and through many other States. And I may here be permitted to say, that this was the first campmeeting ever held in the United States, and here our campmeetings took their rise.''[1]

The campmeeting phenomenon has been a marvelous vehicle for the spreading of the gospel throughout America. The old Methodist circuit riding preachers and evangelists would reach multitudes with the message of salvation and holiness at these meetings.

Grandma Harper has often told us about the old campmeetings that she attended as a little girl in Kentucky and Indiana during the 1840's and 1850's. She remembers seeing the women dancing in the Spirit, their long braided hair snapping like a buggy whip as they shook under the power of God. Soon great Holiness campmeetings would be held all across the United States. And later, when the Pentecostal fire fell, it was common for it to spread abroad among these people that were seeking the Lord, and it was natural for Pentecostal people to start holding campmeetings themselves.

During the Summer of 1907, a great campmeeting was sponsored by the little Azusa Street Mission. People ask today, ''Whatever happened to the Azusa Street Mission and why did conditions change there? Why isn't the Glory Cloud still hovering over the old mission?'' I believe the answer to these questions rests upon the fact that when the Glory fell, it set people on fire and they literally radiated out like shooting stars from the old mission. The original workers went as missionaries, workers and evangelists, beaming the glorious Full Gospel message to the ends of the earth. Once they were filled with Shekinah and souls were aglow with heavenly fire, they could only burn like flaming stars for His Glory. They went forward with whatever ventures the Lord placed upon their hearts. And new generations of workers had to be raised up to take their places.

One such venture was this great summer Campmeeting. The crowds had been growing and the old mission could no longer contain the multitudes that were seeking God. The Lord's leading was simultaneously revealed to several of the Azusa workers and it was clear that He desired expanded facilities for the summer. And so the old mission closed down during the day and moved out to the campgrounds for the whole summer, although a small group of saints returned to maintain worship each evening at Azusa Street. At the campmeeting, hundreds received the Pentecostal blessing and went forth bearing precious seed back to their own worlds. Rachel Sizelove told us the story many times while we were children, and later on sent me some notes on it. I wrote them up and published them in one of the old issues of *Word and Work*. Here is the story substantially as I published it in January of 1936.

### Azusa's First Campmeeting
#### By the Editor

''At the time of the marvelous outpouring of the Holy Spirit in 1906 and 1907, Rachel Harper Sizelove was living in Hermon, California. While she lay asleep one night, she dreamed of seeing many little white tents pitched at the Arroyo Seco, at the foot of the hill there in Hermon. When she awoke, she pondered as to the meaning of the dream.

'Oh Jesus!', she said, 'can it be possible you will let us have a campmeeting right here near my own people, the Free Methodist Colony?'

They were the people with whom she had

labored for twenty years and ministered as an evangelist, traveling and preaching all through Oklahoma, Kansas, Missouri, Arkansas and Indiana. She was delighted to discover that it seemed to be the will of the Lord to have a campmeeting there so that the Free Methodist people could receive the light on Pentecost and receive the Baptism of the Holy Spirit according to the scriptures.

She arose early and told her husband of the dream. Then she hastened down into Los Angeles to the Azusa Street Mission to tell the saints what the Lord had revealed to her about the campground. Brother Seymour and the saints had been praying about a campmeeting and had been looking for a place for the summer. The Azusa Mission could not hold all the people, for they kept coming from all parts of the earth to see and hear of the wonderful outpouring of the Holy Spirit as on the day of Pentecost.

She arrived at the Azusa Street Mission early in the morning and went into the office. Some of the consecrated workers were already at work folding and mailing out the Azusa papers. Before the papers were sent out, the saints would lay on their hands and pray over them and many were healed when they received the paper, so strong was the faith, as in the days of the apostles, when they prayed and laid hands on aprons and clothes and sent them to the sick. The faithful saints worked here without receiving money for themselves.

Brother Ruben Clark was working in the office. He was a Civil War veteran, and received a pension and was able to devote his time to this work. According to the February-March, 1907 issue of *The Apostolic Faith*, Brother Clark was secretary of the Azusa Street Board of Trustees. He was such a pillar in the office to see about sending out the papers. He was never married. Brother Tommy Anderson, who is now a missionary in South America, was also there. Sister Lum was also there that morning. God surely had chosen her. She took down so many of the testimonies at Azusa in shorthand, which were published in the Azusa paper. She had never married, and her life was given to the Lord. Sister Mayo and her sister, Mrs. Perkins, were there. All were filled with the Holy Ghost.

Mrs. Sizelove told them what the Lord had revealed to her and asked them where to find Brother and Sister Scott. While they were talking, Brother Scott came into the office. The Lord had also revealed to him that He would bring His people together for a great campmeeting. In the Azusa papers, we read (Vol. I, No. 8, Pg.2): 'He had not been able to sleep for thinking of it and where to have it.' Brother Scott had been a prosperous farmer in Canada, but the Lord had called him to Azusa and into the ministry. He had come with his wife and little daughter, Kathleen, then twelve years of age. The Lord mightily used the little girl. At one time, she gave a message in tongues and a man who had come from Chicago to investigate Azusa understood the language. It was a message to him to come to the Lord. He knew the little girl did not understand the language. He surrendered to the Lord and was saved. Before that, he had been an infidel.

That morning, the people gathered around and prayed for the Lord to direct them where to have their first Pentecostal Campmeeting. Then Sister Sizelove, Sister Lum, Sister Mayo, Brother Scott, and Brother Anderson got on the street car and later got off at 60th and Pasadena Avenue. They went down near the Los Angeles River where there was a large grove of sycamore trees, called the Arroyo Seco at the foot of the hill near the Free Methodist Colony.

In the Azusa papers, Sister Sizelove wrote, '...As we landed there, every step we took seemed to praise God. As we walked down the Arroyo, heaven came down our souls to greet, and we said, 'Surely God is in it.' After wading around through the tall grass and weeds and locating a lovely spot where the camp meeting was to be, they went over to the home of Sister Williams which was close by. In her yard was a well where hung an old oaken bucket. They drew the cool water from the well and all drank for they were thirsty. Then they looked out over the campground-to-be and, according to one of the committee, 'As we began to drink, we thought of how God will water thirsty souls there, and we sang,

> 'By Samaria's wayside well,
> Once a blessed message fell,
> On a woman's thirsty soul long ago.'

They sang in the Spirit until it seemed the old earth was losing its gravity and they would be translated right there. Surely the Spirit of God witnessed to the choice of the camp ground, a place to which many thirsty souls would come and drink of the living water.. . . Surely it looks like the land of Beulah around there. Then they went back to Azusa and told how the Spirit had witnessed to the spot where the first Pentecostal campmeeting should be held. A campmeeting committee was appointed and the meeting was to begin June lst, 1907, and was to last three months or as long as the Lord willed.''[2]

Immediately, word of the coming 'Pentecostal' camp-meeting began to spread. The following description was published on the front page of the May, 1907 issue of *The Apostolic Faith*:

Los Angeles Campmeeting of the Apostolic Faith
Missions

"We expect to have a grand campmeeting in Los Angeles, beginning June 1, and conti-nuing about four months.

The spot selected for it is adjoining the ci-ty limits, several miles from the center of town in a grove of sycamore and live oak trees near Hermon. The fare is only five cents on the electric cars which run every seven minutes. It is only three blocks from where the cars stop to the campmeeting.

We expect to have a tabernacle with seating capacity of about one thousand people. There will be room in the grove for many tents. Free camping grounds. The air is fresh with the sea breeze which comes in from the distant ocean, and there is plenty of good water. You can pray there as loud as you like. There are wooded hills all about which we expect will ring with the songs and prayers of the saints and shouts of newborn souls.

There will be a separate tabernacle for meetings for the children with services daily, so it will be a children's campmeeting as well as a grown up people's meeting. There will be competent workers to teach and help them spiritually. We expect it to be a time of salvation among the children. Mother's meetings are also planned for.

Workers from all missions in and about Los Angeles who are one with us, by virtue of having been baptized by one Spirit into the body, are uniting in this campmeeting. Services will be continued in Azusa Mission every night, just the same as ever, a band going from the campmeeting to carry on the work. Other missions will also carry on their work.

A large band of Holy Ghost workers, men and women, whom God has equipped for His service will be present to carry on the meeting, under the guidance of our blessed Redeemer whom we honor as the great Leader and Manager. Much prayer is going up to God that He will make this a time of visiting His people with salvation and an outpouring of

Pentecost such as we have never witnessed before. The business part of the work is being arranged in orderly and systematic shape. Proper officers will have charge of the grounds; putting up tents, etc.

The workers from the different missions first met to counsel together about the campmeeting. We got down to ask the Lord for the money, and the witness came that prayer was heard, the Spirit was poured out upon us. We arose and decided to lease the grounds for four months. Before the meeting was over, the power of God so filled the room that one fell under the power and the meeting turned into a Pentecostal Service.

A number are willingly giving their services in clearing and preparing the grounds. No collections have been taken, but several hundred dollars have already been offered for the campmeeting. God hears prayer and is putting His seal on it.''[3]

Brother Scott wrote a letter to the public and it was published in the same issue of *The Apostolic Faith*, on page two.

The Lord's Leading for the Campmeeting

''God has just awakened me and said: 'Get up and write. My people must be called together. I have called this mighty campmeeting that I might get a chance to speak to My people. I am coming soon and I have great things to show them.' Glory to His Name!

Dear ones, I expected to be back in Winnipeg, Canada, ere this, and would have been had not God spoken so plainly to me on the night of April 6, just after coming through three days of fasting and praying that God

98

would show me what I was to do. About midnight, I heard a rap at my door. I awoke and listened, and while listening, Jesus appeared in a door about six feet wide and eight feet high, standing, it seemed, between me and heaven, with His arms stretched out and a most beautiful mantle covering Him to the tips of His fingers, and said to me: 'It is not my will that you should take your family back to Winnipeg just now.' And He disappeared. I then fell asleep, but again the same knocking as before came on my door and awoke me. This time, I was more certain than ever that someone was at my door, and as I listened for the knock to be repeated again, Jesus appeared in the same position as He had just disappeared, only this time, more beautiful than these eyes can behold, and as I saw past the edge of His mantle, oh, such a light, man cannot imagine or eyes behold, oh, how pure and white -methinks I yet can see - and with outstretched arms He said to me: 'Go, tell My people, behold I come quickly;' and again disappeared as before. Oh, glory to His Name. Behold, He comes so soon. Oh, get ready, dear ones. Oh, how God had blessed me and my dear family since the last issue of the paper.

On the night of April 23, I could not sleep. God talked to me all night about a big camp-meeting that would bring His people together from far and wide, that He might talk to them. I found on reaching the Mission, He had also been talking to two sisters, saints of God, who were waiting when I got there, to tell me. So we at once started to the proposed grounds, and as I stepped on the place we have now selected to erect the large Tabernacle, my heart seemed to stop and my bosom filled - Oh, glory, glory, to God - and I said to one of the party: 'This is the place,' but one of them said: 'No, there is a nicer place up the creek on the other side.' So up we went, crossing the creek, but no other place seemed to have any charm. We went down the creek and crossed back, coming up the other side. I must confess, they had me lost, but as we went up the bank of the stream and came to a most beautiful cluster of oaks, my heart seemed to stop again, my bosom filled with joy, as I again remarked to my friend: 'Oh, this is strange, why this seems to be the place.' and he looked at me and said: 'This is the same place.' Then my heart seemed to say: 'Glory, glory, glory, O, glory to my Redeemer.' Oh, that is a holy spot. God is breathing down on that site. Every time I go out to it, heaven seems to open. Glory to God in the highest.

Last week, I went out to locate some improvements on the ground, and as we came to one beautiful spot where the dear brethren were working, getting the ground ready, they gathered around us, and as we sang, 'What a friend we have in Jesus', God poured out His Spirit. We knelt down to have prayer, and as we prayed, God opened heaven and spoke through us in unknown tongues as the Spirit gave us utterance. O, glory to God. As we arose from our knees and I looked upon the faces of the dear ones, they seemed to light up with joy, and they said: 'Why, this is a happy place, we would rather be here than even at Azusa Street.' On this spot, we have decided to place our Children's Tabernacle.

Oh, dear ones, come to this campmeeting. If you cannot come, you can help us with your prayers.

Yours in Jesus,
R.J. Scott''[4]

### More Azusa Street Testimonies

We have mentioned the names of several more Azusa Street workers: Ruben Clark, Tommy Anderson, Sister Mayo, Sister Perkins, Brother and Sister Scott. Fortunately, the personal testimonies of some of these saints have been preserved. Let us listen to the expressions of their joyful hearts.

### Tom Anderson

"Beloved, I was saved about seventeen months ago, from a wretched life. When I called on God, He heard my prayer and saved me instantly. What convinced me of the reality in salvation was the peace that came into my heart. The desire for opiates went out immediately, and I was cured of the drug habit. The Lord has also healed many others of the drug habit. And God has healed my body, after being afflicted over six and a half years. When physicians failed, the Man, Christ Jesus, healed me. The devil had me bound hand and foot for years. Thinking myself wise, I became foolish. But beloved, God sent His transforming power through the Blood of Jesus and burst all the shackles, and

101

shook off the handcuffs of hell, and today I am a free man in Christ Jesus. Then He sanctified me wholly and gave me a clean heart. Then He baptized me with the Holy Ghost on Jan. 22, at Azusa Mission. Dear ones, all I live for is Christ. I sold out; body, soul, and spirit to Him. My desire is to point souls to the bleeding Lamb of Calvary that takes away the sin of the world. The Holy Ghost, the third person of the Trinity, speaks through me in the languages of the nations whenever He chooses. And He is now engaged in pulling the rope which rings the joy bells of heaven in my heart. And there is a revival going on in my soul continually, and the choir is singing and praising God in the unknown tongues. The Holy Ghost is the leader and is well qualified. He came from the college in heaven. Beloved, it is no more I, but Christ. To Him be all the glory."[5]

About a year later, Brother Anderson was in Winnipeg, Manitoba, Canada, and he wrote:

"I am here in Winnipeg and the glory of God is upon me. I can feel the Holy Ghost walking up and down in my innermost being and the cloven tongues of fire are burning from my head to the soles of my feet. I feel my nothingness and so unworthy to preach the Gospel, . . . God spoke to me a few days ago and asked me if I would be willing to sit at everyone's feet and be nothing, that He might be glorified, so that is my prayer to get deeper down yet and stay at the feet of Christ."[6]

Brother Anderson soon would go as a Missionary to Ecuador, Bolivia, and Venezuela.[7]

### Mary P. Perkins

By the way, the photograph of the Azusa Street Credentials Committee which has so often been reproduced was owned by Sister Perkins, and she gave it to G.B. Studd to pass on to Rachel Sizelove for publication in *Word and Work* back in 1934-1936 - F.T.C.

> ". . . . When I first came from San Jose here last May, I heard of these meetings and came down to see. I had not been in the house an hour before I knew God's Spirit was here, and I commenced seeking the Baptism with the Holy Ghost. And, glory to God, He came and completely deluged my soul and body, until I hardly knew whether I was in the body or out. And as the Holy Ghost came upon me, I saw Jesus sitting upon a cloud looking at me and at the congregation, and He said He was coming soon. My tongue commenced to move, and I spoke in an unknown tongue as the Spirit gave utterance. In prayer, I often speak in a foreign tongue and at home or in meeting, I often am moved to speak in tongues. Bless God! Glory!"[8]

### May F. Mayo

Sister Mayo had been a worker at the little Peniel Mission Hall at 227 South Main Street in Pasadena. Sister Mayo and Mary Perkins were sisters.

### A Peniel Worker Baptized

"O, magnify the Lord with me, and let us exalt His name together. For He that is mighty hath done to me great things: and holy is His name.' When I was getting ready for my vacation last July 1, I said, 'How I would love to

103

go to a real live campmeeting this summer.' Well, Praise the Lord, I found one and have been in it ever since.

When I went into the little church in Monrovia, the last Sunday in July, I did not know what God had in store for me, but I am glad I went. Some of the Apostolic Faith people were holding meetings there....

I went to the altar and began to pray, 'O Lord, give me the Chinese language.' Some one said, 'Hadn't you better let God have His way?' As I prayed, I found I did not have the witness of my sanctification. I prayed until God gave me the witness that the work was done. The power of God came on me and I was prostrated. I was always afraid of such demonstration, and as soon as I could, I got up. Someone said, 'You have the Baptism, claim it.' But I knew better. I was tired of claiming something I was not sure I had.....

On Thursday, I went to the church again. Soon after I sat down, I began to shake. I said, 'Lord, you shall have your way with me.' Soon I found myself on the floor and for about five hours, the Lord had His way. . . . I cried out, 'O Lord, give me the Baptism of the Holy Ghost, and I don't care if I never speak in tongues.' Soon I felt the power of God upon me in a mighty way and I began to speak in an unknown language and to sing with one of the workers who was praying with me. My hands began to move swiftly over my body, and I knew I was asking for healing, my hands went to my eyes and my glasses were taken off and laid on the floor and I have never had them on since. When I got up, I knew I had the Baptism with the Holy Ghost, and I have it today. Hallelujah! Rom. 8:ll has been fulfilled to me. Praise His Holy Name. 'This is the way I long have sought and mourned because I found it not.' This life in the Holy Ghost is blessed. I never had the joy and freedom and power I have now. The shouts roll without any effort on my part. I have spoken in three languages that have been interpreted. I have seen in a vision the face of a native whose language I speak and I am saying, 'Here am I, send me.'

'He brought me to the banqueting house and His banner over me was love.' I am feasting on the hidden manna and His Glory fills my soul. Hallelujah! I am so glad I have more than one tongue to praise Him with.''[9]

### R.J. Scott

''Eight years ago, I was shown that there was more than justification and sanctification for us; there was a power the disciples had that I must have. Being placed in the position I was, as superintendent of home and foreign missions in Winnipeg, Canada, a city of a hundred thousand, I certainly felt my lack of power. . . . . I got to the point where I must have all God had for me.

Just as I decided to take charge of a church and circuit offered me, the Lord spoke to me and said, 'You must go to Los Angeles and take all your family.' . . Just before leaving for Los Angeles on the train, a friend passed me a copy of The Apostolic Faith. I was much

105

interested and was determined to see for myself, but with the thought that this speaking in tongues was of the devil and I was going to do all in my power to stamp it out. . .

My wife and I attended the meetings and it was not long till we got real hungry for the glorious gift that God has for us, His people. . . Knowing part of different Indian languages and trading dialects used throughout Canada, I said, 'Now God, if you want to convince me that this is of you, just let some of the Christians speak in a tongue that I understand.' Glory to His name. . . He took a young lady from the same place I came from, and put her under the power, gave her the Pentecostal gift and made her sing an Indian song that I had known since I was a boy, and I knew that she never was closer than 1,200 miles from the Indians, and had never been taught by anyone. She then changed into another unknown tongue, which afterwards proved to be the Armenian language. After speaking for a few moments in this tongue, she drew my attention by signs, as her English was gone, to an Armenian man near by who was greatly interested in what she was saying. He replied, 'I no speak your tongue, but that lady speak my tongue and talk to me about Jesus.' The perspiration broke out upon the man like beads, and he commenced to tremble; and this was the means of his conversion. Glory to God, this is what tongues are doing.

. . . .I was determined to have it, so I went in with all my might. But to my surprise, I found I was not nearly as high up the mount as I thought. I found out I did not possess the experience of sanctification, and was a long ways from living the sanctified life, in God's sight. While looking on the lives of others that professed it, I justified myself in thinking I compared with their experience, but this was not what God wanted. I had to be pure and clean in His sight. . . . Now as I got all of self and the rest of the rubbish out of my heart, God gave me the witness to my entire satisfaction. I knew I had a clean heart. Glory to God. Hallelujah to His Name. Are you there, reader? If not, dig down till the old Adam nature and roots of bitterness are out of the way. Then He will breathe on you and you shall receive the Holy Ghost.

I tarried and prayed and in about nine days, He baptized me with the Holy Ghost and gave me the Bible evidence of speaking and singing in tongues. Upwards of half an hour of my language was taken from me and God used me as He saw fit. . . .

I have attended those meetings for nearly three months, and during that time there has been scarcely a day that something has not happened through interpretation of tongues or someone being present who understood what had been said, which brought conviction on someone and started them to seeking God. . .

Thanks be to His Holy Name for what He has done for me and my family since I came down here. I do not know how to praise Him enough.''[10]

By the way, the testimony of Brother Scott's daughter, Kathleen, is given in *The Apostolic Faith*, Vol. I, No. l2,

(Jan. 1908) Pg. 4.

Well, those are testimonies from some of the people that were there in the early meetings at Azusa Street in 1906-1907. These that we have just given were some of the people that the Lord gave a vision to for the great Summer Campmeeting of 1907.

Brother Seymour continued to be marvelously used by the Lord at this campmeeting. At the beginning, he had charge as at Azusa Street. Later in the summer, the Lord led him to leave the campmeeting in the hands of the elders, and make a trip to the East.

While the campmeeting plans were being finalized in late May of 1907, the Lord laid it on the heart of Sister Sizelove to carry the message of the Latter Rain outpouring back to Springfield, Missouri. That trip would lead to the series of marvelous incidents reported on in this book, whose influence will last through eternity.

## REFERENCES

1. **Deeper Experiences of Famous Christians**, by James Gilchrist Lawson, The Warner Press, Anderson, Indiana, 1911, PP. 230-231.

2. "Azusa's First Campmeeting", by Fred T. Corum, *Word and Work*, Vol. 58, No. 1, January, 1936, PP. 1, 4, 5.

3. *The Apostolic Faith*, Vol. 1, No. 8, May,1907, Pg. 1. Reprinted in **Like As of Fire**.

4. *The Apostolic Faith*, Vol. 1, No. 8, May,1907, Pg. 2. Reprinted in **Like As of Fire**.

5. *The Apostolic Faith*, Vol. 1, No. 6, February-March,1907,Pg. 8. Reprinted in **Like As of Fire**.

6. *The Apostolic Faith*, Vol. 1, No. 12, January,1908,Pg. 4. Reprinted in *Like As of Fire*.

7. **Suddenly From Heaven**, by Carl Brumback, The Gospel Publishing House, Springfield, Mo., 1961,

PP. 38-39. (Reprinted as **A Sound From Heaven**, GPH, 1977, PP. 36-37.)

8. *The Apostolic Faith*, Vol. 1, No. 4, December,1906, Pg. 3. Reprinted in **Like As of Fire**.
9. *The Apostolic Faith*, Vol. 1, No. 8, May,1907, Pg. 4. Reprinted in **Like As of Fire**.
10. *The Apostolic Faith*, Vol. 1, No. 6, February-March,1907,Pg. 6. Reprinted in **Like As of Fire**.
11. *The Apostolic Faith*, Vol. 1, No. 12, January, 1908, Pg. 4. Reprinted in **Like As of Fire**.

# Chapter VII

## THE CALL TO SPRINGFIELD

". . . go and go quickly, for I am with you."

**W**hile the plans for the Azusa Street Mission Campmeeting were being completed, Rachel Sizelove became convinced that she must go to Springfield, Missouri, and bring the Latter Rain message. For it was in Springfield where her younger sister, Lillie, and her brother-in-law, James J. Corum, were living. Rachel sensed a great desire to share this new blessing with them. Aunt Rachel wrote up the events surrounding her call to Springfield for me many years later and I published them in *Word and Work* in June of 1934. Here is part of what she said:

> A Call To Carry The Message
> "In May of 1907, the Lord showed me I must go back East and tell my mother and brothers and sisters what the Lord had done for me and bring them the blessed message. My mother was living with my sister and her family in Springfield, Missouri. I hurried down to the Azusa Street Mission and had some of the saints pray with me for the Lord to make His will plain to me. The evidence came so clearly, 'My child, you may go and go quickly, for I am with you.' The saints gathered around me and laid their hands upon my head and prayed that the blessing of the Lord would go with me. The brethren in charge gave me a minister's license, which I still possess. I had a license with the

Methodist Church for many years, but they now rejected Pentecost.

On my trip, on the same train I traveled, was a dear black sister who had been to the Azusa Street Mission. She was on her way to carry the glad message to Africa. We talked with everyone we could about the mighty outpouring of the Holy Ghost and told them that Jesus was coming soon. For almost the first interpretation that everyone had when they spoke in tongues was that, 'Jesus is coming soon.' The conductor gave us permission and we held services on the train. The people listened intently and many were convicted.

### The First Pentecostal Meeting in Springfield, Missouri

On arriving in Springfield, Missouri, as I was greeted in the home of my sister, the Holy Spirit spoke through me in tongues and then gave the interpretation, 'The Holy Spirit as a dove shall hover over this place.' Soon the neighbors came in to see me and inquire of the great Pentecostal revival being poured out in Los Angeles. After telling them how the Lord baptized me with the Holy Ghost I said, 'We have been talking of the wonderful works of God, let us kneel down and pray before you go away.' And while I was praying, the Holy Ghost prayed through me in other tongues and when my sister heard me praying in tongues, she reached her hands toward heaven and cried, 'O Lord this is You and I want the Baptism of the Holy Ghost.' And she was slain under the mighty power of God. The meeting lasted all night. My sister received the Baptism of the Holy Ghost and spoke and sang in tongues. How precious and how holy the very atmosphere seemed to be with the presence of the Lord. She was the first to receive the Baptism of the Holy Ghost in Springfield. This was on the night of June 1st, 1907. From that time on, the power began to fall and has been falling ever since and will continue until Jesus comes. Hallelujah!

My sister said she would go over in town and try to get a place for me to preach while I was there. I said that I just wanted the Lord to direct and lead and that I did not try to do anything of myself. We had cottage prayer meetings. I had a great desire to see the Lord have His way in Springfield. The seed was sown and began to grow, but my sister can relate better about the early struggles and growth in Springfield.''[1]

We would like to tell about those early struggles to establish a Full Gospel work in Springfield, and how the Lord caused the work to prosper. But before we do, we must relate Mother's experience of the Baptism in the Holy Spirit.

## REFERENCE
1.      ''A Sparkling Fountain for the Whole Earth'', by Rachel A. Sizelove, *Word and Work*, Vol. 56, No. 6, June, 1934, PP. 1, 11, 12.

## Chapter VIII

### MOTHER RECEIVES THE BAPTISM OF THE HOLY SPIRIT

". . . one word stood out surrounded by God's glory.
BLOOD! O! What a word! No wonder it is so
highly exalted."
L.H.C.

In an earlier chapter, we told how Rachel Sizelove brought the Pentecostal message to Springfield, Missouri, in the latter part of May, 1907. Many years later, while I was editor of *Word and Work* in Framingham, Massachusetts, I got Mother to write up her experience of the Baptism of the Holy Spirit. I published parts of it in the *Word and Work* and also issued it as a small tract. Below is an excerpt.

"My Experience of the Baptism of the Holy Ghost"
By Lillie Harper Corum
"On June 1, 1907, the Lord Jesus so wonderfully baptized me in the Holy Ghost, that I wish to put it in tract form for the benefit of hungry souls, who may read it.

I was converted when I was seventeen years old, in the year of 1887, in a Methodist church of southern Indiana. The Lord had done wonderful things for me many times in answer to prayer, healing my body and others as we prayed for them. But my hungry soul would cry out many times to be filled with all the fullness of God. So in the year 1906, I had a letter from my sister, who was living in

113

California, telling of the great outpouring of the Holy Ghost as on the day of Pentecost. She also sent me a little paper called, 'The Apostolic Faith', which the Pentecostal people had begun to print. The heading read in big letters, 'Pentecost Has Come.' O! how my hungry heart leaped for joy, and a new hope sprang up within me as I read of the many who were receiving the Holy Ghost. From that moment, I began to seek the Lord for my inheritance. Of course Satan tried to oppose.

I was seeking and praying earnestly for the Baptism of the Holy Ghost from the early Fall of 1906 until in the late Spring of 1907. I began to pray for the Lord to send someone to my home at Springfield, Missouri, with the experience. Praise God who hears our faintest cry. My sister in California wrote that she was coming East and would visit me. While there, she would preach this gospel. That was an encouragement to my hungry soul. In due time, Sister Rachel Sizelove arrived, her face shining. She gave the message of this wonderful latter rain outpouring and soon coming of Jesus. O, what joy; what anxiousness filled my soul! I must have the Baptism of the Holy Ghost. I felt that light had come, and I was lost unless I walked in the light. My neighbors came in, and my sister gave us the Word of God. She told me how she had met with the saints at the Azusa Street, Los Angeles, meeting to inquire of the Lord about coming East. He had told her to go and to go quickly. While I was praying for Him to send a messenger, I never thought of my sister coming. He works at both ends of the line. O, the questions I asked her as I would point out the testimonies in the little 'Apostolic Faith' paper. What wonderful answers she would give, the half had not been told in the paper. My sister said, 'Come, go to California and get the Baptism.' I said, 'Rachel, the Lord is here as well as in California.'

How faith began to spring up in my heart at that moment. She gave the message each night as my neighbors would come into our house.

Late one night, Sister Sizelove led us in prayer and, after praying a few moments, she began to speak in another tongue as the Spirit gave utterance. The Spirit lifted me up from where I was sitting. I started toward her, but suddenly stopped. I felt the presence of God so near. I said, 'Could it be for me?' 'Yes', she exclaimed, 'it is for you.' 'O!', I said, 'I'm unworthy.' As my tongue uttered some sounds, Sister thought it was the evidence of the Baptism, but Satan was there, and he said to me, 'You are trying to take it by faith.' Just as I was gently falling to the floor, I said within myself, 'I will never move a muscle until the Lord lifts me up.' I knew it was real, and He was the Baptizer. My sister told me to be clay in His hands, and to keep my eyes on Jesus. It seemed the power had left me. I thought, 'Oh, if she would only lay her hands on my head and pray.' Then the scripture came to me, 'Work out your own salvation with fear and trembling' (Phil. 2:12). As I looked to the Lord by faith, I felt I must

115

have this Baptism of the Holy Ghost if it took all the flesh from my bones. I knew Jesus was the Baptizer. (John 1:33). O, how I longed for his touch. Satan would say, 'What if you are deceived, or get a false baptism?' Scripture would again come to me. 'If you ask for bread will He give you a stone?' (Matt. 7:9-11). I then felt I could get up, but I was just waiting for God to complete the work He had begun. It pays to wait on the Lord. He is the author and finisher of our faith.

As my sister would sing and praise God, I would feel the glory of God. Without an effort, my right hand went up with power and the warm cleansing Blood from Calvary was flowing through my hand, going all over my body. What joy it brought! What power! The devil is small when we are covered with Jesus' blood; mind, body, soul, and spirit. Then as it were, my heart began to expand, making room for the Holy Ghost to come in and occupy it. My tongue was shaken loose. The utterances began to come, and He, the Holy Ghost, was singing in many kinds of languages. I wanted ten thousand tongues to praise my Lord in. He lifted me up in His mighty power while myriads and myriads of Angelic hosts sang with me as the Spirit gave utterance. I remembered Matt. 4:11. O! I was sealed to the day of Redemption. It was four o'clock in the morning. Mother said, 'This is the shortest night I ever saw.' Sister Sizelove began to sing, 'The long, long night has past.' O, the joy and rapture just overwhelmed me. We went to our beds, sleeping

116

and resting as it were a whole night of refreshing sleep. I arose at 5:00 a.m., all my old nervous troubles and sickness gone. I felt so rested and well. My soul was basking in the heavenly sunlight of God's eternal love. Taking the Bible, I opened it, and O, the glory of God just blinded my eyes to every thing, but one word stood out surrounded by God's glory. BLOOD! O! What a word! No wonder it is so highly exalted. It is our only hope of eternal salvation for without the shedding of blood, there is no remission of sin. Heb. 9:22. O, how the Holy Spirit will discern between the false and the true. He will have clean vessels to dwell in, cleansed by the precious blood of Jesus.

As the Holy Spirit would tell me again and again, Jesus is coming soon, my very heart would leap for joy. Praise God, He abides still, and is just as real as at the beginning. His peace passeth all understanding.

Looking for His soon-coming."[1]

### Aunt Rachel Returns to Los Angeles

Sister Sizelove had previously committed herself to the work of Azusa's first campmeeting. Consequently, after bringing the precious message of the Latter Rain to Springfield, she hurried back to California, to assist the saints at the campmeeting. When she got back to California, she looked out and saw . . .

> ". . . More than three hundred tents were pitched on the campground. Surely, her dream had been fulfilled.
>
> After a glorious time for two months, Brother Seymour was called to Chicago and

117

the East. The camp was then placed in charge of different ones and when they were called to other fields of labor, the committee met and appointed Mrs. Sizelove in charge and it seemed the meetings could not come to a close even when the cold, chilly nights of autumn began to creep on, because the people kept coming. It seemed that they came from every part of the world.

Many souls were born into the Kingdom of God. The Holy Ghost was poured out as a great flood tide. Joel's prophecy of the latter rain outpouring of the Holy Spirit was fulfilled. As people received the Baptism of the Holy Ghost and spoke in tongues, the first interpretation almost always was, 'Jesus is coming soon!' Many were called to labor in the great whitened harvest fields of the earth, and the message has been carried to all countries of the earth. This movement has so often been called 'God's last call to mankind.' "[2]

A review of the campmeeting was published in *The Apostolic Faith* entitled:

"Everywhere Preaching The Word"

"This is a time as never before when the baptized saints are scattering abroad everywhere preaching the Word. They have gone out from Los Angeles far and near, carrying the sweet message that the Comforter has come. Some have gone to Canada, some East, some South, and some are on the way to foreign fields.

Many of the campmeeting saints are gathered back to the old 'manger home' at

Azusa. The pillar of fire still resting there. Meetings went on here all summer, souls seeking and finding the Lord.

The Lord taught His people at the campground and gave them some practical experiences that will stand them in good stead on the field. The enemy came in as an angel of light, and we had a battle with the powers of darkness; but it was turned into victory after all. The Spirit was poured out and many souls baptized. God only knows the number. They were slain about the altars and in the 'upper room tent', and came through speaking and singing in tongues and rejoicing in God.

Many were saved and sanctified. Over l00 were baptized in the stream near by. The baptismal services were sweet and heavenly. Numbers of children followed Jesus in baptism, and came out of the water praising God. Many testified to healing. The Lord performed some real miracles. Praise God!

There were over 200 living tents in the camp, besides a number of large tents; the big tabernacle where God met with us graciously; the 'upper room tent' where many sought and obtained the Pentecost; the children's tabernacle where they were taught the Word and many of them found the Lord, and we shall never forget that spot for it was so sweet to hear the children praying and praising the Lord. Then there was the dining tent, where hundreds sat down to the tables and no charge made except as the Lord laid it on them to put into the box. We enjoyed some blessed times in the Spirit there, and also in the workers' dining tent, before we got to the big tabernacle on the 'all things common' line. One morning while at prayer after breakfast, the power of God so came on us that ten of the workers were slain and we did not get away till noon. We had a foretaste of heaven.

The hills around would sometimes ring with prayer and praises. Some sought and found the Lord on the hills, and came down with faces shining.

The early morning meetings before breakfast, when the saints met, will never be forgotten. The Lord met with us. There were three other services in the big tabernacle during the day, which often ran into the night, if not till morning. The altar workers were very faithful. They would stay and pray with seekers all night.

People came from hundreds and thousands of miles seeking Pentecost, and went back with the rivers of salvation. The songs from the camp could be heard distinctly up in Hermon. One sister, who had been told it was all the power of the devil, was up in Hermon listening, and she said to herself, 'So, that is the devil. Well, the devil has some sweet singers.' She came down and the result was she went to the altar and received the Baptism with the Holy Ghost.

From Hermon, one sister saw fire issuing out of the tabernacle, as it were a tongue of fire. Her daughter also saw it. And a little boy who was in the power of the Spirit in the tabernacle, saw a ball of fire in the top of the tabernacle which broke and filled the whole

place with light. God surely did send the fire.
Many were the heavenly anthems the Spirit
sang through His people. And He gave many
beautiful messages in unknown tongues;
speaking of His sooncoming, invitations to
come to the Lord, and exhortations from the
Word.

We had some precious saints' meetings,
feasting on the Word. One blessed thing was
the unity of the ministers and workers in the
doctrines of the Bible, so plainly taught by our
Lord. The Lord put His seal upon it. Those
who were not present will find the doctrines
in this paper as they were taught there. Our
power in this Gospel is in standing in the
Word. O, how precious it is when we are in
the Apostles' doctrine and fellowship.''[3]

How we long for this spiritual unity today among the
ministers and workers. As in those days, our power is in
standing on the Word. Spiritual victories seemed to
abound in Los Angeles, but in Springfield, the battle was
only beginning.

## REFERENCES

1.    ''My Experience of the Baptism of the Holy Ghost'',
      by Lillie Harper Corum, Tract published by The
      Christian Worker's Union, Framingham,
      Massachusetts.

2.    ''Azusa's First Campmeeting'', by Fred T. Corum,
      *Word and Work*, Vol. 58, No. 1, January, 1936, PP.
      1, 4, 5.

3.    *The Apostolic Faith*, Vol. 1, No. 10, September,
      1907, Pg. 1. Reprinted in **Like As of Fire**.

# CHAPTER IX

## EARLY STRUGGLES AT SPRINGFIELD

"Let them alone. If it's not of God, it will soon fall through, but if it is of God, it will stand."

When Mother received the Baptism, she received great power to witness and to tell others about the Lord. It was a marvelous experience and she was sure that others would want this precious experience also. We were attending a small Baptist Church at the time, where Dad was the Sunday School Superintendent (as he had previously been at the little Baptist Church where Mother and Dad had first met back in Artemus, Kentucky). Mother and Hazel (who was ten) went to see the Pastor and tell him of the wonderful experience which she had. She thought that he would be joyful that the Holy Spirit had fallen again and that she had received the Baptism of the Holy Ghost. Surely others that loved the Lord would receive the Holy Spirit too. Instead, he ridiculed her and scoffed at this precious experience, completely rejecting the Baptism of the Holy Ghost. Dad was quite baffled and hurt by this response and resigned from the church. By the way, that pastor was later expelled from his denomination and that church, in fact, is no longer in existence. Over the years, many Godly people were denied their heritage because their leaders rejected God's blessing.

Mother was now full of the Holy Spirit, but we had no church to belong to. So Mother called on all the neighbors and had prayer meetings and the neighbors also began getting the Baptism. Our next door neighbors, the Boyd family, attended the Presbyterian Church in Springfield. Mrs. Florence Boyd loved the Lord and she came and brought her children; Janet, Ruth, and Paul. Sister Boyd soon received the Baptism (in 1907) and she and Mother became great prayer warriors for a church in Springfield. Sister Boyd joined with my Mother and they started a church in our house. This was the pioneer effort which has grown into Central Assembly in Springfield, Missouri. Sister Boyd's daughters, Janet and Ruth, both came into Pentecost. Although he rejected it at first, several years later, at one of Mother Barnes' tent-meetings, Brother Boyd came into Pentecost. I can still see him lying in the straw shaking under the mighty power of God and then later, standing with one arm around Sister Boyd and the other raised toward heaven, and tears streaming down his cheeks, speaking in heavenly languages.

Mother would gather all the children of the neighborhood into our living room on Sunday mornings and have Sunday School. Many of the children were from poor families that had very little. One little girl that came had never heard about Jesus. She had heard of the devil, but had never heard of God or the simple plan of salvation.

Another little boy (about 6 or 7 years old) named Fred Beeman came. He was from a poor family in the neighborhood. I believe that the only spiritual instruction that he had ever received was from my Mother in that little Sunday School. His family moved to another part of Springfield and we lost track of him. Many years later, in the mid 1920's, Mother got a call from Fred Beeman for help. I think that it was Sister Hoy who found him and brought the message to Mother. In his teenage years, he had run with a fast crowd, engaged in all kinds of illegal activity and now in his mid-20's he lay sick and dying with syphilis. His body was covered with sores, his sight was almost gone and the doctors told him that he would soon be dead. He never went to school and he had never really had a chance in life, but there on his death bed he remembered hearing about Jesus and he wanted to go to heaven. Mother was the only one that had ever told him about Jesus - and he begged for ''Sister

Corum" to come. I was attending Harvard Law School at the time, but Mother told me how he got wonderfully saved and called in all his buddies and told them to become Christians before it was too late. It was only matter of a few days when Fred Beeman, with a heart whiter than snow, went to be with the Lord, to join the blood-washed throng where the pure in heart are ever about the throne.

Well, the Sunday School began to grow and we continued to hold a cottage prayer meeting. The neighbors began to come and many received the Baptism. Mother would talk to anyone that came to the house and although we had a small fellowship started, we had a terrible time trying to start a church going.

In July of 1907, a band of Pentecostal workers from Joplin, Missouri, came to Springfield. Sister Lula France and her husband came. She was just a young lady at the time, but the dear Lord used her to preach most of the messages. She was really endued with power from God.

Brother Bert H. Doss, who was just a young man, had been saved from a very sinful family and was so filled with God that he preached with power. Others in their group were Arthur Gilfillan, and Lillie and Kate Russel. And they would shout and sing. Mother's notes say, "We bought goods and made a tent which was pitched on Central Street, near the Boulevard." I'm sure that this is the tent meeting referred to in Brother Brumback's book.[2] Mother continues, "Large crowds attended these services and wondered at the so-called new doctrine, among them being students of Drury College, and ministers of the denominational churches." A group of the men in town said, "Why this is a terrible thing to be doing in the name of religion. That's no religion." And they wanted to get a posse and run the Pentecostal people out of town. (We were "Pentecostal" then. The Assembles of God was not formed for another seven years.)

There was a man named Tom Thomas from the First

Baptist Church who said, "No. Let them alone. If it's not of God, it will soon fall through, but if it is of God, it will stand." Well, it has stood and you can go and see what has happened in Springfield.

In the latter part of July, Aunt Florence Taliaferro came from Mammoth Springs, Arkansas, to attend these meetings. Aunt Florence ( my mother's sister) had been wonderfully saved years before back in Indiana, and her heart was open and hungry for more of God. She began to wait upon the Lord for the Baptism of The Holy Spirit. Mother writes, "At this time, she was healed of heart trouble and sanctified by Jesus' blood. She was slain in the Spirit and had a marvelous vision of the cross of Christ. One night after we came home from the meeting, while she was leading out in prayer, suddenly the Holy Ghost fell upon her with signs following and she spoke in tongues as the Spirit gave utterance." Mother's sister, Aunt Mary Crandell, came from Lawton, Oklahoma, and she received the Baptism of the Holy Ghost too. Well, the Lord was moving. Sister Lula France was preaching her heart out and many were saved and filled with the Holy Ghost during these meetings.

### Brother Geisler

There was a man named Geisler who had been an alcoholic in Springfield. Much to Springfield's shame, around this time, we had a lynching of two black men. They were dragged out of the old jail house and were lynched; in the middle of the square on the Statue of Liberty, if you can imagine that. And their bodies were burned. That was on the Saturday before Easter, and the morning was Easter Sunday. Every preacher in town lamented about this terrible lynching that had taken place in Springfield. I believe that it came out later that the two men had, in fact, been innocent. But this Mr. Geisler had stood along side shouting, "Hang 'em! - Hang 'em! - Hang 'em!" Now, he happened to go to Joplin,

Missouri, and as he was walking along the street, he heard a man preaching. This street preacher said, "Everybody that gave their consent for the killing of these Negroes was a murderer and has committed murder." And Mr. Geisler thought, "Am I a murderer? Have I killed somebody?" So he followed the preacher into a Pentecostal mission and he got saved and he got the Baptism of the Holy Spirit and after that he never ceased talking in tongues. He never let up. He talked all the time! He returned to Springfield. He was a tall man. I can see him yet with his hands up, speaking in tongues. Our meetings would just go on as usual. We didn't think anything about it. He would talk in tongues so much that he would get up and go out and kneel down in the bushes and praise the Lord. The little boys would all gather around him to see and hear for it was still something new.

Soon it was Autumn, and the weather began to get cold. Most of the Joplin workers left. We were called Apostolic Faith people then, or just Pentecostals, and we continued prayer meetings in our homes. We didn't have a church and couldn't seem to get one started. Sometimes we would worship with the Holiness people. Brother J. E. Ellis, a long white-bearded, Holiness preacher, was holding services in Bethel Chapel on Campbell Street near Calhoun. We used to call it Noah's Ark. It was an old wooden chapel with houses all around it. It had wooden benches and straw all around the altar. They later took the land and built Pipkin High School on the spot. Bethel Chapel stood on what is now the playground behind Pipkin Junior High School. Ellis was not a Pentecostal man, but some of us were teachers and workers in his Sabbath School, and we were made welcome and we had freedom and liberty to witness about the Baptism of the Holy Ghost. These were wonderful days, but we still believed that the Lord wanted something special for Springfield, and we just couldn't seem to get a place started where people could worship the Lord in the beauty of holiness and the freedom of the Holy Spirit. We just couldn't get a Pentecostal church started. The only Pentecostal Church in Springfield at this time was our living room on Division Street, where our small band continued to meet.

## REFERENCE

1. "The Pentecostal Church of Springfield", typed notes by L.H. Corum, n.d., circa 1921.
2. **Suddenly From Heaven**, by Carl Brumback, The Gospel Publishing House, Springfield, Mo., 1961, Pg. 283, (Reprinted as **A Sound From Heaven**, GPH, 1977, Pg. 105.)

# Chapter X

## THAYER, MISSOURI

. . . the Lord was reaching out around the congregation with great arms of love and drawing them unto Himself.

We would like to tell about the great move of God that occurred at Thayer, Missouri, while we were struggling to get a start at Springfield. But first we must tell about a dear Pentecostal Brother named Joe Duke.

Thayer, Missouri, was a railroad junction. The train crews would change at junctions, like Thayer, all over the country. At many of the Frisco railroad junctions there were hotels and nice restaurants called "Fred Harvey Restaurants", and Joe Duke ran the hotel and Fred Harvey Restaurant near the Thayer, Missouri, railroad station. But he was an alcoholic. One day he was up in St. Louis on business and happened to be out walking the streets. He passed a little mission and heard the singing and went in. He was wonderfully saved and the Lord delivered him from drink and he got the Baptism of the Holy Ghost. Mother (Mary) Barnes ran the mission. It was one of several that she had in St. Louis. After this, Joe Duke went into "partnership" with the Lord, giving 50% of his business income to Christ. He had printed on his business cards, "The Lord and Joe Duke". He said, "The Lord came first."

Joe Duke went back to Thayer, Missouri, and at this time, Thayer was just a small town, much smaller than Springfield. Joe begged Mother Barnes to come down and hold a meeting. And so she came. But things were altogether different in Thayer than in Springfield. She had a good sized tent, many workers and was well-organized. Harry Bowley and Bennett Lawrence were there. They were just young men then and the Lord had mighty ministries ahead for both of them. The Lord poured out His Spirit in a marvelous way. Well, it stirred the whole town. And God saved the people. In just a short while, not only did they build a beautiful church, but also sixteen churches sprang up in the surrounding area as a result of these meetings. It seemed like in Springfield no one was stirred and we were on the wrong side of the tracks, but in Thayer there was no class distinction; many of the leading people of the town came into Pentecost, and God saved and filled them all. I've often wondered if a part of that great harvest grew from seeds which were sown by Rachel and Josie Sizelove while they labored through that region a decade earlier.

Well, we must tell you how it was that we got there to see the meetings. Uncle Charlie Taliaferro was an engineer for the passenger trains on the Frisco Railroad and he, Aunt Florence, and our cousins, Laurel and Virginia, all lived on a farm of around 160 acres just over the State line in Mammoth Springs, Arkansas. In fact, it was the original land that Rachel and Josie Sizelove had homesteaded years before. It was now a beautiful farm. Uncle Charlie had his own bees, a small herd of cattle, a new farmhouse and so forth. When they heard from Joe Duke that Mother Barnes was going to come to Thayer, they were very excited, for at that time there were very few Pentecostal people in the area. Later on, we heard that when the tentmeeting started, the Spirit of the Lord came upon Aunt Florence and she gave a ringing testimony and message in tongues which stirred the whole camp. Mother Barnes, who had believed that no one in the area had even heard of Pentecost, was surprised and greatly encouraged and the Spirit of the Lord began to fall. Aunt Florence wrote to us that God was doing great things in Thayer, and could we please come for a while. Dad was able to take a week's vacation (he was the telegraph operator for the Frisco Railroad in Springfield). I was just eight or nine years old at the time and I believe that Hazel had just had her twelfth birthday.

I remember seeing Uncle Charlie's new farmhouse back up on the hill surrounded by willow trees. Uncle Charlie had a four wheel wagon and a new team of mules named Kitt and Kate. He put some straw in the back of the wagon to make it comfortable for us, and we rode along bumpy roads, over a creek, and on into Thayer where Joe Duke had put up a big tent.

I remember the singing. Mother Barnes was a little Irish woman and had a great deal of Irish wit. She would have the crowds bursting at the seams with laughter one minute and weeping the next. But oh, how she could preach souls into the kingdom of God. Rex Humbard's mother, Martha Childers Humbard, tells a little about Mother Barnes and her marvelous ministry in her book, **Give Me That Old Time Religion**.[1] Martha Childers was saved under Mother Barnes' ministry. I'm sure that a whole book could be written about Mother Barnes and the great impact that her ministry had upon Pentecost. Perhaps one will be written someday.

Surely God met us all at the Thayer tentmeeting. People were slain under the power of God all over the tent. A dear old Holiness preacher named Brother Bliss received the Baptism and later started one of the churches near by. The Pentecostal message penetrated the whole town. Bennett Lawrence and Mother Barnes did most of the preaching, and Harry Bowley would give the altar call. I remember Harry Bowley as a flaming evangelist. While Brother Lawrence would preach, aglow with Holy Fire, Brother Bowley, sitting near the front, would weep and pray in the Spirit. His whole being seemed to be interceding for the people that were listening to the preaching. Then, when the message was over, Brother Bowley would leap to the platform and deliver the altar call. It seemed as though the Lord Himself led the altar call through Brother Bowley. It was as if the Lord was reaching out around the congregation with great arms of love and irresistibly drawing them, saint and sinner, unto Himself.

On one occasion, Brother Bowley gave a message in tongues and a German women jumped up and said that he had spoken in High German and told what she had done when she was a girl, and she ran to the altar. I remember one Sunday afternoon when a woman that was operating a brothel house in Thayer came to the meeting. She got under conviction while Mother Barnes was preaching and rushed to the altar and fell on her knees before God. She was gloriously saved and later gave a marvelous testimony of God's redemptive power. On another occasion, some people operating as a band of horse thieves came to see what was going on, got saved, and straightened out.

It was very hot and very humid on the Fourth of July. We had all perspired through the afternoon service. They had three meetings a day then. I remember that Harry Bowley called on Joe Duke to dismiss the afternoon meeting. He held up his hand and prayed for rain to come and cool the atmosphere. We had all brought picnic suppers and just about the time we were finishing dessert - it began to rain. It didn't rain hard, but it did rain steadily. It was like air conditioning! And then it let up, and when we came out of the tent at the close of the evening service, the stars were out. I should tell you that that night was the first time that I heard the Heavenly Choir. The whole congregation sang and worshipped in tongues and truly we had a foretaste of what it will be like, someday, when we sing and worship around the heavenly Throne of God.

I remember riding back to Uncle Charlie's farm in the wagon that night. Uncle Charlie had a low, gruff voice and Aunt Florence had a high, sweet voice, and along with Mother and Dad, we all sang in the night as our wagon rolled through the hills. The rain was over and I think the moon came out. Hazel often tells about falling asleep in the back of the wagon and every time that it went over a bump, she would bump her head and wake up. But I can still hear them singing as it echoed back over the hills, along about three o'clock in the morning. I remember that most of the songs were about Christ coming back and the rapture:

"When Jesus comes to claim His Bride
And steal away the sanctified;
Someday we'll drink the King's new wine
And then we'll sing the new, new song,
Wait a little while, Wait a little while
And then we'll sing the new, new song."

When we got to English Creek, Uncle Charlie stopped the mules and stepped out on the wagon tongue and released the neck strap so the mules could drink, and then we wound our way up the hill to their farmhouse. This may all sound very picturesque to some people today, but I assure you that human beings are still the same today, in 1982, while I am writing this, as they were back in 1908 or 1909 when these events occurred. By the way, that old farmhouse has been restored up in those old Ozark Hills.

Now, I must tell you about one of the most thrilling things that happened at the Thayer tentmeeting. We told you above that they had three meetings each day. On weekdays, the afternoon meeting was usually spent in prayer and worship. One afternoon, the people were all down at the altar rail praying, and Brother Bowley rose up and said, "We're going to hear the Angel Choir." And they heard the Angels singing - way, way off in the distance. And by and by, they came nearer until they were just inside the tent poles around the edge of the tent; singing. Then they came down into the midst of the tent, hovering over the people. This was a miracle and filled the people with awe. The people quit praying at the altar and began to join with the Angels singing praises to God. Wouldn't you have loved to have been there? The power of God was so strong the people wept for joy. Uncle Charlie loved the Lord, but over the years his religion was up and down. When the Angelic Host dropped within the midst of the people, Uncle Charlie wept, ''My God, my God, I can't take this'', and he got up and ran out of the tent to pray in the bushes outside. The presence of Glory was just too much for him. The music was glorious. How wonderful heaven must be - for all of heaven must be filled with this song.

Well, these were glorious meetings. We were just children. Hazel, Artemus, Paul, and I would fall asleep on the benches some nights, and sometimes in the straw under the benches, but Mother and Dad, who were young in Pentecost, were thrilled with the glory of God and the beauty of this salvation. My fondest memories of these meetings are of the afternoon meetings where fifty to a hundred people would be gathered around the altar singing - such beautiful melody - singing in heavenly languages. Many people don't understand Pentecostal people, and consider them to be eccentric. But when you have experienced the miraculous, your life will never be the same.

REFERENCE

1. **Give Me That Old Time Religion**, by Martha Childers Humbard, Logos International, Plainfield, New Jersey, 1977.

# Chapter XI

## JOE DUKE

Sister Flint: "What shall we do now, doctor?"
Dr. Culp:    "Keep on praying."

**W**hile the meetings up on the hilltop at Thayer were going on, another miracle event occurred down in the town. Joe Duke, the restaurant owner, had a cook named Joe French. And, he died. And Joe Duke said, "Nobody in my house shall die unsaved." The doctor had already pronounced Joe French dead, and while the funeral arrangements were being made, they prayed and God raised Joe French from the dead. Joe French later married Martha Childers' sister, Hattie Childers, and started a large restaurant near the corner of St. Louis Street, at the square in Springfield. And so Joe French was to become Rex Humbard's uncle. ...While I was on the staff of Word and Work, we published an account of this marvelous miracle, Vol. 52, No. ll, Nov. l930. It had earlier been published in The Latter Rain Evangel:

"Raised From the Dead"
by Joe Duke

(Pastor Harry Bowley of Dallas, Texas, who was one of the Evangelistic Band of Thayer, Missouri, at this time, was an eyewitness to this remarkable death and resurrection, and corroborated the story. He writes that Joe afterwards gave a vivid account of his terrible experience in hell for a few hours, which made an indelible impression upon him and no doubt led to his salvation.)

"In the month of June, 1908, I was in charge of the Railroad Hotel in Thayer, Missouri, on the Frisco Lines. One evening about five o'clock, while sitting on a veranda, a little Irishman walked up to me and asked to see the manager. I replied that I was he. He then asked if we were in need of a cook, and on being told that we were, he at once presented himself for the job. He said that he had been chief cook on ocean steamers and had been around the world about five times. I was surprised at this, as he had the appearance of a mere boy. However, this is typical of the Irish, as they generally carry their age well. I hired the young man, whose name was Joe French.

This was just prior to the great revival that broke out in Thayer. When God began to work, the whole country side became mightily stirred. The band of saints who came from St. Louis to hold the meetings, were entertained at my hotel. They were five in number; Mother Barnes and her daughter, Sister Flint, who conducted a charity hospital in St. Louis, Bennett Lawrence and Harry Bowley. They all enjoyed Joe's cooking and inquired especially as to who made the delicious biscuits. I informed Mother Barnes about my Irish cook, and she being Irish also, was eager to see Joe. She found her way to the kitchen, introduced herself to him and at once began to praise his good cooking.

Joe was not accustomed to hearing people praise the Lord and as everyone in the hotel did this, he thought us a most peculiar crowd of people. He was soon prevailed on to attend the meetings, and one Sunday evening when he was present, the speaker referred to the different churches (Catholic included) as being below the Apostolic standard. Joe, being a Catholic, instantly became stirred up and the next morning when I entered the kitchen, to my surprise, I found him breathing out threats of slaughter against that preacher for daring to say anything against the Catholic Church.

After some little explanation, the matter was adjusted. I assured Joe that the preacher loved him and that we all were very fond of him and would do anything in our power to make him happy.

The following day, after the train dinner had been served, Joe was suddenly stricken down while in the kitchen. When the two ministering brethren entered, they found him in a state of utter collapse and looking as pale as death. They summoned me and I at once ordered him taken to the main part of the hotel, these men carrying him upstairs to one of the best rooms of the house. Joe asked me to get him the very best doctor we had in the town, so I called Dr. Culp. After a thorough examination, he pronounced the case to be malignant typhoid fever which he said was so fatal that very few ever recover from it.

Sister Flint, on being told of Joe's condition, felt condemned because she was the only one in the band that had failed to speak to him concerning his soul's salvation. Being a professional nurse, she at once volunteered to nurse him. For eighteen days, she faithfully ministered to Joe's wants. On account of her profession, she was not strong on Divine Healing and administered faithfully all the drugs that the doctor's prescription called for, which were many. About five days after Joe was taken sick, the marshall of the town came into my office and said, "Mr. Duke, I understand that you have a sick man in this hotel and that you are letting him die for the want of a doctor." I told him that his informant had not told the truth, that I had called a doctor at the very outset and not only that, but that I also had a trained nurse in Joe's room from the beginning. I insisted that he come up and see for himself, which he did. He was dumbfounded when he saw that he had been sent on a fool's errand.

As time went on, Joe became worse. By this time, God was working mightily in the meetings. Great crowds looked on from night to night as sinners were saved, devils cast out, the sick healed and numbers baptized in the Holy Ghost, speaking in other tongues.

One morning while in prayer about Joe's condition, I took my Bible and asked God to give me a passage of Scripture regarding his almost hopeless case. It came in a flash, "I am the resurrection, and the life: he that believeth in Me, though he were dead, yet shall he live." John 11.25. I seemed to be able to draw only one meaning from this, as the doctors, in a special consultation, had pronounced Joe's case utterly hopeless and told me to notify his people to that effect. Try as I would to believe otherwise, there was no alternative but the solid conviction that Joe would surely die but that God would raise him from the dead. The three doctors had emphatically declared that Joe would die before morning, but I informed them that I knew that several days ago, as God had clearly shown me this from His Word.

That same evening, we had one of the most remarkable meetings in the tent that I have ever seen. People were slain everywhere under the power of God. My wife and I returned to the hotel about eleven o'clock and retired for the night. At about half past one in the morning, I was suddenly awakened by the nurse who was weeping and saying that Joe was dead. I arose and quickly dressed and on going to Joe's room, found that he was already washed and laid out for burial. I was quite composed in spirit, and walking close by the dead man's side, I felt his hand and put my ear close to his heart. There was no sign of life. I turned to Sister Flint and asked her if she was sure that Joe was dead. "Dead," she replied. "Have not I seen one hundred and fifty of them die? And don't I know when a man is dead?"

The Spirit instantly took my tongue and repeated the promise of Scripture God had given me, "Though he were dead, yet shall he live again." She instantly became so agitated that she derided me and turning to Mother Barnes, whom I had not noticed, she said, "What do you think of this man?"

Mother Barnes said, "I believe that he believes God." At this, the mighty power of God came upon me and before I knew what was happening, I was on my knees at the dead man's head, holding him by the hair and rebuking in tongues, the interpretation of which was, "I rebuke this death demon in the name of Jesus, and command the spirit to return to this body."

Instantly, life reentered the body and Joe's frame shuddered. He opened his eyes and looked straight at Sister Flint. In a short time, Joe became very hungry and as I had already told the nurse to give him anything he asked for, she was ready and when Joe said, "I am so hungry," she asked, "Joey, what can I get for you." He called for two poached eggs on toast and a glass of milk. This order was quickly brought and he devoured it heartily.

Sister Flint read the Bible to him during the remainder of the night and talked to him about his soul, which resulted in his conversion.

In the morning, while all were rejoicing over the good news, the doctor stepped in. He had no medicine case this time, but instead, a death certificate. Joe was sitting up in bed with a heavenly smile on his face. When the doctor saw him he was speechless. We all looked at him and Sister Flint said, "What will we do now, doctor?" He gulped at the lump in his throat, and backing toward the door muttered, "Keep on praying." He then went out.

This was on Friday, and on Sunday, Joe was at the meeting seeking the Holy Ghost.

139

The Lord subsequently filled him with His Spirit. He went back to Ireland and gave himself up to the authorities, confessing a crime of murder and giving the details, but they would not take any action, so Joe was clear.

He preached the Gospel there and his father, mother, and two sisters were saved and filled with the Spirit. He is now in this country, still happy in the Lord. We heard from him recently. It is useless to state that this miracle stirred the town of Thayer and the surrounding country. It put a living faith in my heart that remains to this day. "Why should it be thought a thing incredible with you that God should raise the dead?"[1]

I assure you this was a true event. Well, God did marvelous things at Thayer. Another thing that happened at the Thayer tentmeeting was the conversion of a fiddler and dance-caller named John Davis. We will have more to say about this dear man in the next chapter.

## REFERENCE

1.    "Raised From the Dead", by Joe Duke, *The Latter Rain Evangel*. Reprinted in *Word and Work*, Vol. 52, No. 11, November, 1930, PP. 16, 21.

Fig. 1  This is the Old Azusa Street Mission where
the fire first fell in April of 1906.

Fig. 2  Letterhead used by the early saints at Azusa
Street Mission.

Fig. 3 This is a group photograph of the Azusa Street
workers. Seated (from left to right) are Sister May
Evens, Brother Hiram W. Smith, Brother William
J. Seymour, and Sister Clara E. Lum. The little girl
seated in Brother Smith's arms is Mildred Crawford
(Sister Crawford's daughter). Standing (from left to
right) are an unidentified woman, (perhaps one of the
readers of this book can identify her), Brother G.W.
Evans, Sister Jennie Moore, Brother Glen A. Cook,
Sister Florence L. Crawford, Thomas Junk (?), and
Sister Prince. The insert is Rachel Sizelove. The
twelve (not including the little girl formed the creden-
tial committee at Azusa Street, and after a ministerial
candidate had been approved, they would lay hands
on the person and pray as did the apostles of old.

Fig. 4    This is Frank Bartleman as
I knew him in the late
1920's. He was born
December 14, 1871 and
died August 23, 1936. He
received the Baptism at his
Eighth and Maple Avenue
Mission in Los Angeles on
August 16, 1906.

Fig. 5  This is a photgraph of the first person to receive the Baptism of the Holy Spirit in Springfield, Missouri. On June 1, 1907, Lillie (Harper) Corum was filled with the Holy Ghost.

Fig. 6  This is Lillie Corum and daughter Hazel just about the time that they went with Fred and Sister Benedict to the saloon keeper to get permission to put up a tent at Campbell and Calhoun Streets. The spot today is on the site of the Pentecostal work in Springfield, Missouri, which has come to be known as Central Assembly.

Fig. 7 This a photograph of Lillie and James Corum taken in 1928, around the time that they came up to Framingham, Massachusetts to assist with the Christian Workers Union.

Fig. 8 This is dear Sister A.E. Benedict who fasted for a year on bread and water for the city of Springfield, Missouri.

Fig. 9   This is Rachel (Harper) Sizelove about the time she received the vision of the great sparkling fountain issuing from Springfield, Missouri.

Fig. 10

This is Joe Duke. This picture was taken around 1910, and this is just as I remember him.

Fig. 11 I believe that this is a picture of the afternoon group at the Great Thayer Tentmeeting. As I look through the photo, I can see Joe Duke, John Davis, Mother Barnes, Harry Bowley, Hazel (age 12), myself (age 9), Mother (Lillie Corum), Aunt Florence, Uncle Charlie Taliaferro, Virginia Taliaferro, Bennett Lawrence, Grandma Harper. (The author is the little boy sitting at the feet of Mother Barnes.)

Fig. 12 This is Charles Taliaferro (Uncle Charlie) dressed for business (R). He was an engineer for the passenger trains on the Frisco Railroad. That's his fireman, standing on the left.

Fig. 13 This is the Thayer Church. When Harry Bowley started to build it back in 1909, he had only 25 cents and a lot of faith.

Fig. 14 This is John Davis, Ozark Pentecostal
Preacher - just the way I remember him. He
would go out in the woods and pray all night
before he would preach.

Fig. 15 This is a snapshot of our
friends at Mother Barnes'
short term Bible School at
Eureka Springs, Arkansas.
The girl on the far right is
Martha Childers. The pic-
ture was taken just about
the time that she met Alpha
Humbard.

Fig. 16 This is Martha Childers and
her roommate, Eva
Bartley. Eva later married
Laural Taliaferro.

Fig. 17 Some of the youth group with sister Boyd.
Left to right: Janet Boyd, Berneice, Clarence
Trueblood, Lois Jackson, Sister Boyd and
Brother Boyd.

Fig. 18 Janet Boyd and Sister Boyd

Fig. 19 This is Mother Barnes and Bennett
Lawrence's son in Eureka Springs, Arkansas.
I believe that he was later killed in an airplane
crash.

Fig. 20 Some of the young people: Among them I can see Martha Childers, Virginia Taliaferro, Hazel Corum, Snowdie Sizelove. I don't remember the names of all the rest, but I can remember the boy on the right lying in the straw under the power of God when we were meeting in the wooden tabernacle across from the courthouse. Just ordinary young folks growing up in the Ozarks - yet they felt "the touch of His consuming fire".

Fig. 21 This is Paul about the time he received the Baptism and just a few years before he said, "Lets claim it all: from Boonville to Calhoun and Division to Campbell."

Fig. 22 This was our first "real" church building. We just called it "The Pentecostal Church" then. Today, it's known as Central Assembly of God. The picture was taken on the day of its dedication in 1920. That's our Brisco ("the car with a million dollar motor"), standing in front. A few years later, Paul used it to drive Aimee McPherson from the colonial Hotel down to Convention Hall each day while she held meetings in Springfield.

Fig. 23 This is Fred about the time we got permission to put up a tent on a vacant lot at Campbell and Calhoun Streets.

Fig. 24 This picture was taken sometime after the time that the Gospel Publishing House moved to Springfield. This is the Flower Family visiting us. Sister Flower is there and her father, Brother Reynolds, is in the back. Hazel is there and Mother is in the center. Sister Flower brought her Father and her children out to visit us many times (Adele, Susan, Roswell, David, George, and Joe. Joe used to be in the Sunday School class that Fred taught).

Fig. 25 This is a snapshot of Lillie N. Corum walking the streets of Springfield before a revival. Jesus is coming. Get ready!

Fig. 26 This was our farm house out on Division Street in 1909.

Fig. 27 Harry Bowley and J.J.
Corum in the 1930's.

Fig. 28 This is Harry Elwood
Bowley in the 1920's. The
picture is from *Word and
Work*.

Fig. 29 This was part of our young people. The picture was taken around the time of the New Year's Eve prayer meeting. That is Bennett Lawrence, Central's second Pastor, standing third from the left. Fred is on the right.

Fig. 30 Another snapshot of our young people. Bennett Lawrence (second from the left) and Fred Corum (second from the right).

Fig. 31 This is "White City" as it appeared just about the time it was claimed for the Lord and the spreading of the Gospel. We regarded it as a den of iniquity where only the devil and his crowd would want to be.

Fig. 32 This is part of White City as it looks today.

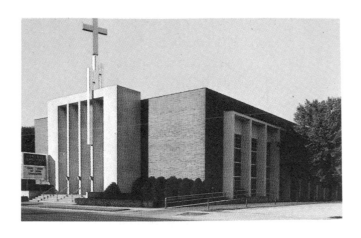

Fig. 33  This is the other end of White City as it looks today.

Fig. 34  This picture was taken when Bert Williams came out to visit us. That's dear Brother Williams (top right), Mother (center), Dad (lower right), Hazel, Herman Harvy and his wife (in the upper left). This picture was taken about the time that CBI was started.

Fig. 35 This is Mother, Hazel, Grandma Harper, and our old dog, Dee Dee. The picture was taken just about the time that the church was dedicated. (Note the Brisco automobile again.) This is the house where Pentecost started in Springfield, and for several years, this house was the only Pentecostal Church in Springfield, Missouri.

Fig. 36   This was used as a handbill for the Smith Wigglesworth rally in Springfield, but it was taken when the tent was up at Campbell and Calhoun and Bert Williams preached the revival that shook Springfield.

Fig. 37   This is the other side of the handbill. I think Herman Harvey was then the pastor, and of course this is Smith Wigglesworth. Brother Wigglesworth used to say, ''I'm bigger inside than I am outside!'' While watching Niagara Falls, he was heard to shout, ''Like that, my God, like that in me!''

Fig. 38 This is Bert Williams (L) and my Dad, J.J. Corum (R). It was taken sometime after Brother Williams had left *Word and Work* as editor and returned to the evangelistic field.

Fig. 39 This is Brother Stanley H. Frodsham and his daughter, Faith. The picture was taken while Brother Frodsham was editor of *Word and Work* in the late 1920's. The story of Alice Frodsham's homegoing, "Jesus is Victor", was published in *Word and Work*, July 1929, and in **Prophet with a Pen**.

Fig. 40 This is when the Argue Family came to visit us at the Christian Workers Union, while I was first preparing the manuscript for this book in the early 1930's. (R-L) A.H. Argue, Eva Argue, Zelma Argue, Hazel Corum, James J. Corum, Fred T. Corum.

Fig. 41 This picture was taken down at Mammoth Springs, Arkansas, at the time of the "Pentecostal Fountain" (L-R): Hazel Corum, Josie Sizelove, Rachel Sizelove, Lillie Corum, Florence Taliaferro.

Fig. 42 This is Fred Corum just about the time that Brother Bell gave him some advice that helped him win the state oratorical contest.

Fig. 43 This is Rachel and Joseph Sizelove baptizing a group of young people down in the Ozarks.

Fig. 44 Mother Barnes around the time that she came and held a tentmeeting for us in Springfield.

Fig. 45 Our neighbor, Brother Boyd, in 1922.

Fig. 46 Rachel and Josie Sizelove in 1915.

Fig. 47 An early tentmeeting held by Mother Barnes.

Fig.48 Sister Boyd (center). I believe that is "Grand-mother" Flower on the left and Sister Reynolds on the right.

Fig. 49 Paul Corum about the time of the shotgun accident.

Fig. 50 Laurel Taliaferro and Fred Corum, 1919.

Fig. 51 Group photo of the Thayer Church when it started. Mother Barnes is fourth from the left in the second row. John Davis is standing second from the right in the back row. (Courtesy of the Thayer Assembly of God.)

Fig. 52 Evangelist A.H. Argue, 1917.

Fig. 53 CBI's first year. Front row left to right Mrs. and Mr. Willard Pierce, Miss Ruth Campbell, Mr. and Mrs. D. W. Kerr, Miss Helen Atkinson. Hazel is standing behind and to the right of Miss Ruth Campbell. (courtesy of the Assemblies of God)

Fig. 54 Digging the foundation for CBI's first building. (Courtesy of the Assemblies of God).

Visitors and delegates at the organizational meeting of the General Council of the Assemblies of God, April 2-12, 1914, Hot Springs, Arkansas. Kneeling in front are members of first Executive Presbytery. Inset, Grand Opera House where meetings were conducted.—*Reprinted by the Assemblies of God Archives, Springfield, Missouri*

Fig. 55 Hot Springs Arkansas (Courtesy of the Assemblies of God Archives).

# Chapter XII

## JOHN DAVIS

"We will meet our loved ones at the Marriage Supper of
the Lamb."
A Tombstone in Thayer, Missouri

One of the most remarkable converts to come out of the
great Thayer, Missouri, tentmeeting was a fiddler and
dance-caller from Arkansas. He had been a drunkard and
the craving was so great, that he had to sleep with a jug of
whisky beside him at night. He heard the commotion and
came to Mother Barnes' tentmeeting to see the show. He was
gloriously and thoroughly saved and filled with the Holy
Ghost. Back in those days when you got the Holy Ghost,
it put the "go" in your feet and John Davis became a
preacher. He just started preaching and relied on the Holy
Spirit to show him what to say. Uncle Charlie loved him,
as did many others, and he would travel many miles just to
hear John Davis preach. Joe Duke recognized the stamp of
God upon Brother Davis' ministry and bought him a tent to
hold meetings in. John Davis held tentmeetings all over
Arkansas. The picture we've included of Joe Duke in this
book was a postcard mailed to John Davis back in 1912, and
the message Joe Duke sent was to encourage Brother Davis
and to let him know that he was praying for him.

Once when Uncle Charlie was very sick, he sent for John
Davis, and he came and prayed. Uncle Charlie was gloriously
healed and never forgot the great faith of this precious
evangelist.

John Davis was holding a brush arbor meeting down in
Yellville, Arkansas, and the power of God began to fall. By
the way, a brush arbor was made by stringing wires back

and forth between tree limbs. Then leaf-filled branches would be placed over the wires to form a covering to keep out the sun and rain. He was just a plain old Arkansawyer with very little religious training, but he was clay in the Master's hands. He would go out in the woods and pray all night before he preached, and then ministered in the power of the Spirit. Well, people began to get saved and healed and filled with the Holy Ghost. Soon opposition began to arise. One day, a group of denominational preachers announced that they were going to come in and take over the meeting to hold a debate with John Davis and show him all this Pentecostal preaching was error. Brother Davis didn't know what to do. He wasn't a debater. He had very little education and no formal Bible training. Brother Brumback tells about this incident in his book :

> "Davis was distressed, for though a firm believer and preacher of the message, he did not consider himself able to defend it against these sharpshooters. He went to prayer, lying all night before the rough altar (just a few years before, he had spent many nights lying dead drunk in the road before a saloon). The next night, even before the meeting was formally opened, the Lord baptized twenty in the Spirit, and the slain of the Lord were many."[1]

People were praying all over the place and God had intervened and taken control, and the fire was falling from heaven. While Brother Davis was busy ministering at the altar, several of the denominational preachers showed up dressed in long-tailed black coats and sat on some of the benches near the back, waiting for the opportune time to interrupt and start the debate. The power of God fell with great demonstration and grew in intensity as the evening progressed. You can't debate with God. When Brother Davis looked up from the altar, he saw the last of the seven preachers

142

slinking away in the bushes outside the brush arbor. As with Jehoshaphat's battle against the invading armies of Moab, 'Ye shall not need to fight in this battle', for the debate was the Lord's (II Chronicles, Chapter 20) and the meetings were not even interrupted.

Later a group of workers from Joplin, Missouri, came down to Springfield to hold meetings for us. They believed that God had called them to Springfield, but it seemed like all of their efforts were in vain. A message came in tongues one night, ''Your work in Springfield is finished. You have preached with foolish jesting and I could not use you. Go to Yellville, and there I will use you.'' So they went from Springfield down to Yellville where John Davis had preached. God used them and a great work was done in that place. Later someone told my Dad, ''All you have to do is shake a bush in Yellville, and out will pop a bunch of holy rollers.'' Part of this band of workers were T. B. Ashley and his wife, Everett and Opal Wiley, Homer Wilson and Ethel Write. Ethel Write later married Howard Goss, who was one of the five ministers that called the General Convention at Hot Springs, Arkansas, in April, 1914. Brother Goss pastored the host church at Hot Springs. His testimony of the early days is given in Bennett Lawrence's book, **The Apostolic Faith Restored**[2] and his wife, Ethel, later wrote a book, **The Winds of God**.[3] In it, she tells about the gospel bands that went out from Parham schools and how they ministered.

John Davis was filled with the joy and glory of the Lord and he proclaimed it wherever he went. One day, he saw an old friend walk down the street and turned into a saloon that Brother Davis had often frequented before he was redeemed. Brother Davis went after him and as he stepped up on the sidewalk in front of the saloon, the power of God came on him and he fell prostrate. He had a marvelous vision of the Marriage Supper of the Lamb and the glories that are yet to be. When he was lost, he had spent many nights

143

dead drunk at the same spot. But oh, the glorious transformation that had taken place in his life, and he often told of this vision of the Marriage Supper of the Lamb.

Uncle Charlie said that if he ever died, he wanted John Davis to preach his funeral. Years later, I believe it was in the early 20's, while I was attending Drury College, Uncle Charlie died in the Frisco Hospital in St. Louis. They brought his body back to Thayer for the funeral. I believe that John Davis was out of the ministry and working on the railroad when he received the call to preach the funeral. But oh, how he could pray.

Uncle Charlie had been a Mason, and the Masonic Order came in dressed in their regalia, and performed their ceremony. And then it was John Davis' turn. This was the last time that I ever saw John Davis. He was just a plain Arkansawyer, but he had been out praying in the woods all night. And when he spoke, the fire fell and a revival broke out, right at the funeral. He only talked ten to fifteen minutes. He said he'd see Uncle Charlie again in heaven, and asked the question, "Will I meet you at the Marriage Supper of the Lamb?" Dignified men and women began to weep and pray and seek the Lord. It had been almost 15 years since the great Thayer revival but the sweet Spirit of God swept over glowing coals, and revival fires spread through that litle community one more time.

If you go to the cemetery today in Thayer, back up on a hill, near the old entrance, you can find Uncle Charlie's and Aunt Florence's tombstone. On it you'll find the inscription, "We will meet our loved ones at the Marriage Supper of the Lamb."

John Davis was a great man of prayer, and when he reached the throne, his ministry had marvelous results. His widow sent me the picture that we've enclosed in this book. My clearest remembrance of John Davis, however, was when he was at the city-wide tent revival that Bert Williams held for our church in Springfield. But the memory of him which I cherish most was seeing him praying away, pressing the battle at the altar.

## REFERENCES

1. **Suddenly From Heaven**, by Carl Brumback, The Gospel Publishing House, Springfield, Mo., 1961, Pg. 283, (Reprinted as **Like A Mighty River**, GPH, 1977,Pg. 141.)
2. **The Apostolic Faith Restored**, by Bennett F. Lawrence, The Gospel Publishing House, St. Louis, Missouri, 1916, PP. 53, 60-68.
3. **The Winds Of God**, by Ethel E. Goss, Word Aflame Press, Hazelwood, Missouri, 1958. Revised, updated and reprinted 1986.

# Chapter XIII

## HARRY E. BOWLEY

"We spent a month in strong supplication before God... the revival was born in our hearts."

Harry E. Bowley

I t is difficult for me to describe on paper the spiritual power of this wonderful man of God. He was very responsive to the leading of the Holy Spirit, and his burning desire was to point souls to the manifested love of God at Calvary. He had a glorious ministry in the Spirit. I'm sure that there are many people that could tell you much more about Brother Bowley than I. Brother Flower wrote of Brother Bowley,

"He had a deep spiritual life and he had a great influence upon many young people who were inspired to follow his example in their consecration to God and His service."[1]

During the Autumn of 1933, I was able to arrange to get Brother Bowley to conduct a series of meetings in the Northeast, and I wrote a short article about him in the December issue of *Word and Work*.[2]

Harry Bowley had first heard of the Latter Rain outpouring of the Holy Spirit in the Fall of 1906 when he was just a young man working in a print shop in Illinois. I believe that Charles F. Parham and one of his evangelistic bands went to Zion City, Illinois, and it was in these meetings, according to Brother Brumback, that Harry Bowley, F. F. Bosworth, Fred Vogler, and Edith Banger received the Baptism.[3] Less than a year later, Brother Seymour would write, "People here at Zion City received the Baptism in their pews while the service was going on, and sometimes scores of them received it. It is the sweetest thing you want to see. . . This is another Azusa.''[4]

The Richey family was at Zion City at this time also, and I believe that Raymond T. Richey's father was, at one time, the Mayor of Zion City. By the way, J. Roswell Flower had previously been at Zion with his parents, and soon Brother Flower, Brother Vogler, Harry Bowley, and Bennett Lawrence would engage together in pioneer ministry. In June of 1911, Brother Bowley would serve as best man at J. Roswell Flower's wedding with Alice Reynolds in Indianapolis.[5]

After receiving the Baptism of the Holy Spirit in 1906, Harry's soul was on fire to preach the Word and let others know about the great love of God. It was while he was on his way to Kansas City in 1908 or 1909, that he visited Mother Barnes in St. Louis and learned of Joe Duke and the call to Thayer, Missouri. According to a Pentecostal Evangel article by Brother Bowley:

> ''. . . We spent a month in strong supplication before God, which lasted sometimes all night, and the revival was born in our hearts.
> . . . Supernatural things happened those days.
> (Brethren, we have missed God's will somewhere. He wants to do the same thing today. Why shouldn't we expect miracles and wonders as great and glorious today - and even more glorious, for isn't this the end time.
> Thirty-five and forty years ago, we heard from God, and He said, 'Jesus is coming soon; prepare to meet Him.' That was the message which the Spirit gave the people when they received the Baptism. Friends, we don't realize how near we must be to the time of His coming.) . . . One day we went to the tent and stayed there all day, not leaving until two or three o'clock in the morning. We

147

> didn't even leave for meals at noon. People
> all over the place were receiving the Baptism;
> others were getting saved, the sick were be-
> ing healed, and demons were being cast out.
> When one person would get saved, he would
> go back and tell the news, and someone else
> would come running. We had no need of
> advertising. God took care of that. The place
> was crowded with folk who wanted to know
> the Lord.''[6]

In the photograph that I've enclosed of the great Thayer
tentmeeting, you can see Bennett Lawrence, Harry Bowley,
Mother Barnes, Joe Duke, John Davis, Joe French, Charles,
Florence, Virginia and Laurel Taliaferro, James, Lillie,
Hazel, Paul, Artemus and Fred Corum (I'm sitting at Mother
Barnes' feet), Grandma Harper, Brother and Sister Sloan,
Sister Flint, Mother Moise[11], Imogene Barnes, Rufus
Cooper, and of course, many others whose names I do not
recall. I guess we were just children then, but those meetings
have stayed with Hazel and me all our lives. So many
wonderful things happened there. I remember one of the
young people giving a message in tongues. I believe that it
was in Spanish. Brother Bowley has reported the incident.

> ''...There was a backslidden missionary who
> had fallen into deep sin. He wandered into
> town and asked someone, 'Have you a show
> where a person can go and have some fun?'
> 'Yes, the biggest show in town is up there at
> the 'rag meeting house''. He came up. In the
> midst of the meeting, one of our young peo-
> ple stood up and spoke in the most beautiful
> Spanish. This man had studied Spanish and
> understood it. She told him of every sin in his
> life - what he was doing, the wives he was

148

living with, how he had covered up his life - and called him to repentance. After it was over, he stood up and said, 'I planned to come and make fun. Here an innocent child comes to me with a message, telling me that the gifts and calling of God are without repentance. If I'm going to be ready to meet Him, I must get out of my sin and shame. What on earth do you have here? This girl has spoken in the pure Spanish language, telling me everything I've ever done wrong in my life.' "

That is the kind of thing that happened in the meetings in those days."[7]

At the close of the meetings, Brother Bowley was chosen to pastor the newly formed church at Thayer.

". . . During the whole revival, I had spoken only twice. Brother Lawrence, being a wonderful preacher, was able to give out the Word; but when it came to the altar services, it seemed that God mightily anointed me for that. The unction and power of my prayer life was so upon me that during the meeting, I would lean over on the front seat, and while he preached, I would weep. When he finished preaching, I would leap to the platform, and in less than fifteen minutes, the altars would be jammed with men and women weeping and seeking God.

To my great consternation, I was chosen to be the pastor of the new-born church. I felt so incapable. I had little education. I was limited in Bible knowledge, and I was a very poor preacher."[8]

And so, Harry Bowley found himself the pastor of a congregation, but they had no place to meet. The Lord brought in enough money to purchase a lot on the corner of Fifth and Walnut Streets for the church, but when they started to build, the church's financial resources amounted to twenty-five cents . One of the brethren said to Brother Bowley,

> "Man, you can't build a church on twenty-five cents. . . If I didn't have faith in your prayers, I'd lay down my tools right now. But we'll build the church."[9,10]

And so, Harry Bowley took the church's total finances and

> ". . . he bought twenty-five cents worth of nails to start with, but before the last nail was driven there was a thousand feet of lumber on the grounds and enough money to buy nails and pay four carpenters at the end of the week. In sixteen months, sixteen Assemblies had grown up in that vicinity. After preaching around for about two years, he suddenly found himself pastor of a large Assembly in southern Missouri, while just in his early twenties."[11]

Sometime after building the church at Thayer, Harry Bowley went as a missionary to Africa for several years. Subsequently, he returned to this country to work on the evangelistic field and later pastored churches in Dallas, Texas, and Tulsa, Oklahoma.

While he was visiting us in England, back in 1933, and preaching at a rally, he stated that

> ". . . He envied the young men today and longed to start over again. He never had the opportunities of attending Bible School as Pentecostal young people have today, but was trained in the school of hard knocks. [He said] . . 'The need today is a vital, living, personal touch with God. . .. A tragedy in the Pentecostal Movement today is that thousands

150

have come into the movement, but there is no longer such a passion for a lost world, and hunger for God, no touch of God on their lives. . . We need a spiritual sensitiveness. . . . The sweetest thing in all the world is to walk with Jesus. Not by schools and mastering of books can you attain, although they are helpful, but success comes from the personal touch with God by putting Him first.''"[8]

Concerning the intercessory prayer life that rested upon him during the Thayer Revival, Brother Bowley later wrote.

''. . . May God bring us back to such a life again. We never will have the revivals and the supernatural working of God in our churches until we press into that place where we will let God have His way regardless of cost. We are in the time of the last outpouring of God's Spirit. The last call is going out. It is the day of God's visitation. What are we going to do about it? Are we going to be careless and fail the Lord, or are we going to rise to the opportunity and press in until God can again pour out His Spirit and send miraculous signs and wonders to confirm His word?''"[6,7]

During the time that I knew him, Harry Bowley was one of the most Spirit-led men that I have ever known. He was very sensitive to the movings of the Holy Spirit and knew the secret of ministering in the Spirit. He was a very humble, but brilliant speaker - always preaching under the anointing of the Holy Ghost. I believe it was John Wesley that said, ''God is only limited by our prayer life.'' Harry Bowley was a great man of prayer and a precious instrument in the hands of the Lord.

Harry E. Bowley

## Editorial Comments

On July 5, 1982, three of the authors traveled to Thayer, Missouri, and had the opportunity to speak with Vernon Aileen Green. Brother Green, now eighty years old, was seven years of age when he attended the Thayer Campmeeting, and he is a charter member of the original Pentecostal Church at Thayer. He remembers Brother Bennett Lawrence, Brother Bowley, Joe Duke, Joe French, John Davis, and Mother Barnes quite well. Brother Green took us to the spot where the tent sat, on the corner of Fourth and Chestnut Streets. The spot is now a large grassy lawn surrounded by tall trees, beside an old Junior High School, built on a hill overlooking Thayer, Missouri. From the hill, you can look across Thayer, and the railroad, on up to the cemetery where Uncle Charlie and Aunt Florence are buried.

Brother Green, who became an ordained minister, recalled that, "Sister Sloan got the Holy Ghost first, and then Sisters Lucy and Bessie Johnson. As many as seven at one time would get the Baptism of the Holy Ghost. People would get saved and sanctified all over the tent, and would be slain in the Spirit for hours. Brother Bowley had a mighty anointing upon his life and God used him to minister to the people's spiritual needs."

We also met Reverend Wayne Smith, who is the current pastor of the Thayer Assembly. Brother Smith pointed out the rich heritage of the Thayer Church, whose pastors included not only Mother Barnes and Harry Bowley, but also Bennett Lawrence, W. T. Gaston, Joe Rosselli, and many other famous Pentecostal brethren. Brother Ralph Riggs received the Baptism of the Holy Ghost and the call into the ministry there in 1913.

## REFERENCES
1. Tribute, by J. Roswell Flower (*Pentecostal Evangel*)
2. "Harry E. Bowley", *Word and Work*, Vol. 55, No.

12, December, 1933, Pg. 13.

3.  **Suddenly From Heaven**, by Carl Brumback, The Gospel Publishing House, Springfield, Missouri, 1961, Pg. 72, (Reprinted as **A Sound From Heaven**,GPH, 1977, Pg.70.)

4.  *The Apostolic Faith*, Vol. 1, No. 9, September, 1907, Pg. 1. Reprinted in **Like As of Fire**.

5.  **Grace for Grace**, by Alice Reynolds Flower, Springfield, Missouri, 1961, PP. 46, 48.

6.  "The Great Revival at Thayer, Mo. - Part 1", by Harry E. Bowley, *Pentecostal Evangel*, June 12, 1948, PP. 3,-.

7.  "The Great Revival at Thayer, Mo. - Part 2", by Harry E. Bowley, *Pentecostal Evangel*, June 19, 1948, PP. 5, 12-13.

8.  Reference 2 (Word and Work, Dec. 1933)

9.  "The Great Ozark Mountain Revival", by Harry E. Bowley, *Assemblies of God Heritage*, Vol. 2, No. 2, Summer, 1982, PP. 1,3.

10. "The Great Thayer Revival", **Thayer Assembly of God- 70th Anniversary**, 1979, PP. 2-4.

11. "Mother Moise", by Wayne Warner *Assemblies of God Heritage*, Vol. 6, No. 1, Spring 1986, PP. 6,7,13,14

# Chapter XIV

## CONTINUED STRUGGLES AT SPRINGFIELD

"There shall be no Alps!"
A. E. Benedict

T he Thayer, Missouri, tentmeeting was a turning point for Pentecost in the Southern Missouri-Arkansas region. My Father was so enthused and blessed by these meetings that we stayed a second week. When we finally got back to Springfield and Dad returned (one week late) to his job as telegraph operator at the Frisco Railroad, his boss, Mr. Dritt, fired him for staying away the second week. Well, we were back in Springfield, and it was a different world than Thayer. There were great spiritual battles before us. This was a period of time when many men were out of work, and employment was hard to get. However, Dad was soon hired to be Chief Supervisor of the freight office, but with a thirty-five dollar a month decrease in salary.

The Lord did a wonderful work in Thayer, but still Springfield seemed so hard. Then some preachers came along and held some meetings for us and they said, "It's an old burnt over field and God's never going to work in Springfield."

The next years were difficult for us. Mother would go and rent various little buildings around Springfield and conduct church. She also would hold street meetings and it seems as though every summer we would hold tentmeetings. There were no wealthy people in the church. We rented store fronts all up and down Boonville Street and Commercial Street. Different preachers would come through, and they didn't have any finances either. We had an eight room farm house and when visiting preachers or missionaries would come, they would always stay with us and it meant that we boys would be sleeping on the floor. Our little Pentecostal band was gradually increasing, but we were still struggling. And then the Lord brought a marvelous woman into our little band.

### Amanda E. (Alice) Benedict

We want to tell how God brought a mighty prayer warrior and faithful soldier of the cross into our midst. This is an inspiring story of a dependable and faithful servant of the Lord, who knew how to fast and pray and hold on to God until results followed. Oh, that there were more of her caliber in these days! God gave her a vision of a mighty revival coming to Springfield long before the General Council was formed. Mother wrote this story up and I published it in *Word and Work* in July, 1934.

### "How A Handmaiden of the Lord Kept the Army in Rank"
#### by Mrs. J.J. Corum

"It was a warm, sunshiny day there in the Ozarks and Amanda E. Benedict, for such was her name, had walked many miles. I met her at the door of my home and she smiled cheerfully in spite of her weariness. She was glad to come and sit down in the chair I offered, and she began to show me the little things she was selling. I felt that I just must tell her how precious it was to know the Lord as a Saviour.

After she had shown me what she had to sell, there was a pause, then she spoke of the large Bible on my center table and asked if I loved to read it.

I replied, 'Yes, especially since I have received the Baptism of the Holy Ghost.' 'Oh', said she, with her eager, heavenly look, 'have

155

you the Baptism? I want you to pray for my healing.'

I sent my little girl, Hazel, for a neighbor who had also received the Baptism, Sister Boyd, and we then went before the Lord in prayer. When Miss Benedict prayed, so wonderful was her communion with God, that I marvelled that she had not received the Baptism of the Holy Ghost, but it was all so new to us at that time. How glorious it was to revel in the presence of our mighty Baptizer! She appeared as one that talked face to face with the Lord as did Moses.

'Now Father Dear,' she would say as she reminded Him of her longings. My little son remarked afterward, 'Mother, she asks God for everything in the world.' The depths of my heart were moved as she so wonderfully exalted the Blood of Jesus.

What sweet fellowship we had with this sister in Christ, no longer a stranger. I felt at once, here is another dear one who Jesus will baptize with the Holy Ghost and fire to add to our little company of believers.

### Pioneering in Springfield, Missouri

We were then the early pioneers in Springfield. The Lord was selecting the foundation and the pillars upon which to build. We had our little prayer meetings in our homes in those days and it was marvelous how God would meet us and pour out His Spirit as we waited before Him. Some would hear about the manifestations of God's power and would come to see. Often fear would fall upon them and they would be convicted that God was the author of this movement. Others said we will wait and see if it stands, for if it is of God, it will stand.

### Sister Benedict Receives The Baptism

One day, Sister Benedict said to me, 'The Lord has said to me that He will baptize me next Sunday.'

On that day, I went to our cottage meeting and she was under the mighty power of God and the precious Holy Ghost came into the clay temple testifying of Jesus. I felt she would surely preach the Gospel as she had a splendid education. Her native home was in New York. She was not ignorant of the devil's devices, but was a trained soldier of the cross. She had conducted a rescue home for girls in the city of Chicago and had been connected with a faith home for children in Iowa. However, the Lord kept her right in her place as an intercessor, enduing her with the mighty power of the Holy Ghost. She had a burden for lost souls and that God might do a work in Springfield.

### Vision of the Heavenward March

One day, as she waited before the Lord, she had a vision of a mighty revival coming to Springfield and she saw an awful darkness and was made very sad, as many in the heavenward march were unable to keep step with the soldier on either side and the one in the front and the one in the rear. Many fell by the way, and it was sad to behold, but thank God many

157

kept in the ranks and pressed the battle to the gates.

She told us of her vision and as we continued our march, there were many joyous victories. We have also beheld the sad part, for many that joined in the march fell out of rank by the wayside.

### A Tattered Tent

Brother Frank Landis, who was seeking the Baptism, donated a gospel tent to us one summer. I believe this was in 1911. It was old, but of a good size and suited our purpose. It was a 'two pole tent', that is, it had two big poles in the middle with a lot of tent poles around the edges. We decided to erect it on a vacant lot located at Campbell and Calhoun Streets which was then owned by a saloon keeper, named Kirby. He operated the Kirby Saloon near the square on Commercial Street. My little son drove Sister Benedict and I in our four-wheeled buggy. Hazel held the horses and we went into the saloon and met the owner who willingly gave us permission to use the land. A group of young ministers from Arkansas came and cleared off the property, piling up all the shrubs and branches on our wagon. My son hauled it away.

We had good meetings, but in our absence, boys began to damage the tent, and then to annoy and persecute during our meetings. They would jerk the ropes and slide down the canvas. On the last day of our meetings, the old Gospel tent stood there in tatters. About all that was left was the end that covered over the platform. It was a Sunday morning and

Brother S. F. Wishard of Denver, Colorado, was in our meetings. He had been a cowboy out in Colorado and he told us that once when he was on a cattle drive, a great electrical storm came up one night. The lightning would jump from horn to horn and play on the horns of the cattle. He was a Spirit-filled, old, Holiness preacher that was holding meetings with the Holiness people on Commercial Street at the time. Some were discouraged and thought it was the end, but the old saints felt a song of triumph. Brother Wishard said our tattered tent reminded him of a soldier's parade he had attended in the East. He said that while the people were admiring the soldiers with their bright flags and music, an old tattered flag that had been in many Civil War battles came by, carried by old men, some of whom had been wounded, some were crippled, and some were on crutches. He said when the old, torn and tattered flag, full of bullet holes passed, there arose a great cheer from the crowd and there was more cheering for it than all the parade. So he believed there would be more cheering in Heaven over our tattered tent in which we were worshipping God.

The next day, early in the morning, we went back to take down our old tattered tent at the corner of Calhoun and Campbell Streets. We found that the tent had already been torn down (what had been left of it) by the boys.

### The New Church

It was a determined little force that day which claimed the land and even claimed the

159

city for Christ. Oh! if we could have looked down through the years and seen how God honored our humble efforts. For in after years, when our assembly had grown larger and we wanted to build our own place of worship, Brothers E.N. Bell, J.W. Welch and other brethren had already secured the same land the saloon keeper had owned, and it was purchased by the assembly. The beautiful church building was built while Rev. J. R. Elsom was our pastor, and stands today as a monument to the faithful effort of those early saints. It stands on the very spot where unfurled to the breeze, stood our torn and tattered tent.''[1]

[Remember that this was written by Mother in 1934. Today, Central Assembly covers almost the entire block from Boonville Street to Campbell Street. Many thousands have found God on the place where this old tent stood. The trees under which Sister Benedict would go and pray all night during this tent meeting, stood where the choir, pulpit, and altar rail of Central Assembly now are. Surely, God answered her prayers.]

Just after this tentmeeting, we followed Brother Wishard, who was holding meetings with Brother Moore, for the Holiness people on Commercial Street. Brother Wishard was Spirit-filled, but the Holiness people let him preach full salvation. This was in 1911. However, after Brother Wishard left to hold meetings elsewhere, the Holiness people also left and so we kept the building to hold services in. It was during this period of time that Sister Birdie Hoy came into our assembly. She was a beautiful woman with a wonderful singing voice. Sister Hoy used to jump up in our meetings and say, ''I feel like a Jericho March!'' And she would start singing ''The Fight Is On'' and be off and marching with the

160

rest of us following behind. She often did this over the years - especially if the preaching got flat. We will have more to say about Sister Hoy in a later chapter. She, Mother, and Sister Benedict became a powerful prayer band for the church. Sister Benedict used to say, ''A threefold cord is not easily broken.'' But, let us continue with Mother's article about Sister Benedict.

### Fasting and Prayer

''Hast not the Lord said, 'Am I not thy God? Is there anything too hard for me?' Sister Benedict believed that promise. She was brave and fearless, going into the hard places, shielding others. How great was her courage! I have seen her smile in the face of seeming death, because there is no defeat in the ever-present One who is the Resurrection and the Life.

Never have I met a person who prayed as she prayed, fasting from food and from sleep, praying all night, yet looking as bright and happy in the morning and never appearing to be fasting.

It was laid on her heart at one time to fast and pray until a loved one was saved. For fourteen days, she neither tasted any food or drank any water, yet she kept on her feet working for the Lord. Of course, the loved one was saved. All heaven is moved by such prayer. She became a marvelous Christian worker and has been instrumental to a great extent in building up a large assembly in another city and also instrumental in guiding policies of the Council. After leaving Springfield for a long time, she continued to

> send her tithes to our little struggling
> assembly, which was of great help to us.''[1]

After holding meetings in the building on Commercial Street, we rented a place to meet in Maple Grove on East Division Street. Our little Pentecostal band continued to meet regularly. Here a man by the name of L.H. Pruett came and preached with great demonstration. But the Lord showed us that he was a deceiver. Our place of worship moved to Boonville Street near Pacific Street. I've often wished that we had kept photographs of all those little places where the ''Pentecostal Church of Springfield'' pressed the battle. About this time, it was late in 1911, a rather overbearing woman named King came from West Plains, Missouri, and stirred up trouble, and our little assembly began to be torn by the devil. Sister Benedict, who lived on Phelps Street, came to our home out on the edge of Springfield very early one morning and told us that God had said that the saints should fast on bread and water until victory came. She said that as she had walked along in the early hours of dawn, an angel came on either side of her and helped to bear her along. She had prayed all night. And so Mother and Sister Benedict began to fast and pray.

Then, when this Mrs. King and Mr. Pruett heard about our pledge to fast, they said they'd starve us out. That night, I drove Mother down to Sister Benedict's house on Phelps Street in the buggy, and they prayed all night. They prayed and prayed that God would protect and save the church. Around midnight, I fell asleep on the hard board floor in Sister Benedict's house. As the first rays of dawn began to show in the window, I was awakened by shouts of victory from Mother and Sister Benedict. The room was filled with glorious victory. I knew that they had reached the throne and that God had answered their prayers. Without even asking, I got up, went out and hitched up the horses. I knew that we could go home.

162

Mrs. King left before nightfall that very day, and Mr. Pruett left within the week. They had been running the church (ruining it would be more descriptive). We later found out that they were keeping the offerings and had been living together.

Thank God for the faithfulness of Sister Benedict, and Praise God who giveth us the victory through Our Lord Jesus Christ.

Back in those days, it seemed natural for people to fast and pray. Mother gave her heart to the Lord in an old-fashioned Methodist meeting in Marengo, Indiana, on Thanksgiving Day in 1878. She was seventeen years old then and she never grew weary of witnessing to God's wonderful grace and the power of the Blood. After that, she always fasted on Thanksgiving Day, yet preparing a feast for the rest of us.

Sister Benedict would fast and pray for days on end. Back in those days, she sought God for the city of Springfield, and He laid it on her heart to fast and pray for Springfield for a year - fasting only on bread and water. I can remember her being at our house many times, and while we ate our meals, Sister Benedict would have only a piece of bread and glass of water. She made no open show of it, but she would not compromise either. And, for over a year, she was on her face before God, pleading the promises and ministering in the Spirit for the city of Springfield and for its Pentecostal Church. It is no wonder that glorious victory was coming our way.

> "Many were the labors of this dear saint
> of God. She continued to work and pray for
> souls to be saved and believers filled with the
> Spirit. She lived to see the General Council
> formed and the work prosper."[1]

Years ago, Mother wrote the following in her notebook:
"Many times I have heard her say, like

163

Napoleon, 'There shall be no Alps!'

Pentecostal saints were few at Springfield in those early days. There were three of us sisters who stood together in the faith [Sister Benedict, Mother, and Sister Hoy]. We prayed much for God to do a great work in Springfield. As we did so, she would often say, 'A three fold cord is not easily broken'. She loved preachers, but was brave and would expose a sham as an untruth, seeing that God's work should not suffer from any hypocrisy. As we kept under God's banner of love, I have seen her weep and pray for a weak brother or sister until some would ask to have the demons cast out. It was wonderful to see one delivered after a desperate struggle and filled with the praises of God.

We had a small hall rented on Commercial Street where we had services. She would go before anyone else got there so she could pray. I believe by her presence there so early, pleading with tears to our Heavenly Father, that the atmosphere was cleared and God's presence was in our midst." L.H.C.[2]


### Trail Blazing

"In 1915, she moved to Aurora, Missouri, into new fields of endeavor where she began another Pentecostal work. Later, students from Central Bible Institute often went with us to assist her there. She bore many hardships at that place, but God used her to blaze the way for the Full Gospel to be proclaimed there."

On Saturday nights, Stanley Frodsham would take a train

164

from Springfield to Aurora, preach Saturday night and two meetings on Sunday, and return to Springfield on Sunday night. It was here that Brother Frodsham met Sister Benedict. Brother Frodsham's daughter, Faith Campbell, wrote,

"Miss Benedict's tremendous burden was that God would make Springfield a center from which His blessings would flow to the ends of the earth. My father believed that the church [Central Assembly], Central Bible College, and the Gospel Publishing House were largely the results of her fervent, effectual prayers"[3]

### Work Follows On

"In 1925, God saw fit to promote Sister Benedict to her glory. Her body was brought to Springfield for burial, and we held her funeral in the Assembly of God church. Rev. D.W. Kerr was our pastor at that time. He was the first Dean of C.B.I. and is now in glory. During the service, he gave us the privilege to testify. A holy hush prevailed over the people, as one by one, old-time friends and students of Central Bible Institute spoke of what her life had meant to them. It had been such an inspiration, such an example of indomitable courage, of prevailing prayer. Mention was made of her all-night prayers, how that when others fell asleep, she held on until dawn. Mention was made of the old tent that had stood on that spot where the assembly was cradled and how there were a few bound by a chain of love that never broke. Some spoke of how branches of the Springfield work now

165

reached practically the whole earth and God
alone knows how much of that success is
traceable to her prayers.''[1]

There was a funeral report published in the Pentecostal
Evangel, April 9, 1927.

By the way, I have a copy of perhaps the last letter that
Sister Benedict ever wrote. It was postmarked only a few
days before she went to be with the Lord. It is too long to
reproduce here, but let me give the closing lines:

". . . Pray, fight, hold, till hell gives way,
till the real power, the power of His might,
of our real God shall fall with such invinci-
ble force, that sin shall go down before it and
the Christ that saves from sin shall be lifted
up. That bodies may be healed and devils cast
out. Keep praying for the preachers - we must
put up a resolute, winning fight on their
behalf.

Our fighting force is small, but it's gain-
ing ground. Every forward step is hotly con-
tended, but our flag is flying, our bugle is
sounding an advance to our forces; a retreat
to the foe, and my heart cried out incessantly
during last night's meeting, 'Take us over the
top, Lord, take us over the top!' A.E.B.

(Letter to Sister Lillie Corum written from
Aurora, Missouri, April 14, 1925.)

This was the indomitable spirit of prayer that had earlier
broken the powers of darkness over Springfield. Surely, the
gates of hell could not prevail. Before such seasoned warriors, helpless demon powers must tremble, break ranks, and
flee for cover! God had an army and it was marching through
the land.

"We have heard it many times remarked
that very few anywhere could pray as she

166

prayed. Thank God for this soldier of the cross who was faithful unto death - dear Sister Benedict. 'At rest with Jesus from toil set free, yet still thy works are following thee.' ''[1]

Lord, do it again. Oh Lord, take us over the top.

## REFERENCES

1. "How A Handmaiden of the Lord Kept the Army in Rank", by Mrs. J.J. Corum, *Word and Work*, July, 1934, PP. 1, 10.

2. "The Pentecostal Church of Springfield", typed notes by L.H. Corum, n.d., circa 1921.

3. **Stanley Frodsham - Prophet with a Pen**, by Faith Campbell, Gospel Publishing House, Springfield, Missouri, 1974, Pg. 64.

4. "Abundance For All", by A.E. Benedict, the Pentecostal Evangel, March 19, 1927, pg. 5.

# Chapter XV

## REINFORCEMENTS COME TO SPRINGFIELD

"... saved, filled with the Holy Spirit, and brought out into a life of blessing in God."

**M**other Barnes held tentmeetings for us several times. Along about 1910 or 1912, she came with a small "two-pole" tent and held meetings for us during the summer. Joe French, John Davis, and Joe Duke were there. The true date could probably be set because this was very likely just about the time that Harry Bowley went to Africa as a missionary. And many others were there too, whose names have slipped away over the years. It was a marvelous meeting, but did not have the great effects that occurred in Thayer. I remember, late one night after the meeting was over, Brother Duke was letting the tent flap down and saw someone standing in the shadows. Brother Duke said, "My, isn't this glorious!" The man looked at him and said, "You ought to be hung. You're insane."

I remember Dad getting up and testifying one night. I can still see him by the light of the old gasoline torches in the wooded grove. He spoke of the importance of winning the lost, the horribleness of a lost soul, and that someday there would be shining stars for the crown of the soul winner. My Dad loved the Word and loved to hear it's great themes expounded by able Bible teachers. Both he and Mother were interested in souls. However, they were not proselytizers looking for another hide to nail to the Pentecostal barn door. They loved to talk with people about the riches of this great salvation and they were anxious to share. That night, Dad spoke of the shining stars. There is an old song that goes:

"Oh joy it will be when His face I behold
Living gems at His feet to lay down.
It would sweeten my bliss in the City of Gold
Should there be any stars in my crown."

Over the years, I've often thought of the rich heritage that children have whose parents love the Lord and are filled with His Spirit. I can see them yet, Mom and Dad, praising God in that old tent in the wooded grove.

Laurel Taliaferro, who was just a youngster at the time, gave a message in tongues and an interpretation one night. The interpretation was that Jesus was coming back and would stand on Mount Zion. After the service, a number of the other youngsters made fun of him for what he had said. Mother spoke up and told us that what he said was true, and that the old prophets, Zechariah and Joel, had talked of the Lord returning someday to Mount Zion.

This was only one of several tentmeetings that Mother Barnes held for us. Later, she came back again, around the time when Bennett Lawrence became our pastor. At that time, she had a very large tent and created quite a stir in Springfield.

### Joe French Comes to Springfield

In 1911 or 1912, Joe French and his wife, Hattie (Childers), came to Springfield from West Plains, Missouri. This was the same Joe French that had been raised from the dead at the great Thayer tentmeeting several years earlier, in 1909. Brother French opened a large restaurant, near the Square on St. Louis Street. I remember he made the best chili in town - for five cents a bowl. Martha Childers Humbard mentions it in her book, **Give Me That Old Time Religion**[1], and when she used to come to our church to help out with the meetings, she would stay with her Sister Hattie and Brother French. In fact, when Joe French first came, he held

169

meetings for us and preached for several weeks. Here we heard the gospel from one who had been raised from the dead. Brother French has often repeated the terrible experience which he had when he died at the Hotel in Thayer. For he passed into the region of the lost and sank into a place of awful torment. He saw the great door through which all the unsaved must pass into a great fiery abyss and he heard the horrible cries of those who have been eternally separated from the peace of God. Brother Bowley later wrote about Joe French, and describing his condition before this remarkable event, said:

> "He was one of the hardest men I've ever met. He had fifteen scars on his body from fighting. It was said he had murdered an English soldier on a vessel. He was a down-and-outer, one of the worst characters I have known. I was reluctant to say much to him because of his hardness; he cut folks off like a snapping turtle; but somehow whenever I talked to him, he was kind to me."[2]

We have already told of Joe French's return to life. Joe testified that a great arm reached down and lifted him out of the flames just when it seemed that all was lost. It was at this point that he was drawn back to the earthly realm in answer to the effectual faith of Joe Duke and to the prayers of Mother Barnes, Bennett Lawrence, and Harry Bowley. I believe that Sister Flint and Sister Sloan were also there and could testify of this unusual event. Harry Bowley later wrote, "This man owed his life to the Lord and knew it. He was glad and happy. It was my personal privilege to see him saved, filled with the Holy Spirit, and brought out into a life of blessing in God." Brother French held wonderful meetings for the little assembly, and he and his wife soon became effective members in our church.

Gary Martin Joins With Us

As I read through Mother's notes, I see that at this time, Brother Collins from Stone County, Missouri, came and held meetings for us too. Brother Ed Deweese and his wife moved here from Texas and they were a great help to us. Mr. Brown, who pastored the United Brethren Church in Springfield, got the Baptism and joined with us. Brother Gary Martin and his family came and joined our assembly. Brother Martin was of great assistance to us. I remember that later on, when the brethren decided to start Central Bible Institute, Brother Martin testified that he had been a horrible drunkard when the Lord marvelously saved him and gloriously filled him with the Holy Ghost. He was a barber and he said he started to testify to everyone that came into the barber shop. One day, he had a man all lathered up in the barber chair ready for a shave. While he was stropping the old, straight-edged razor on the leather strap hanging on the side of the barber chair, he looked down and thought, "Here's a soul that's going into eternity and doesn't know Jesus." As he held the razor up and prepared to shave the man, he paused, looked down and said, "Sir, are you prepared to meet God?" The man took one look at Gary Martin standing there with a straight-edged razor poised over him, he jumped up and ran out of the door and down the street, with his face still lathered up and a red-striped barber's apron over his shoulders. Brother Martin said, "I never did get the apron back." And so, when they were discussing the necessity of Central Bible Institute, Brother Martin said to the brethren, "I need all the education, training, and wisdom I can get to deal with people about their souls." I believe that he was related to the baseball player, Mickey Owen. By the way, Brother Martin lived to be ninety-two years old.

## REFERENCES

1.  **Give Me That Old-Time Religion**, by Martha

Childers Humbard, Logos International, Plainfield, New Jersey, 1977.

2. "The Great Revival at Thayer, Mo. - Part 1", by Harry E. Bowley, *Pentecostal Evangel*, June 12, 1948, PP. 3,-.

## Chapter XVI

### OUR NUMBER SLOWLY GROWS

"I'm the one that threw the egg."

**W**e had been holding meetings up stairs in Woodman Hall on Prospect Street during the Fall and early Winter while Joe French and Brother Collins were preaching for us. When Brother Collins left, we waited upon the Lord to show us where to hold our meetings. We still did not have a church. The Lord showed our little fellowship to go and rent Bethel Chapel on Campbell Street from J. E. Ellis. This was the building which stood where the playground now is behind Pipkin Junior High School. We rented the building, and started having meetings in it on January 18, 1913. The power of God was with us and a sweet spirit of love prevailed over the assembly. Martha Childers came and helped out at this time. She was a beautiful girl and a vibrant Christian. This was the first time that we had met her.

In May, Mother went to visit her sister, Mary Harper Crandell, in Lawton, Oklahoma, for about four weeks. Father and we four children remained at home, for school was not out yet and Father had gotten back his job as telegraph agent for the Frisco Railroad at Springfield. During this time, Sister Sloan of Thayer, who had been holding meetings in California, came and held meetings for our assembly. There was a wooden tabernacle that had been owned by the Holiness people on the other side of Brother Ellis' property. It was on Boonville at Calhoun Street and stood exactly where the front of Pipkin Junior High School now stands. While Mother was gone, our little assembly raised the money and we bought this tabernacle. It had wooden benches and straw all around the altar. Sister Sloan preached and many were saved and

173

several received the Baptism of the Holy Spirit. These meetings continued on until August. Mother returned toward the end of June, and it was during this time that my brother, Paul Corum, received the Baptism of the Holy Spirit at church. Mother's notes say, "July 1, 1913 - Paul received Baptism of Holy Ghost." He would have been 12 years old at this time.

### How the Lord Used an Egg to Make a Preacher

While we were meeting in the wooden tabernacle on Boonville Street, the crowds would often come to find out about Pentecost. We also would attract quite a crowd of rowdies on the outside. They would cut the harness off of our old horses. They would stand at the windows and holler, pound on the walls, and carry on. Often times, the crowd on the outside looking in was almost as big as the crowd on the inside seeking the Lord. In Springfield, we seemed to be regarded as castoffs. But the power of God would come down and it seemed like the Glory Cloud of old would fill the tabernacle.

One night, while Sister Lula France from Joplin was preaching, a young boy ran halfway down the center aisle and threw an egg. It soared through the air, hit the pulpit a perfect bull's eye and splattered all over the platform, the preacher, and those near the front. The young man stood there with a great big grin, pretty proud of his aim. Mother jumped up, ran over to him, pointed her finger at him and said, "I saw you throw that egg." He arrogantly snorted, "What of it." Mother said, "I'm going to pray that you won't be able to sleep nights until you get saved. I'm going to pray that the Lord will make you miserable until you give your life to Christ. I'm going to pray that God will make you a preacher and a winner of souls - that you will lead many to Christ." Well, he just stood there, grinned, then swaggered out of the tabernacle. I can remember Mother praying about this many times afterward.

Years later, after Central Bible College had been started in the basement of our Church (which was located on the same spot where the tattered tent had stood), a tall, well-dressed, handsome, young man came to my Mother one morning and said, "Mrs. Corum, do you remember me?" Mother looked at him and somewhat confusedly said, "No, I don't think I know you." The young man said, "I'm the one that threw the egg." He began to weep and related, "I couldn't sleep nights and I remembered that you said you were going to pray that I couldn't sleep. In my misery, I sought God and He saved me, and I'm here at Central Bible College to become a minister." He later wrote a Bible Commentary and pastored a church in Texas. His name was Finis Jennings Dake. And so, God used a humbling incident to make a preacher.

The Lord dealt with other members of the crowd that hollered in the windows and pounded on the walls of that tabernacle on Boonville Street. There was one little boy that was terribly mean. He wore a yellow shirt and we called him "yellow jacket". He would shout and throw stones at the people at the altar and run and hide. He would torment us any way he could. Martha Childers was a radiant young Christian then. She had a beautiful velvet dress and all the girls were envious of her. Just before church one night, while she was praying at the altar, this rascal threw a rotten egg and hit her in the middle of the back. One of the saints grabbed him and said, "Look here. The Lord's going to get hold of you and use you for His glory." Martha was full of the joy of the Lord and she got up and sang and testified anyway. By the way, "yellow jacket" became a Christian, got the Holy Ghost, and ten years later, he was the contractor that built the first building (Bowie Hall) at Central Bible College. His name was Arthur Dake and his brother was Finis Jennings Dake.

In the mid 1920's, when Mother was visiting Denver, Colorado, she went to the Pentecostal Church there. At testimony time, she jumped up and testified for the Lord. After the service, the church pastor came to Mother and said, "Sister Corum, you don't know me, but I was one of those rowdies that used to torment the folks in the tabernacle on Boonville Street there in Springfield. The Lord saved me and brought me into the fullness of God and now I'm preaching the Gospel."

So the work wasn't in vain. Early in August, 1913, Brother and Sister Sloan returned to their home at Thayer, Missouri, where the fire was still falling and a mighty revival was in progress. Harry Bowley had moved on after praying in the building materials and constructing the mother church at Thayer, and Bennett Lawrence was pastoring there during the Summer of 1913. Ralph Riggs, a future General Superintendent of the Assemblies of God, was his song leader. Concerning these early meetings at Thayer, Brother Riggs has written, ". . . W. T. Gaston came to hold a tent revival. Here I was baptized in the Holy Spirit on August 29, 1913. I can still remember singing, 'Joys are flowing like a river since the Comforter has come.' In the church at Thayer, I also received my call to preach. . ." It was only a few years after this that Brother Lawrence would come to Springfield to be our pastor. Brother Gaston would later pastor the church at Thayer, and then the church at Springfield too (as would Brother Riggs later on). Brother Gaston would also serve several terms as General Superintendent of the Assemblies of God. But at this time, there was no Assemblies of God.

It was also during the Summer of 1913, that a large camp-meeting was held in Eureka Springs, Arkansas. At this meeting, M.M. Pinson, who edited a magazine called *Word and Witness*, joined forces with E. N. Bell who was editing a paper called *Apostolic Faith*. (There were several magazines around the country with that name at this time.) Bell's paper took on the name of Pinson's and Brother Bell continued to publish it in Malvern, Arkansas. In late December of 1913, it's pages would announce the call for a "General Convention of Pentecostal Saints and Churches of God in Christ" to be held in Hot Springs, Arkansas, the following April.

All of the Thayer preachers were at the April, 1914, Hot Springs Conference: Brother Lawrence, Brother Riggs, Brother Gaston, and Mother Barnes. I'm not sure if Brother Bowley was there or if he had already gone as a missionary to Africa.

# Chapter XVII

## THE SPARKLING FOUNTAIN

" . . . God is going to do a mighty work that will issue forth
from this city and will astound the world."       R.H.S.

Towards the middle of August, 1913, just after Brother
and Sister Sloan had returned to Thayer, Aunt Rachel
and Uncle Josie Sizelove made another trip East to
Springfield. They stayed with us for several months and while
they were there, they preached for us. Many souls were saved
and several received the Baptism of the Holy Spirit. I
remember that we held a street meeting down in the city and
Uncle Josie preached. I can still see Aunt Rachel standing
there singing L.L.Pickett's old hymn,

> "I dreamed that the great judgment morning
> Had dawned and the trumpets had blown:
> I dreamed that the nations had gathered
> To judgment before the White Throne.
> From the Throne came a bright shining angel,
> And stood on the land and the sea,
> And swore with his hand raised to heaven,
> That time was no longer to be.
>
> The widow was there with the orphan
> God heard and remembered their cries;
> No sorrow in heaven forever,
> God wiped all the tears from their eyes.
> The great man was there but his greatness
> When death came was left far behind;
> The angel that opened the records,
> Not a trace of his greatness could find.

And O, what a weeping and wailing
As the lost ones were told of their fate;
They cried for the rocks and the mountains,
They prayed, but their prayer was too late.''

Uncle Josie and Aunt Rachel were deeply committed Christians. They would gladly give everything that they had to reach the lost for Christ.

One afternoon, we were sitting in the dining room eating our afternoon meal, when Aunt Rachel came in. We thought that she had been asleep, in the front bedroom. When she came through the living room into the dining room, there was a holy glow upon her countenance. I knew that she had been at the Throne of God - you could see it on her face, and the glow reminded me of when Moses encountered the Glory of the Lord. Aunt Rachel said, "I've been in the presence of the Lord, and I saw the Lord sounding a bugle for the angels of heaven to go and do battle for the city of Springfield.'' She saw the angels come down and battle *and conquer*. And the Lord spoke and said, "I'm going to do a work in Springfield that will astonish the world.'' Then God showed her a great crystal fountain of pure water bubbling up out of the city of Springfield. She told us that in her vision, healing waters flowed out over the whole land. They flowed to the four points of the compass and covered the entire earth. The fountain kept bubbling in Springfield, and she said, "I know that God is going to do a mighty work that will issue forth from this city and will astound the whole world.''

Many years later, I published an account of this vision, written by Rachel Sizelove in *Word and Work* (June 1934) and issued it also in tract form. Here is a portion of Aunt Rachel's testimony:

179

A Marvelous Vision

"In the year 1913, the Lord permitted me to return again to Springfield. By this time, there was quite a good sized assembly of baptized saints. One afternoon, I was alone in a room of my sister's home, and I was carried away in the spirit, and the Lord gave me a vision. There appeared before me a beautiful, bubbling, sparkling fountain in the heart of the City of Springfield. It sprang up gradually but irresistibly and began to flow toward the East and toward the West, toward the North, and toward the South, and kept flowing until the whole land was deluged with living water.

This was before the brethren met together at Hot Springs, Arkansas, and formed the General Council of the Assemblies of God. Because I had had to die out to my own church, the Free Methodist Church, I had been opposed to organizations and churchanity; afraid of getting wrapped up in formality. But when I think of the vision the Lord brought before me of the waters flowing out from Springfield, I have to say surely the General Council at Springfield, Missouri, is of God."[1]

As we sat around the dinner table, we knew that it was God, and that something wonderful was going to happen. I was only thirteen at the time, but I will never forget the wonderful presence of God in our home, and the awesome wonder and great joy which we all sensed. We had heard the bugle call.

Looking back from the present perspective, almost seventy years later, I believe that the reason why we had such a difficult time getting a church started and a work established in Springfield was because, in the spiritual realm, the powers of darkness hovered over the city like nowhere else in the surrounding area. Perhaps they perceived that God was going to do a wonderful work and they were marshalled together in a supreme effort to hold the city. But God's bugle had sounded an advance! The Lord was leading a mighty army forward. The saints had taken authority over the spiritual powers of wickedness and we were going over the top.

### Victory Ahead

On October, 5, 1913, our little church held a water baptismal service in the River Jordan which flowed through Springfield. Mother, being a Methodist, had never been baptized in water and I recall that, among others, she and Paul were both baptized in water by Brother Gary Martin, and Aunt Rachel and Uncle Josie preached.

At this time, our church really had no formal structure and Aunt Rachel, with her strong Free Methodist background, suggested that the church be formally set in order. This seemed good to all the people and so on November 2, 1913, Mother was made pastor of the church and the assistant pastor was Gary Martin, the barber. Mother's notes say, ''We organized a Sunday School with Brother Ed Dewcese as Superintendent, Sister Florence Taliaferro as Assistant Superintendent, and Sister Katie Beckman as Secretary.''

We continued to meet in the little wooden tabernacle on Boonville Street at the corner of Calhoun Street. Mother preached there, Aunt Rachel preached there, Mother Barnes preached there, and many of the Arkansas preachers preached there.

Aunt Rachel and Uncle Josie left and returned to Los Angeles at the end of November. I'll never forget the next Sunday service after they were gone. Only a few of the saints

The Sparkling Fountain

were there and the enthusiasm which we all had only a week
before was now deflated. I think the entire Sunday morning
attendance fit up on the platform. We were singing "Victory Ahead", and we really sounded defeated. Mother
jumped up and said, "Oh, there's victory ahead! I can see
it! I can see it! Can't you Sister Boyd?" Sister Boyd looked
out over the empty tabernacle, thought for a moment and
honestly said, "No, I can't." Mother said, "Well then, you'll
have to take it by faith." I remember Martha Childers (who
later married Alpha Humbard and became the mother of Rex
Humbard) jumped up and said, "Well, I can see it. There's
victory ahead!" And she took a tambourine and started
shouting and dancing all over the church like Miriam of old,
"Glory be to God! Hallelujah!" Sister Hoy was right behind
her, and soon we were all up and dancing for joy and for
the great things that God was going to do for Springfield.
Before the meeting was over, we all knew there was victory
ahead.

This was in 1913. There was no General Council at this
time; nothing at all. It wasn't formed yet because the
Pentecostal people all thought, "Oh, the churches will be
so happy to have this wonderful Baptism of the Holy Spirit."
They had thought that all the churches: the Methodists, the
Baptists, the Presbyterians, the Holiness, the Christian and
Missionary Alliance, the Nazarenes - would all reach out
their hands for the Baptism and hold it to them. But they
all rejected it and turned it down.

And so a denomination had to come into being and in April
of 1914, the Assemblies of God was eventually formed. Truly, coming events cast their shadows before them.

REFERENCE
1.    "A Sparkling Fountain for the Whole Earth", by
      Rachel A. Sizelove, *Word and Work*, Vol. 56, No.
      6, June, 1934, PP. 1,11, 12.

182

# Chapter XVIII

## BENNETT F. LAWRENCE

"Can you not hear the tongues in the golden bells as our
great High Priest ministers?"

B.F.L.

**B**ennett Lawrence was just a young man when he came to Springfield to be our pastor. He had married Mother Barnes' daughter, Imogene, but somehow the match was never right. Brother Lawrence was a dynamic speaker, a brilliant speaker - probably the first real orator that I'd ever heard. He was only a young man, but he possessed wisdom and great leadership ability. He was an anointed preacher, ministering in the power of the Spirit. And we all loved him dearly.

When we heard that E. N. Bell and others had called a conference in Hot Springs, Arkansas, we decided to send our Pastor, Brother Lawrence, down as our church representative. The conference was held in the old Opera House, April 2-12, 1914. Mother Barnes, Brother Gaston, and Ralph Riggs were there as well as many others that have faithfully served Pentecost over the years.

At the conference, Brother Bell was appointed Chairman (the office is now called General Superintendent of the Assemblies of God) and Brother Lawrence was elected as a Presbyter. I believe that he is still the youngest Presbyter ever to serve the Assemblies of God in that capacity. In the large group picture of that conference, you can see Bennett Lawrence in the third row, standing to Mother Barnes' left (look between Cyrus Fockler and Howard Goss). In November of 1914, when the General Council met at the Old Stone Church in Chicago, Brother Lawrence was elected

Bennett F. Lawrence

Assistant Secretary, under J. Roswell Flower.

Brother Lawrence was a gifted Bible teacher and was especially good on Bible doctrine. I remember him teaching on Old Testament types and shadows too. We were all held spellbound while he preached one morning on the bells and pomegranates that lined the High Priest's robes. While he was our pastor, he wrote a series of articles which were published in the *Evangel* and then collected into a book which was published by the Gospel Publishing House. (This was while the Publishing House was at 2838 Easton Avenue, in St. Louis, and before it moved to Springfield.) The book was called **The Apostolic Faith Restored** and it was the first one to trace the history and development of the Pentecostal Movement. It documents the conversions and marvelous experiences of such men as H.A. Goss, M.M. Pinson, D.C.O. Opperman, A. W. Orwig, G.B. Cashwell, and missionaries like A. G. Garr and Max Moorhead. There is even some information about Pandita Ramabai and T.B. Barratt.

In the Introduction to the book, Brother Welch (who was Chairman of the General Council of the Assemblies of God in 1916, when the book was finally printed) wrote the following:

> ". . . the many wonderful events which have occurred during the past decade . . have proven beyond a doubt that God's time piece has reached the dispensational hour in which He had promised to pour out His Spirit in Latter Rain significance."[1]

So often people ask me what those meetings were like in the early days of Pentecost. What stands out in my memory was how anointed ministers preached the Word. Those content-filled messages would burn within our hearts, and while they were yet preaching, we would long to get to the altar to worship and seek the face of God. And oh, how God would meet us around those old altars! I mentioned above

184

how Brother Lawrence spoke on the High Priest's garments. In his book, he gives credit for the idea to an article by Brother Chamberlain who published it in *The Weekly Evangel*. A quotation is given in Bennett Lawrence's book:

"Paul tells us that 'the invisible things of Him (God) from the creation of the world are clearly seen being understood by the things that are', (Romans 1:20), i.e. the things which we can see and comprehend with our finite minds. Thus we are referred back to the type, Aaron, the first High Priest under the law or first covenant, where we find 'Golden bells and pomegranates, beneath, upon the hem of the robe round about, and it, (the robe) shall be upon Aaron to minister; and his SOUND shall be heard when he goeth IN unto the holy place before the Lord, and when he COMETH OUT. Exodus 28:33-35.

The bells were the sign designated by the Lord Himself to give forth the sound when Aaron went in and when he came out, THE SAME SIGN, THE SAME SOUND, at both the ingoing and the outcoming.

'The tongues being God's appointed sign, when Christ, our High Priest ENTERED INTO heaven (the most holy place) before the Lord, we may expect the SAME SIGN, the SAME SOUND, when He cometh out; this is why we have the tongues with us today, pealing forth the sound of His coming. For He is nearing the door. The sound thereof is increasing in volume and will increase more and more until 'the Lord Himself shall descend from heaven with a shout, with the voice of the Archangel, and the trump of God,' (I

185

Thess. 4:16) to gather His loved ones unto
Himself as He promised He would do. John
14:3."[2]

But Brother Lawrence had developed the theme far beyond this. He spoke of Mary Magdalene at the tomb on resurrection morning (She, out of whom had gone seven devils). He spoke of Mary, the sister of Martha and Lazarus. Others came to the Master's feet to receive, she came to offer adoration. He spoke of the golden-covered ark of the covenant and the golden mercy seat whereon dwelt the Shekinah Glory of God. He spoke of the common linen garments which the High Priest wore when he took the blood of the sacrifices and passed within the veil to make atonement. And how the High Priest, when he returned to the Holy Place, was again robed with those wonderful garments of glory and beauty, the beautiful ephod, the jeweled breastplate, and the robe of the ephod which was bordered about with pomegranates of blue, purple, and scarlet ". . . and bells of gold between them round about." Can you not hear the tongues in the golden bells as our great High Priest, Christ Jesus the Lord, ministers in the Holy Place today? When He returns to show Himself to His people, it will be in wondrous garments of glory and beauty, for when He returns for us, Matthew says it will be 'in the glory of His Father, with His angels.'

What he told us was absolutely spellbinding. When it came to Old Testament types and shadows of Christ, Brother Lawrence was an outstanding expositor. What I have written is as mere crumbs compared to a feast which was served; as a patchwork of ragged threads compared to a glorious tapestry of splendid craftsmanship. How our hearts burned within us as he taught us these wonderful things of the Lord. Wondrous things which are only revealed to the Lord's anointed.

## Another Summer Tentmeeting

During the Summer, we sent for Mother Barnes and she came with a tent for tentmeetings. I don't remember whether this was before or after we had made Bennett Lawrence our Pastor. At any rate, he was there and Mother Barnes came with a number of workers and preachers, and together we pitched the tent at Central and Robberson Streets. We got good crowds and many were saved, healed, and filled with the Holy Ghost.

Rex Humbard's mother, Martha Childers, was just a teenager then, and was working with Mother Barnes. I believe that this tentmeeting was the one she told about in her book, **Give Me That Old-Time Religion**:

> "There was always something exciting happening during the years I traveled with Mother Barnes. Once we were in Springfield, Missouri, with a big tent that seated one thousand two-hundred fifty people. Even at that, it couldn't hold all the people that came. They'd line up out on the sidewalk and all around the tent.
>
> One Sunday afternoon, Mother Barnes told me, 'Darling Child, you lead the testimony service this afternoon.' As I was leading the testimony service, I began to talk in a language I didn't know. I wasn't really feeling anything different: no frenzy, no shaking, just talking. I was just standing there talking and listening to myself. It was real enough, but I didn't know a word I was saying. Then suddenly, I quit speaking in that language and went on leading the testimony service. People were getting up and thanking God for the tentmeeting, telling how God had healed them of different diseases.

When Mother Barnes gave the altar call, she told us workers to get down by the altar bench and be ready to pray with the unsaved. So I was standing by the altar bench when a well-dressed woman with beautiful black eyes and black hair came up to me with tears flowing down her cheeks. She said, 'Little girl, you speak my language.' I told her I didn't know what she was talking about. 'But you do,' she insisted, 'How did you know my name?'

'Ma'am, I never saw you before!' But she just kept insisting that I spoke her language. I told her I couldn't even speak my own language too well, and I certainly didn't speak any other.

She kept on, 'Well then, how did you know where I lived?'

'I don't know where you live!' I replied.

'But you know my house number!'

'Ma'am, I only know two streets in Springfield, one of them is St. Louis Street and the other one is Boonville.'

She looked very puzzled, 'But you talked plainly in my language, and you told me my sins. You told me not to confess my sins to a man, but to God. You told me to come to Jesus Christ and confess my sins, that this was my time to get right with God.' Suddenly, I began to wake up to the fact that God had spoken directly through me. I will never forget that woman's look as she spoke with me. The tears were just pouring from her eyes, 'You told me things that no one knew but me and God.'

'Ma'am, that was the Holy Ghost speaking

through my lips of clay, directly to you', I
explained. 'God sure loves you, and you'd
better obey whatever He told you to do. I
don't know what He said.'

When I told her that it was the Holy Ghost,
God's Spirit speaking to her, and that He loved her, she fell on the altar like she'd been
shot. I got down beside her, and she confessed her sins and gave her heart to God.'"[3]

Many wonderful things happened at that tentmeeting. The
services were attended by large crowds and there was much
interest. Many lives were touched, many people were saved
and received the Baptism of the Holy Ghost. Mother Barnes
was a wonderful woman.

Soon the weather began to get cold and Sister Barnes went
down to Eureka Springs, Arkansas, to hold a short term Bible School in a hotel down there. I believe that we next
secured a small wooden church on the Corner of Main and
Webster Streets. (Right across from the old St. John's
Hospital.) And here we continued to hold meetings.

### New Year's Eve

I'll never forget the watchnight service Brother Lawrence
conducted on New Year's Eve. Several years ago, I visited
Springfield and told the story to Brother Cunningham, the
editor of the *Pentecostal Evangel*. He wrote it up and it was
published in the December 31, 1978 issue. Here is a part of
that article,

### An Unforgettable New Year's Prayer Meeting
#### by Robert C. Cunningham

". . . Our little group of Pentecostal
believers in Springfield had just finished the
Watch Night service, and the new year (1915)
[it may have been 1916 - FTC] was just a few

Bennett F. Lawrence

minutes old. Our pastor was Bennett F. Lawrence. We had sent Brother Lawrence as our delegate to the meeting at Hot Springs, Arkansas, the previous April, at which time the General Council of the Assemblies of God came into being. Brother Lawrence was one of the youngest presbyters. Upon his return to Springfield, our church affiliated with the new Assemblies of God Fellowship which had its first headquarters in Findlay, Ohio.

Near midnight, Pastor Lawrence told us the new year that we were about to enter might be the year the Lord would return. The First World War was raging in Europe, and the Pentecostal people were looking for the second coming of Christ.

After the service, there was not room for all of us to ride home in the two-seated buggy, so my brother and I, and three other teenage boys started walking home, a distance of about three miles.

One boy suggested we could save time going from Campbell Avenue to the corner of Boonville and Division, if we cut across White City. This was a large amusement park. It was fenced, but some of the boards were loose, and we crawled through.

The place was deserted by this time. It was a carnival type of park with a large roller coaster. It had a bad reputation as it also had been a burlesque place. Many years later, it was turned into a baseball park.

We knew it was a wicked place, and we felt we were crossing the devil's territory.

One of the fellows said, 'This place is

unclean.'

Another asked, 'Do you suppose it could ever belong to God?'

Then my cousin, Laurel Taliaferro, the oldest of us boys, said, 'Let's claim it for the Lord.'

So we agreed, and there beneath the stars we knelt and started praying.

One boy said, 'How much shall we claim?' Another said, 'Let's claim the whole block.'

My younger brother, Paul, said, 'Let's claim the other block too - from Boonville to Campbell and from Division to Calhoun.'

I spoke up and said, 'We shouldn't take the greenhouse at the corner of Boonville and Calhoun. We sold peaches to the people living there, and they are nice people.'

Laurel said, 'Why not? God will take care of them. Let's claim it all.

There in the early morning, we prayed that all this land should be used for the work of the Lord so that His gospel might go out to the end of the earth from this place.

It was a clear, crisp night. The stars were bright above. One boy remarked, 'Just think; when the Lord told Abraham to look up and see if he could count the stars, they were the same stars we can see tonight.'

Another boy said, 'Let's pray that the gospel will spread over all the earth and reach as many people as there are stars.'

God must have been listening to the prayers of those boys. The spot where they knelt and prayed is now the site of the national headquarters of the Assemblies of God.

Piece by piece, all the land they claimed has come into the possession of the church and is being used for the gospel.

The first parcel was the corner of Campbell and Calhoun. Here Central Assembly was built. Later, the church bought the adjoining lots (including the greenhouse on the corner of Boonville and Calhoun) on which to erect the present edifice.

It was in the old church at the corner of Campbell and Calhoun, in 1922, that Central Bible College came into being. Thousands of young people have gone out from this school to preach the gospel around the world.

For a number of years, White City Ballpark was the home of the Springfield Cardinals, a minor league team, but after the baseball club disbanded, it became a sort of 'white elephant'. In 1945, the Assemblies of God acquired the site and erected the Gospel Publishing House on the portion facing Campbell Avenue.[1]

---

[1]There is another miracle associated with this acquisition. Hershall Hartly, a college classmate of Fred's, told me that when the St. Louis Cardinals decided to sell the White City Ballpark, the Springfield City School Board wanted to purchase it as an athletic field for the schools. However, Tom Watkins, a prominent businessman, was on the school board and also part-owner of the Cardinals. Consequently, there existed a conflict of interest and the School Board could not buy it. God had His own plans for that place, and He answered those boys' prayers - H.E.B.

A few years later, the Assemblies of God erected a four-story office building on the portion facing Boonville and this became its national headquarters.

The Southern Missouri District of the Assemblies of God erected a large office building on the Southwest corner of the same block for its headquarters and purchased a house across the street for its district parsonage.

Business properties at the southeast and northeast corners of the block were purchased and added to the General Council complex.

In 1972, a six-story distribution center was added to the Gospel Publishing House. The fifth and sixth floors house the Assemblies of God Graduate School where more than one thousand three hundred students have already taken courses of study, including approximately four hundred missionaries.

Two apartment buildings on Campbell Avenue were purchased to house students of the Graduate School. Central Assembly purchased additional property for a youth center and parking area.

The last portion of the two-block area to come into the possession of the Assemblies of God was the National Auto Supply, where the attractive new Radiant Book and Bible Center now stands.

When Brother Corum and his wife visited Springfield for the last time in 1972, they saw the transformation that has taken place on the land he and his young friends claimed in the new year's prayer meeting sixtyfour years ago

193

'When I look on this area now and see the General Council headquarters complex, Central Assembly, and the district headquarters all on this property, I am overwhelmed,' he said. 'When I see the presses turning out the printed word, and the missionaries being commissioned, and the radio programs going to the ends of the earth, I know there is a God who hears our sincere prayers. How insignificant one feels to behold His mighty works that are exceedingly and abundantly above all that five teenage boys - or grown folk either - could ask Him to do.'"[4]

How the stars twinkled and sparkled with fire that night! Many times since then, has my heart rejoiced while pointing out the constellation of Orion, or the brilliant, fiery stars Regel, Sirius, or the Pleiades to my own children. The sight of those fiery winter stars and constellations has often recalled to my heart the faithfulness of God. How He longs to hear our requests, and to fellowship with us.

I really can't recall who the other two boys were. I wish that Paul or Laurel was still with us, for they could probably remember. I think that they may have been Claude Martin and Leonard Hoy. At any rate, none of us claim any credit for what the Lord has done on that spot, and we all have been overwhelmed as we beheld the works of His mighty hands.

### Napoleon

Brother Lawrence inspired many members of the church to step out in faith. I remember one challenging message which he gave one night in the old tabernacle, in which he quoted the great emperor, Napoleon.

The French armies had been away from Paris for an extended period of time. Napoleon, upon his return from Egypt, made the legislative chambers of Paris echo with the words, "What has happened to our glorious France? What have you done to her? I gave you victories; I find defeats; I brought you riches;I find destitution! What has happened to the thousands who were my friends, who shared my glory?"

Brother Lawrence said, "What if Christ returned for His church this hour. Would He not see a world unministered to, a world of broken bodies, lonely and empty hearts, and the souls of Adam's fallen sons and daughters reaching out in darkness. As He looks out over His Bride today, is He not saying, 'Where are the ministries of my glorious church? I gave you victories; I find defeats. With the Holy Spirit, I brought you riches and power; I find destitution! What has happened to those that I have washed in My blood and those with whom I have shared My glory?'"

The whole church was stirred by such marvelous messages from this wonderful and precious brother, and we flocked to those rough wooden altar rails to seek the face of God. There in the sawdust; teenagers, old folks, children, young married couples, widows were all on our faces besieging the throne, "Let the Apostolic ministries flow forth from Thy church to fallen humanity; a world going out into darkness and hopelessness. Once more, oh Lord, let the glorious message of hope, joy, and Thy full salvation issue forth to all the world!"

Surely God heard and answered our prayers in Springfield. And yet, Brother Lawrence's message is truer today than it was back then, almost seventy years ago. Let us rush to the altars again to seek His face, for the night cometh when no man can work."

### Receiving the Baptism of the Holy Spirit

I was fifteen years old, and I had been seeking the Lord with all my heart. Though I was saved and had been in Pentecost since my mother received the Baptism of the

195

Holy Spirit in 1907, I had not yet experienced the Baptism myself. I decided to fast and pray until I got through. I didn't tell anyone - I didn't want people to know about my spiritual battle. We lived on a little farm out on East Division Street near what is now the downtown airport. The corn was about waist high out in the back field (we had about an acre of corn), and I took a hoe with me so that it would appear like I was just going out to weed the corn. I took my Bible. Old Dee Dee, our dog, went with me. I would hoe (and pray) for awhile and then go sit under the apple trees and read and pray for awhile. I'd been fasting for three days and it seemed like everything I read kept referring to food and about people eating. I remember reading about the feast of Belshazzar, Nabel held a feast, Abigail brought David two hundred loaves, corn, clusters of raisins, dates, cakes of figs , . . . and I was hungry, but I was hungry for God too. I remember taking the hoe, going out to one end of the corn field and singing:

> "Holy, Holy, Holy is what the angels sing,
> And I expect to help them make
> the courts of Heaven ring,
> But when we tell redemption's story,
> they will fold their wings
> For angels never knew
> the joy that our salvation brings."

They never felt the JOY! It occurred to me that Christ died for me and that I was more important to the Lord than all the angels.

About that time, a mighty wind began to blow across the corn field; wave, after wave, after wave of warm summer air bent the corn down toward the ground. "Holy, Holy, Holy, is what the angels sing!" I was carried away in the Spirit and when I came to, I was at the other end of the corn field shouting, dancing, and talking in tongues. As I read through Mother's notes, I see, "June 12, 1915 - Fred baptized with the Holy Ghost and fire!"[5] Surely, angels have never felt the joy that our redemption brings!

## The New Issue

During late 1915, the "New Issue" or "Jesus Only" doctrine swept through Pentecost. The doctrine taught that all had to be baptized "In Jesus name only" in order to be saved and that the Father and the Holy Ghost are different aspects of Jesus - that Jesus only is God. The Assemblies of God was still very young at the time, and its soul-searching struggles over the issues are documented in several of the well-written histories now available. Many outstanding and well-meaning members of the Pentecostal fellowship embraced this doctrine at the time, and many of those that did later rejected it and returned to the Assemblies or other Trinitarian full gospel fellowships. Mother Barnes was one of those that came to accept the "Jesus Only" teaching and she and her daughter, Imogene, were "rebaptized in water in Jesus Name". Though Bennett Lawrence was rebaptized and went with the Jesus Only group, I don't believe that he ever really accepted it. And this is why. When he came back from the revival where he had been rebaptized, he was still the pastor of our church and he began to teach it. Needless to say, it caused quite a commotion. Mother and Father were strong Trinitarians, as were most of the people in our church, and said they just couldn't accept this new teaching as scriptural. However, everyone in the church dearly loved Brother Lawrence and, in fact, Sister Hoy said, "I don't care whether I can understand it or not. If Brother Lawrence says that it's so - then I want to be rebaptized." And so, when she went down into the water to be rebaptized, Bennett Lawrence said, "No, I can't do it. I can't do it." And he walked back up out of the water without rebaptizing anyone. I tell you this because I want you to know how dear Brother Lawrence was to all of us in the church and how much we all admired this young man.

Brother Lawrence resigned as our pastor, dropped his credentials with the Assemblies of God, resigning as presbyter, and took up with the Jesus Only movement - with the blessings of his wife and in-laws. For awhile it maintained harmony in the family, but I believe that his wife later left him and that he dropped out of the ministry. I've witnessed many tragedies since then in my fifty-five years of legal practice, but I've always felt that somehow the defeat of this precious brother was one of the Pentecostal movement's greatest losses. Brother Lawrence was a flaming messenger, and a fiery, shooting star. He ministered with a special anointing and while he was in Springfield, he accomplished great things for the Kingdom. We all loved him. But I recall Sister Benedict's admonition, "Pray for the preachers - we must put up a resolute winning fight on their behalf . . ." Perhaps if we had all hung on to the horns of the altar for Bennett and Imogene Lawrence, many things would have been so very different. If he had stayed in the General Council, I know that he would have been Chairman, but his heart was sidetracked and his hand was lifted from the plow before his work was done.

## REFERENCES

1.  **The Apostolic Faith Restored**, by Bennett F. Lawrence, The Gospel Publishing House, St. Louis, Missouri, 1916, PP. 7-8.
2.  Reference 1, Pg. 31.
3.  **Give Me That Old-Time Religion**, by Martha Childers Humbard, Logos International, Plainfield, New Jersey, 1977, PP. 49-51.
4.  "An Unforgettable New Year's Prayer Meeting", by Robert C. Cunningham, *Pentecostal Evangel*,

December 31, 1978, PP. 10-11.

5. ''The Pentecostal Church of Springfield'', typed notes by L.H. Corum, n.d., circa 1921.

"With golden bells the priestly vest
And rich pomegranates boardered round,
the needs of Holiness expressed,
And called for fruit as well as sound."

"Holiness on the head,
Light and perfection on the breast,
Harmonious bells below, raising the dead
To lead them unto life and rest:
thus are true Aarons dressed."
George Herbert
(Exodus 28)

# Chapter XIX

## E. N. BELL

"How I cherish the memory of that grand old man."
Rev. Harry E. Bowley *Word and Work*, December, 1933

**C**hildren and young people so often have the ability to see through sham and hypocrisy in adults, and to sense true spirituality where even the religious leaders fail to recognize it. The events which occur in the twenty-first chapter of Matthew follow the triumphal Palm Sunday entry of Christ into Jerusalem and the second purification of the Temple. Why were the Pharisees so annoyed with Jesus? Was it because of the public ministry of Jesus and His Disciples? Was it because they were jealous of His triumphal entry and popularity? Had their ire arisen because he had just overturned the money changer's tables and driven them from the temple? What was it that "sore displeased them"?

As C.M. Ward has pointed out, it was because they saw the wonderful things that He did, and the children crying in the temple saying, "Hosanna to the Son of David". Oh that we, like those children, would be motivated by such pure and simple faith.

Next to my father, E. N. Bell was the greatest man I've ever known. Brilliant, perceptive, well-educated, farsighted, a counsellor to those in authority - he was truly a prince among men. Yet, he had the heart of a child. Words fail when describing this Godly and anointed Pentecostal statesman. When looking for someone to compare Brother Bell to, Stanley Frodsham could only find Mr. Great-Heart in Bunyan Pilgrim's Progress. In the mid 1920's, Brother Frodsham wrote of Brother Bell,

"Humility was the outstanding feature in
200

the life of this modern Great-Heart. Many a time as he definitely humbled himself under the mighty hand of God, has he been seen to break up and weep like a child . . . Many a time has he been heard to testify in the local assembly at Springfield, Missouri, of which he was a member during the last years of his life, and as he would begin to rejoice in the Lord, those of us in the assembly would catch the infection of his holy joy and would become free in praising, adoring, and magnifying the Lord . . .''[1]

I thank my Lord that I was privileged to be there and be part of that assembly at that time. These words are true.

I first met Brother Bell when I was a teenager. At the time, Bennett Lawrence was our pastor and we were meeting in the stucco church building on Grant Street where Central Bible Institute is now located. The General Council had already met. Our pastor, Brother Lawrence, had been elected as one of the Presbyters (in fact, I believe that he is the youngest presbyter ever elected) and Brother Bell had served as Chairman (the position in now called General Superintendent) of the Assemblies of God until the Second General Council which met November 15-19, 1914, in the Old Stone Church in Chicago. At this meeting, Arch P. Collins, a former Baptist minister from Fort Worth, Texas, had been elected as the second General Superintendent. If I recall correctly, Brother Bell was now pastoring a church in Little Rock, Arkansas.

It was a Sunday morning, and I had just finished teaching the boys class and we were now assembled in the main sanctuary. Along with Brother Lawrence, who was then our pastor, six other men sat on the platform. It was clear to all of us that even though he said very little during the morning, Brother Bell had a special anointing upon him. We were

E.N. Bell

about to conduct a series of "protracted meetings", as we called them, and Brother Bell had come to introduce five young preachers from Arkansas. I remember that during his introduction he said, paraphrasing Nathaniel's comment to Philip about Jesus, "You ask, can any good thing come out of Arkansas? I'll tell you what Philip told Nathaniel - come and see!" Oh, how those Arkansas preachers could preach! And the Glory Cloud would come down on our little assembly 'till we could only fall on our faces around the altar and weep for joy and worship the Lord.

E. N. Bell was born at Lake Butler, Florida, on June 27, 1866. He had attended Stetson College in Florida and a Southern Baptist Seminary in Louisville, Kentucky. He had also done several years of graduate work at the University of Chicago. Although it was obvious to all who knew him that he possessed great natural authority, he was very gracious, very humble, and very kind. He regarded his formal training and natural talents as offerings to be dedicated to the Lord on the altar of sacrifice. Though surrounded by less-educated men, he never boasted of his talents.

Brother Bell had served for seventeen years as pastor in the Southern Baptist Church at North Fort Worth, Texas. He began to hunger for more of God. He heard that the Lord was filling people with the Holy Ghost at Brother Durham's North Avenue Mission in Chicago, Illinois.

William H. Durham had been to Azusa Street, and after tarrying almost three weeks, he received the Baptism of the Holy Spirit at 1:00 AM on Saturday, March 2, 1907. (See *The Apostolic Faith*, Vol. 1, No. 6, Pg. 4) Brother Durham returned to Chicago and the Lord used the North Avenue Mission as a great Full Gospel lighthouse.

Brother Bell, who had attended the University of Chicago, was familiar with the area, and so while his heart was hungry, he sought the Lord about a return trip to that city. He wanted the fullness of the Holy Ghost and he would not be content

202

with anything less. His church granted him a leave of absence. He journeyed to Chicago and after tarrying for eleven months, received the desire of his heart on July 18, 1908.

In this same series of meetings, many other future leaders in Pentecost also received the wonderful Baptism in the Holy Ghost.

### What Were The Chicago Meetings Like?

Brother A.H. Argue and his precious wife, Eva E. Argue, had been laboring in Winnipeg, Canada. Their lives had been deeply affected by the ministry of that great Holiness teacher, Dr. George D. Watson, (after whom their son, Watson Argue was named) and the founder of the Christian Missionary Alliance organization, Dr. A.B. Simpson. However, when he heard of the moving of God at Chicago, Brother Argue quickly arranged his business for a trip to Brother Durham's Mission. Years later, his daughter, Zelma Argue, wrote describing his experience at the North Avenue Mission:

". . . he was convinced that the power of God was in the midst of the people. . . God's glory, like the cloud that filled all the tabernacle in the days of old, settled down upon the worshipping people. Folks were testifying with radiant faces to having received the Baptism of the Holy Ghost. . . . How their faces glowed as they praised God!"[2]

This was the same scene that Brother Bell would soon pray through in.

After tarrying for twenty-one days, the fire fell. Brother Argue telegraphed home, "Received Baptism of Holy Spirit; coming home on first train." This was in April, 1907. Soon the fire was falling in Winnipeg and spread abroad. (See *Apostolic Faith*, Vol. II, No. 13, May, 1908, Pg. 4 ) And spread abroad it did! Over the years, we, like so many others, were always blessed by the wonderful ministry of Brother and Sister A.H. Argue and their precious family.

Many others received mighty manifestations from the Lord in the meetings at Brother Durham's Mission in Chicago, and they were to have a profound effect upon the future of Pentecost. In January of 1908, Brother Durham would write, "God is wonderfully working here . . . We have stood by the simple Gospel from the very first, preaching only Jesus Christ and Him crucified. And as we have done this, the Holy Ghost has fallen upon them that heard the Word, so that tongue can never tell what we have experienced. Praise the Lord!'' (*Apostolic Faith*, Vol. I, No. 12, Page 1)

Jennie E. Moore, who was one of the Azusa Street elders, visited Durham's Mission during 1907 and had this to say about its meetings, "Truly beloved, the Mission . . . is a blessed place - many Spirit-filled men, women and children. They have more children than at Azusa and they are filled. Beloved, I would you could see them." (*The Apostolic Faith*, Vol. I, No, 12, Pg. 1)

Brother Bell always spoke warmly of his deep experience at the old Mission at 943 W. North Avenue in Chicago, and the anointing which he received while he sought the Lord there rested upon his ministry to its final hours.

After writing this book, we received a copy of Ethel Goss' *The Winds of God*, which is about H.A. Goss and the early Pentecostal movement. Concerning the Chicago meetings, they wrote:

"Brother Bell, in relating incidents concerning the Durham Mission, reported that the top third of the huge auditorium was often filled with a thick, blue haze. When this haze was present, people entering the church would often fall in the aisles, under the power of God, before they could even reach their seats. According to Brother Bell, miracles took place around the clock, with hundreds receiving either the Baptism or divine healing.''[3]

Later, H.A. Goss and E.N. Bell would labor together (it was Goss and Bell that signed the call to Hot Springs in 1914, which resulted in organizing The Assemblies of God). Goss characterized him by saying, "Brother Bell was a man of good judgement, great wisdom and deep spirituality. He became a blessing to everyone."[4] And, concerning the Chicago period in Bell's life, Brother Goss wrote, ". . . he became so filled with God that he abundantly overflowed in other tongues. Because of this precious time spent on his knees studying God's Word, he later became one of the Movement's great teachers, and a blessing to thousands."[5]

### The Great Commoner

While I was a teenager, William Jennings Bryan was very popular and because of his close relationship with the farmers, laborers, and common people of the country, he was called "The Great Commoner". Bryan was a remarkable man, not only for his farsighted political principles, but also because of his deep religious convictions.

By way of comparison, Brother Frodsham has said, "Brother Bell was a commoner in the truest sense of the word. To the high or the lowly, he was just the same. He would stop in his work, no matter how pressing or urgent its character, to counsel with the most humble who sought his help."[1]

When I was a Freshman at Drury College, I prepared an oration entitled "the Progress of Democracy".[6] After pouring my heart into the oration, I felt that in spite of the logic, something was still missing. I went to Brother Bell's office on the second floor of the publishing house one day and spoke with him about it. He was very busy, but when he learned what kind of assistance I needed, he encouraged me and said, "Bring it over to my home tonight".

That evening, by the light of an oil lamp, he patiently went over the oration with me for two or three hours. He showed me that an oration should have a rhythm and cadence to match its logic. He suggested several modifications, and I knew that I had a winning oration.

I would go out to the barn at night for almost a month and practice giving the oration, while milking the cows. By the end of the month, old Bossie knew it as well as I did. Not only did I win the local competition and represent Drury College at Westminster College (where Winston Churchill later coined the phrase, "The Iron Curtain"), but I also won first place in the State of Missouri. Subsequently, I represented the State of Missouri in an interstate competition in Nebraska.

After church on Sunday morning, dear Brother Bell came by our car and congratulated me. He had read about it in the newspaper. As I look back through the years, it was not the prize nor joy of winning, but the gracious encouragement of this precious man that has had the greatest influence upon my life.

Countless others can point to similar experiences with Brother Bell. Many years later, Harry Bowley wrote to me about this dear man and I published his comments in *Word and Work*, Vol. 55, No. 12, pg. 13, December, 1933.

> "Young people need fathers and mothers today. How well I cherish the memory of that grand old man, Rev. E.N. Bell. I worked with him when he published a religious magazine, and he often worked until four in the morning. One night, I asked him to explain a certain doctrine that was bothering me. He was very busy and cut me off. After finishing his task, he called me to his desk and apologized for speaking sharply to me, and for two hours past midnight, in the early morning hours, unfolded the Scriptures to me. As I look back

now, my question was insignificant and of little importance, but Brother Bell was certainly a father to many ministers, with his sympathy and understanding and deep learning in the Scriptures.''(Harry E. Bowley)[7]

### A Miraculous Healing

In 1922, after graduating from Drury College, I started teaching high school in Lamar, Oklahoma. The local school board offered me the position of high school principal. One day, while performing a demonstration to a class in general science, a mixture of concentrated sulphuric acid and potassium permanganate exploded in a test tube, shooting the acid into my eyes. The pain was intense and my eyesight was gone. Several students rushed me to a nearby doctor, who bathed my eyes. He wanted to inject the eyeballs with cocaine. He said that my eyes were permanently damaged; I would never see again and that the injection would stop the burning - but I refused to let him do it. Someone must have telegraphed my folks back in Springfield.

When Brother Bell heard of my condition, he stopped the presses at the Publishing House and gathered all the workers into one room for prayer on my behalf. At that time they were having a strike on the railroad and my father had a terrible time getting through to Lamar. He fired off a telegram to me and told me that they were praying for me at the Gospel Publishing House. When I heard this, my faith sprang alive, and I knew that God would answer. The next two days I was in great pain, but I knew that the answer would come. I promised the Lord that instead of taking the principal's job, I would go to study Law as I had started out to do. I shall never forget the early morning hours of the third day. As the darkness began to dissolve into dawn, I could see the streams of morning light. My eyesight was completely restored and there wasn't even a scar! I never needed glasses until I graduated from Harvard Law School years later. By the way, my father finally got through, and I met him later that third day at the Lamar Railroad Station - with my eyesight perfectly restored.

Oh, how Brother Bell could pray. When he would pray, it sounded like one of the ancient prophets. He had authority and kindness, and with quiet dignity, he talked directly to God. He was very tolerant, and a born leader. Even in the presence of men who held higher positions in the church political structure, it was evident that Brother Bell was really the leader.

### Brother Bell Prays for Springfield

When Brother Bell and his wife first came to Springfield, I remember they had the youth group come over to their home on Christmas Eve. I remember that he explained what swaddling clothes were, and the Christmas Story took on a special meaning in the hands of this anointed man.

On another occasion, in those days before the General Council moved to Springfield, Brother Bell called all the young people of the church to his home one evening. Brother Bell loved Springfield. His daughter, Anna, had bought a home here and he used to visit her and preach for us quite often. He was very kind and liked the young people of the church, and that night twelve to fifteen of us gathered in his home on Lynn Street. He told us that the next day, he was going to the General Council meeting in St. Louis and that he believed that it was God's will for the Council to move its offices from St. Louis to Springfield. Apparently some of the brethren wanted it to remain in St. Louis and some wanted to move the headquarters to Kansas City. A.S. Copley published a paper at Kansas City called *The Pentecost*. Brother Bell said that no one else wanted to move the General Council to Springfield, but he believed that this was where God wanted it. He asked us to pray that God would give him the wisdom to say the right words to persuade the brethren to come to Springfield. We prayed till after midnight. I can't say that the Lord brought the General Council to Springfield solely in answer to our prayers that night, for all the brethren were seeking the mind of the Lord, but I can say that if you stood today on the spot where Brother Bell and the young people prayed, you would be standing in the middle of the Assemblies of God complex in Springfield, Missouri. (The actual spot is halfway between Boonville and Campbell Streets on the North side of Lynn Street). Remember, that at this time, the church was meeting opposite the courthouse in a tabernacle on Central Street, quite a ways away from Brother Bell's home. We never even dreamed that the Lord would answer by using the very ground that we kneeled upon while we were praying.

### The New Issue

I've read several accounts of Brother Bell's experience with the "Jesus Only" Issue in 1915. However, I do not believe that the episode has ever been accurately reported. In fact, I'm rather puzzled by the accounts given by some authors. One historian states that Bell, ". . . acknowledged that he had been swept away out of fear of losing influence rather than out of Biblical conviction."[8] On this incredible statement, I must differ in the strongest terms possible. In my opinion, it would have been impossible to have motivated Brother Bell at all with the plum of influence. Influence was something which radiated from his being, but something which he never sought. While several others were jealous of this natural talent, the majority of the brethren gladly acknowledged his leadership qualities. In fact, even after this episode was over, the brethren returned Brother Bell for a second and third term to the position of General Superintendent of the Assemblies of God (1920, 1921). He held this office until the time of his passing on June 15, 1923, when

209

he died in Brother Welch's arms.

I believe that his action was not one of intellectual assent, but rather, in keeping with his childlike humility, it reflected his sincerity and willingness to obey the dictates of his great heart - even if it meant the loss of his position.* (He had labored to build up a magazine called *Apostolic Faith* which merged with Brother Pinson's magazine and the name was changed to *Word and Witness*. This magazine had joined forces with Brother Flower's *Christian Evangel* and became the *Weekly Evangel*, now the *Pentecostal Evangel* ).

Shortly after being rebaptized, he resigned as editor. I do know that he had been overworked publishing the *Evangel*, both as editor and as a printer-mechanic. And he was terribly under paid - five dollars a week was all he received, and keep in mind that he had a wife and family and was probably the most competent and educationally-qualified man in the Pentecostal movement at the time. He was truly a servant washing the feet of his brethren. It is difficult for me

---

*Perhaps we are not stating this strongly enough. Although Hazel says that he was rebaptized, Fred has said, on many occasions, in the strongest terms possible, that he does not believe that the reports were accurate. The event is reported to have occurred at a camp meeting in Tennessee. Father was 15 at the time. Certainly, the following comment by Dr. Blumhoffer, in her recent article, does reflect his opinion of Brother Bell,

> "Bell had never really endorsed the unorthodox inclinations of Oneness. Rather, he had sincerely hoped to experience more of God by accepting baptism according to the Apostolic formula."[9]

Father always maintained that other jealous preachers had made much of this incident. - JFC

to believe that his temporary embrace of the "Oneness Doctrine", if it really happened at all, reflects anything more than a period of brief human intellectual weakness in a time of sincere spiritual desire. ("Burnout" is a popular term used today to characterize this kind of physical and emotional overwork.) Considering his personal condition, the events which were occurring in Pentecost at that time, and the fact that many other dear brethren were similarly motivated (Brother Goss, Brother Opperman, Brother R.E. McAlistar, many of the Canadian Pentecostal preachers, Mother Barnes, and my own pastor, Bennett Lawrence), I believe that many of the brethren have been overly-critical of this isolated event in his life. Certainly, he emerged as one of the most eminent and outspoken critics against the "Jesus Only" doctrine. His great humility and life of anointed service surely reveals that he was a special instrument in the Master's Hands. After this period, he ministered to many others yearning for more of God and was able to guide them through to deeper lives, while avoiding wanderings in a spiritual wilderness.

Brother Bell used to write the "Question and Answer" page in the *Evangel* and what I believe to be among the clearest and most succinct refutations of the "Oneness Issue" were written by him in answer to readers' questions, and published in this column. In answer to the question, "Is Jesus the Mighty God?" Bell said,

> "He is the Mighty God. . . But the false teaching slips in by saying Jesus ONLY Is God. All such is untrue, for the Father is God, the Son is God, and the Holy Spirit is God; yet there are not three Gods. . . But Jesus is the only person in the Trinity in whom the Godhead or Deity dwells BODILY. . . .They are one in essence, in nature, in Deity, in Godhead, yet they are clearly distinct. The Father is not the Son, and the Son is not the

211

E.N. Bell

Father."[10]

When asked to give a baptismal formula, Brother Bell responded:

"In the strictest sense of a fixed expression which cannot be taken from nor added to without destroying its efficacy and breaking some command, I do not believe there is such a formula in the New Testament in regard to anything. . . In a larger sense, and with such additions as the minister in charge sees fit to add, Matt. 28:19 is generally regarded as the best and most scriptural. . . For myself, I have for many years used the following: 'In the name of Jesus Christ, I baptize you into the name of the Father, and of the Son and of the Holy Ghost.' Or, 'I baptize you in the name of the Lord Jesus Christ into the name of the Father, and of the Son, and of the Holy Ghost.' Justin Martyr, who lived in Samaria early enough to have seen and talked with the apostle John, says to the emperor at Rome that it was the custom of the early Christians to baptize 'in the name of God the Father, maker of the Universe, and of His Son, Jesus Christ, and of the Holy Ghost.' This quotation shows that the formula used in those early days followed in general the Trinitarian outline as given by Jesus in Matt. 28:19: and shows in the second place that these early Christians did not regard Christ's expression as a fixed and invariable formula, but took the liberty to add such explanatory words as they felt were needed. I believe in the same liberty of the Spirit."[11]

After the "Jesus Only" episode, Brother Bell pastored

several assemblies; one in Little Rock, Arkansas, and then the joint assemblies of Joplin, Missouri, and Galena, Kansas. Stanley Frodsham writes that, "In 1917, he received a unanimous invitation from the Presbytery of the General Council to become editor of the *Evangel*. He accepted this invitation and for two years longer, edited the paper. In the Fall of 1919, he was elected Secretary of the General Council and in 1920, he was elected Chairman of the General Council of the Assemblies of God and he continued in this office until the day of his death."[12] It was during this period of time that I knew this marvelous man of God.

By the way, J.T. Boddy succeeded Brother Bell as editor of the *Evangel* from 1919 to 1920, and Stanley H. Frodsham formally became editor in 1921. (Frodsham held that position until 1928, when he came up to Framingham, Massachusetts, to be the editor of *Word and Work*. He returned to again edit *The Evangel* in December of 1929 and continued in that position for the next twenty years.)

### Building the Church

Brother Bell had the great desire that the young people going as missionaries and into the ministry have the best full gospel training and education possible. I know that the credit for the development of Central Bible College belongs to many Godly people, but if one were to trace Central Bible Institute back to its original conception, it would be in the hearts and minds of only a few men. I have personally regarded Brother Bell as the original founder of Central Bible Institute. While I was editor of *Word and Work* in the 1930's, Brother Welch wrote an article for me about Brother Bell and said the same thing. I would like to tell how we finally got a respectable church building where Central Bible College started its operation.

I believe that it was in the Summer of 1919, that W. T. Gaston became our pastor. We were meeting in a wood-frame tabernacle on East Central Street, opposite the Green County Courthouse and we held a tent meeting at the corner of Central and Rogers Streets in Springfield where he spoke. There was a great deal of interest and the crowds began to come. After the tent meeting closed, we moved into the old city hall, up stairs, on Boonville Street. It got so that we couldn't hold the crowds that came. Late in the Fall of 1919, the men of the church met in a meeting room in the city hall with E.N. Bell presiding. Brother Bell expressed the need for a church building and told us that he and Brother Welch had two lots on Calhoun and Campbell Streets. The men of the church enthusiastically agreed that this would be an appropriate place to construct a church building. My father, James J. Corum, was the church Treasurer at the time. He timidly pointed out to the brethren that our current finances weren't quite up to constructing a whole new church building. Brother Bell responded, "We'll get to that problem in a moment", and he proceeded to determine what the brethren thought we should include in the new building. They discussed how many Sunday School rooms were needed. Other facilities were discussed; a kitchen, offices, and so on. Again my Dad interrupted, "Hold on, that costs too much. We can't ever do that. We don't have the money for it." (No one in the church was even making a hundred dollars a month then.)

I remember Brother Bell putting his hand up and saying, "Brother Corum, we'll get to that later. What we want to find out now is just what it is that we need. What do we believe God wants us to have?" And the business of specifying what we desired continued. Brother Bell was especially concerned about the basement of the church, as he wanted it large enough and with sufficient facilities to serve for a Bible School. This impetus for a Bible School during Brother Bell's term as General Superintendent of the Assemblies of God led to the creation of Central Bible Institute.

Finally, after we had all run out of suggestions for the

proposed building, and everyone had spoken, Brother Bell, who was now sitting, asked, "Is that everything?" Well, we had gone as far as our vision could take us. Dad spoke up and said, "That's going to cost an awful lot of money." Brother Bell then turned to my father and said, "Now Brother Corum, we'll take up your problem. Let's go to the one that's got the money." With that he slipped down from his chair onto his knees and began to pray. It was like Abraham or Moses of old talking to God - and I'll never forget it. Soon all the men of the church joined him. He was truly a mighty man of prayer and he was praying for the finances to raise up facilities to match our vision. When we all left that night, we had confidence that it would go up. I remember riding home with Dad, and we knew we would see it. By the way, it was up and paid for within a year.

Well, the Brethren started drawing up plans and someone suggested Fred Voegler as a builder. Building materials were scarce because of World War One. Brother Voegler was a Pentecostal preacher and he had been a carpenter. A book could be written about Brother Voegler in his own right. He was pastoring a church in Kansas at the time. He later became District Superintendent for the State of Kansas and held national offices in the Assembly of God. At any rate he was a better preacher than carpenter, for after we moved in, the walls of the church bowed out and the brethren installed steel rods across the sanctuary above the windows to draw the walls back in and strengthen the structure. Central Bible College was then housed in the basement of our church, which came to be known as Central Assembly. Brother Bell was able to get D.W. Kerr and his son-in-law, Willard Pierce, to come (from California, I think) and formally establish the school.

We've enclosed a picture of the church on the day of its dedication. That is our Brisco automobile in front of the church. (The car with the million dollar motor - or so the

215

ads used to say.) We dedicated our little white church with the word "Pentecostal" over the door on July 1, 1920. Brother Gaston was still our pastor when the church was dedicated, but evangelistic fire was burning in his bones. That Summer, he held a powerful camp meeting in Russellville, Arkansas, along with Arch P. Collins, who had served as General Superintendent in 1914-1915. Brother Gaston was himself destined to eventually become General Superintendent in 1925-1929. In his early days, he was a wonderful speaker. He would pray all night before he spoke. Several of his children went on to become preachers and evangelists in the Assemblies of God.

I cannot adequately express the deep personal loss which I felt upon Brother Bell's passing. For, to many others like myself, Brother Bell had been a wise councilor. He was perceptive and patient, and he walked in kindness and quiet dignity - yet he had the heart of a child. Concerning his death, Brother Flower later wrote:

> "Back in 1923, while Brother E.N. Bell was serving as General Superintendent, he was sent to the Rocky Mountains District on official business.[2] For sometime, Brother Bell had been suffering in his body without knowing the true cause of his trouble. He was compelled to cut short his ministry and return to his own home. Brother Welch, filled with concern, called on Brother Bell and they opened their hearts to each other. While they were sitting in conversation, in the front room of Brother Bell's home, suddenly Brother Bell

---

[2]Brother Frodsam had earlier reported that it was the Southern California District, and the dates were June 8-10, 1923. (Reference 1, Pg. xi)

was stricken with a heart attack and slumped to the floor. Brother Welch tenderly gathered him in his arms and there the spirit of Brother Bell slipped away to be with Christ. A short time later, I arrived on the scene. I shall never forget the expression on Brother Welch's face and the tone of his breaking voice as he told of Brother Bell breathing his last in his arms."[13]

And so he fell asleep in Jesus on Friday, June 15, 1923, at 8:15 P.M. Brother Welch was soon elected to succeed Brother Bell as General Superintendent in 1923 and so the torch was passed on to another great leader.

["Uncle Will", or "Daddy Welch" as many of us called him, was also a wonderful man of God. He was Chairman of The General Council from 1915 to 1920, when once more the Council elected Brother Bell, and from the death of Brother Bell, in 1923, until 1925. He was a great organizer, and when he died on July 14, 1939, Brother Flower wrote,

"Daddy Welch had a clear vision of the principles of cooperative fellowship and his influence went far in those early days for the laying of a sound foundation in the building of the Assemblies of God.

He was a great lover of men. I shall never forget the day when a report reached us of the awful failure of one of our younger preachers, how he fell on his face by his desk and groaned and wept before God. No censure of unkind criticism - just a broken heart and a tender compassion. Such failures happen in any church fellowship, they are to be expected, and yet when they did come, the effect was always the same - a broken heart and a cry for mercy from God.

217

His vision for the development of the fellowship was great. He was years beyond his brethren in these matters.''[14](*Pentecostal Evangel*, July 29,1939) ]

These were the sort of men that the Lord used to lead the Assemblies of God in its critical formative years. But, when it comes to anointed leadership, E.N. Bell will always stand out in my mind.

Brother Bell was the wisest and most gentle leader that I've ever known.

Brother Frodsham wrote, ''After his death, many suggested that Central Bible College should be looked upon as a memorial to Brother Bell, since it was largely through his efforts as Chairman of the General Council that this project was started''. . . this project so dear to Brother Bell's heart.[15]

Certainly over the years, many of the great leaders of the Pentecostal movement have echoed this sentiment. With Harry Bowley, I too, ''. . . cherish the memory of that grand old man''.

## REFERENCES

1. **Questions and Answers**, by E.N. Bell, (Pulpit and Pew Full Gospel Series), The Gospel Publishing House, Springfield, Missouri, n.d., PP. vii-xiii.
2. **Contending For The Faith**, by Zelma Argue, Messenger of God Publishing House, Burnaby, B.C., Canada, 2nd revised edition, 1928, PP. 20-23. (Previously published as **What Meaneth This**, 1923).
3. **The Winds Of God**, by Ethel E. Goss, Word Aflame Press, Hazelwood, Missouri, 1958. Revised, updated and reprinted 1986, Pg. 201.
4. Reference 3, Pg. 200.
5. Reference 3, Pg. 242.
6. **The Progress of Democracy**, by Fred T. Corum,
7. ''Harry E. Bowley'', *Word and Work*, Vol. 55, No.

no. 12 December, 1933, Pg. 13.

8.  **Anointed to Serve**, by William W. Menzies, Gospel Publishing House, Springfield, Missouri, 1971, Pg. 118.

9.  "The Great Oneness-Trinitarian Debate", by Edith Waldvogel Blumhoffer, *Assemblies of God Heritage*, Vol. 5, No. 3, Fall, 1985, PP. 6-8.

10. Reference 1, PP. 15-16.

11. Reference 1, PP. 22-23.

12. Reference 1, Pg. xi.

13. "A Great Man in Israel", by J. Roswell Flower, *Pentecostal Evangel*, July 29, 1939, Pg. 2.

14. Reference 13, Pg. 2.

15. Reference 1, Pg. xiii.

# Chapter XX

## MOTHER'S VISION OF A PENTECOSTAL CHURCH IN SPRINGFIELD

"I saw God's great arm stretched out . . ."

It is difficult for us to place a date on the following event, but it occurred after our tentmeeting on the corner of Campbell and Calhoun Streets where our tent had been so torn and tattered, but before Joe French came to Springfield. So it must have been about 1911 or so that we had all gone down to visit Uncle Charlie and Aunt Florence Taliaferro again at Mammoth Springs, Arkansas. While we were waiting for a train back to Springfield, we visited with one of the saints that had a home near the Thayer, Missouri, railroad station. Back in those days, you didn't just visit, you got down before God together and prayed. Mother had a great burden for a Pentecostal church in Springfield. She believed this message was so wonderful that everyone would want the fullness of God. While Mother was praying, the Lord revealed to her that the Springfield work would prosper. He gave her a vision and showed her where the church was to be located. Mother had always believed that the church should be near the center part of the city, but now the Lord was showing her that this was indeed so. I have an old scrap of paper before me in Mother's own handwriting and this is what it says:

> "I saw God's great arm stretched out and
> His power rising as a gray mist from Camp-
> bell and Calhoun Streets. The Hand of God
> was so big and powerful. He spread it out over
> Springfield, picking up folks from the East
> and the West, the North and the South. They

220

all came to this one place. He then sprinkled
them with the blood of His Son, Jesus. He
then passed His hand over their heads, seal-
ing them to the day of redemption.''

The Lord showed her that the church was to be located
on the spot where the tent had been torn down. Remember,
that this was in 1911, when we were still struggling to
establish a church in Springfield.

Now there are such things as self-fulfilling prophecies,
where some misguided person will dream up a prophecy and
then proceed to do something to make it happen themselves.
Mother's vision occurred around 1911. I've heard her tell it
many times. When Aunt Rachel had her vision of the Sparkling Fountain in 1913, our hearts had been especially thrilled
for it called Mother's vision back to the remembrance of us
all. But when the Publishing House people came seven or
eight years later, they had never heard of it. In fact, when
we had the business meeting that we told about in the section of Chapter XIX called "Building the Church", no one
even thought about Mother's vision. At that time, only Dad
and I were in Springfield. Mother and Hazel were out visiting
Aunt Rachel in Los Angeles. What is remarkable is that, in
the meanwhile, Brother Welch and Brother Bell (who lived
one block from the property) had unknowingly bought the
very land where the tent had stood, and they offered it to
the church. And so our first "real" church building was to
be on the same spot that the Lord had shown to Mother in
the vision many years before, the very land that had been
sanctified by Sister Benedict's prayers.

When Mother and Hazel returned from California several
weeks later, Dad told them about the new church we were
going to build. He told how Brother Bell was "raising" the
money, and where the church was going to be built. We all
could only weep for joy and wonder at the marvelous
faithfulness of our precious Lord. As we said before, the

221

church served as the first home of Central Bible College, and was paid for within the year. Furthermore, it has been the mother church for eighteen other Assemblies of God churches in Springfield. Slowly and surely, God has brought all of these things to pass.

By the way, I have always wondered about the gray mist. Many years later, someone gave me a copy of Josephus' **Antiquities of the Jews**, and I was pleasantly surprised to read of the manner in which the Shekinah Glory entered into the Tabernacle. For, Josephus declares that there was a thick mist over the tabernacle, and ". . . from it there dropped a sweet dew, and such a one as showed the presence of God to those that desired and believed it." (Book III chapter 8, also see Exodus 40:34).

## Chapter XXI

## THE GENERAL COUNCIL MOVES TO SPRINGFIELD

"Homemade benches and a sawdust floor. . ."
Faith Campbell

everal outstanding histories of the formation of the General Council of the Assemblies of God have been written, and they describe the spiritual and political efforts associated with its genesis. However, I believe that we owe it to Brother Bell's leadership and spiritual sensitivity that the Publishing House was moved to Springfield, instead of any one of several other places which might have been equally suitable. I will explain why in this chapter. Surely, the hand of the Lord guided all along the way.

In 1917, we had leased a small lot opposite to the Courthouse on Central Street (near to where the post office is now), and we built a wooden tabernacle to hold services in. It had, as Faith Campbell recorded in her book about Brother Frodsham, "Homemade benches and a sawdust floor."[1] At this time, Bennett Lawrence was our pastor. He had just recently had his book, **The Apostolic Faith Restored**, published by the Gospel Publishing House which was then located in St. Louis. With the publication of his book, he began to be in great demand as a speaker and he was away quite often. It was during this time that he came under the influence of the Oneness doctrine and resigned from the Assemblies of God. We kept a Sunday School and prayer meeting going, however. Brother Rufus Cooper came and did the preaching for us. He had been converted in the great Thayer Campmeeting years before. Oh, how we missed Sister Benedict, who had moved on to Aurora, Missouri, in 1915 to pioneer a work up there. But God was moving in our midst.

223

Mother's notes read,

> "In May of 1918, the Gospel Publishing
> House folks, coming into our Assembly,
> found us on fire for God as they confessed.
> We were also glad to welcome them into our
> midst."[2]

In June of 1918, Stanley and Alice Frodsham and their
daughter, Faith, moved to Springfield. We had them out for
dinner and he told us about Smith Wigglesworth in England.
(Brother Wigglesworth would later come and hold meetings
for us, staying in the home of Brother Frodsham). This was
the first time that I had met Brother and Sister Frodsham.
(I was eighteen years old at the time and little did I dream
that we would later work together in Framingham,
Massachusetts, on the magazine *Word and Work*, and a missionary outreach called the "Russian and Eastern European
Mission". It was in Framingham where Alice Frodsham
passed away.) Brother Frodsham had rented a house in
Springfield big enough to share with several other Publishing
House families, and Sister Frodsham over saw the operation of it. Brother and Sister Welch came, and Brother and
Sister Flower and their family all came down to live in
Springfield. I believe that Brother and Sister Flower rented
a separate house. We used to have them out to our home
quite often and years later, Brother Flower wrote the following kind words:

> "In the year 1918, I was entrusted with the
> task of moving the Gospel Publishing House
> to Springfield, and in 1919, was moved to
> Springfield to develop the new office of Mis-
> sionary Secretary. Many pleasant hours of
> fellowship were spent in the Corum Home and
> the hospitality of the Corum family was most
> generous and helpful. They were particular-
> ly noted as prayer warriors."[3]

We have included a picture of one Sunday afternoon when the Flowers visited with us. Sister Flower's Father, Brother Reynolds, a wonderful man of God, was visiting at the time and you can see him sitting on the porch. Joe Flower, (now Secretary of the General Council of the Assemblies of God), is standing on the right. I believe that he was in Fred's Sunday School class at the time. All of Brother and Sister Flower's children have given their lives to the service of our precious Lord, and reflect the wonderful faithfulness of their parents and grandparents.

When the Publishing House moved down from St. Louis, they bought an old grocery store building on the corner of Pacific and Lyon Streets. The picture of this building is shown in many of the Assemblies of God histories. The Publishing House was quite different in those days. They brought their equipment and machinery down with them from Saint Louis. Most of it was old and secondhand. None of them had any money, for they had all given everything into the work of the Lord. Brother Frodsham wrote, "If those early workers had not sacrificed, the Gospel Publishing House would have gone on the rocks."[4]

We had a little five and a half acre farm out on East Division Street, out beyond Glenstone, and Mother would take them milk and eggs. Fred would kill chickens, from among his state fair prize-winners, and dress them for the workers. We had a large peach orchard and a big garden. We would take vegetables, peaches, and other fruit to help the Publishing House workers all that we could, for this was a time of financial hardship for everyone. I think that Paul was just starting at Drury College around this time, and Fred and Artemus were studying as upper class men. But this was also the period of time when Brother Bell and the church "raised" the money to build a real church building for the Pentecostal Church in Springfield.

As we pass through the halls of the Headquarters

225

today, and think of the prayers and sacrifices of those early Gospel Publishing House workers, we can't help but recall the line from Baring Gould's old song, "Brothers, we are treading where the Saints have trod."

They had the vision for the marvelous outreach that lay before them. It is true that when they came, they had little money. But they were living in victory, and in the distance they could see the glorious ministry which exists today.

## REFERENCES

1. **Stanley Frodsham: Prophet With a Pen**, Faith Campbell, Gospel Publishing House, Springfield, Missouri, 1974, Pg. 59.
2. "The Pentecostal Church of Springfield", typed notes by L.H. Corum, n.d., circa 1921.
3. Funeral notes by J. Roswell Flower, mailed to J.F.C. by Alice Reynolds Flower.
4. Reference 1, Pg. 58.

# Chapter XXII

## BERT EDWARD WILLIAMS

"Jesus - that one word expresses all the love of God."
B.E.W.

The tide was turning in Springfield. We now had a real church and many dedicated prayer warriors were in our midst. Sister Flower was now here. Men like Brother Bell, Brother Welch, Brother Flower, Brother Frodsham, and so many of those dear and precious Publishing House people were now attending the Pentecostal Church in Springfield.

One Summer, we held a city-wide revival. Bert Williams had been the Assistant Pastor of a large Baptist Church in New York City (I believe that it had around four thousand members). He received the Baptism of the Holy Ghost with speaking in tongues and was relieved of his position, and so he went into the Pentecostal evangelistic field. Ours was his first Pentecostal revival meeting. He was a brilliant speaker and a very dignified man. He was very well educated for Pentecost in those days, holding several degrees from the Ohio State University.

This was the first really big tentmeeting that Springfield ever had. I believe that our pastor was then Brother Herman Harvey.

The Brethren put advertisements on the front and back of the trolly cars all over Springfield and I remember that they pitched a large tent next to our new church building on Calhoun and Campbell Streets. (You can see the edge of the tent in the church picture shown above. The hand bill was issued in 1923, when Smith Wigglesworth came and held meetings for us, but the picture of the church was taken while

227

Bert Williams was holding the tent revival.) We put the tent on the Campbell Street side of the church. I remember that Brother Frodsham suggested that after the services were over each night, we set up a prayer room in the church basement so that there would be less distraction. Brother Williams said, "No, we have nothing to hide. We'll put up an altar rail in the tent and let the people pray through right there."

Well, Brother Williams preached with great power and anointing. It was hot and he would preach in his shirt sleeves. And God began to move mightily. The daughter of one of the bankers came and got saved. After she had wept and prayed through down at the altar, she took out her compact and began to powder her face and arrange her lipstick. Well, our church people had all been raised not to wear makeup and for this to happen at the altar was more than some of the older women could take. I remember that several came running to my mother and said, "Sister Corum, go down there and get her to stop." Mother said, "No, leave her alone. The Lord's dealing with her and He will take care of that." Well, she got the Baptism of the Holy Spirit and her folks got very angry with us. One night her sister came and jerked her up while she was praying and cursed us right at the altar. I believe that most of the family later came into Pentecost.

Well, the rowdies came too. They would stand around the back and holler, shake the tent ropes, and try to torment us. Once when a girl got saved, her cousin came in and said he was going to drag her out. He started down the center aisle and when he got about half way down, Brother Williams, who was ministering at the altar, turned toward him, raised his right hand, snapped his finger at him and said, "That's far enough." The Spirit of the Lord knocked him down and he rolled around and crawled back out of the tent not knowing what had happened.

Before the meeting had gone on very long, someone made

threats against the evangelist. There was a threat that someone would kill Brother Williams. Vandals pulled out the electric wires and we were in darkness for awhile. Later, I heard that they were going to cut the tent ropes. Then one night, the Ku Klux Klan came out all dressed in their regalia, with robes and hoods and all. When they sat down, they took up a whole bench. (The Klan was supposed to help religious services - if you can imagine that.) They said, "We are guarding this." Well, the police were afraid of trouble and so after this, they would bring our evangelist, Bert Williams, to the meetings every night with a police guard and drive him up in the paddy wagon. After the meeting was over, the police would form a guard around Brother Williams and escort him back into the paddy wagon and take him home. He sure looked funny sitting back in there. Well, God used that, and it attracted much attention to the services. The crowds really began to grow and soon the rowdies disappeared.

One night, there was a man that came in from Thayer, Missouri, when they had held a district meeting, and he really knew God! During the preaching he would just sit there, perhaps looking like he was asleep. But when the altar call came, he would get astride the altar rail, start praying - and he would really go to it! The Power of God began to fall and it just stirred the whole town. Now, this was one meeting that really stirred Springfield. And a lot of people that were saved and received the Baptism have gone out from that meeting as preachers, missionaries, and evangelists. It has been said by many that these were the best meetings that Springfield has ever had. As many as twenty one would receive the Baptism in one meeting. That man could pray and pray! When he prayed, it sounded like a steam shovel going to work. While he was praying like that one night, Bert Williams (who was being ushered out by the police guard) came over to my father on the side of the tent and

said, "Brother Corum, who in the round world is that man?"
Dad responded, "It's John Davis." (See Chapter XII.)

That was the way I remember John Davis. He was a great
man of prayer. He would pray alone all night out in the
woods, and when he touched the Throne - the Power of God
would fall.

So the tide had turned and God greatly blessed these
meetings. I believe that more people joined our church as
a result of this revival than any other we have ever held.
Not only did it bless the church, but many people that felt
the call of God on their lives needed a Bible School education. As a result, ten or fifteen acres were eventually acquired
in the northern part of Springfield and buildings started for
what is now Central Bible Institute.

Many years later, Bert Edward Williams would succeed
Stanley Frodsham as editor of *Word and Work* in Framingham, Massachusetts, (a position which I subsequently held
after Brother Williams returned to the evangelistic field).
Brother Frodsham went back to Springfield to return as editor
again of *The Pentecostal Evangel*.

Would you like to know what Brother Williams' preaching
was like? I have before me excerpts of a marvelous message
that Bert Williams published in the pages of *Word and Work*
in September of 1931, concerning "The Loving God and the
Suffering Savior". I can see him yet. . . It is a warm summer night and Brother Williams, in his shirt sleeves, stands
before an old gospel tent, packed to capacity. Listen as he
speaks:

> "It is wholly impossible to measure the
> power of love. There is no limit to its depth
> and its height reaches to the skies. It stretches
> out its strong arms and embraces the whole
> world in its grasp.
>  . . . Jesus - That one word expresses all the
> love of God.. . . When we look at Jesus, we

see Jehovah's heart.

. . .Christ, the Lamb . . . had ever before His gaze the darkness of the valley through which He must pass. Which ever way He turned, there fell upon His path the shadow of a cross. Toward that cross, each day of suffering and abuse brought Him so much nearer.

See Him in the Garden of Gethsemane...
...Listen to the agony of His being . . See the blood oozing from His body and dripping down to the ground. . . On Him were laid the iniquities of us all . . . not far away, the scenes of His trial, Peter's unfaithfulness, Judas' treachery, the cowardice of all the apostles and the tragic doings of Calvary - the Father who had delighted in Him from eternity, who had smiled on angels, and whose countenance of love gave radiance to creation, was soon to lay His hand upon Him.

Christ suffered. He swallowed the bitter cup of the whole world's sin. . . Oh the awful bitterness of that cup! And your sin was in that cup. He bore our sins in His own body on the tree, and by His stripes we are healed.

Come and avail yourself of the salvation which He purchased for you. Come and reckon your sins to be borne away from your soul in the precious broken body of Christ.

Why? Why this life of suffering? Why this terrible death? Why? It was all to manifest the love of God for us. To prove by an undeniable infallible evidence that God really loves us.

And is it possible that so much humiliation and sorrow, so much suffering and anguish, so much pain and grief should count for

Bert Edward Williams

> nothing in your eyes? Is it possible that so
> wonderful and so magnificent a sacrifice of
> love could be made for you,- and you not ac-
> cept it?'' . . .

I can still hear Brother Williams' voice as he delivered such marvelous messages as this. Times haven't changed. Burdened hearts still yearn to hear the glorious message, and come and be set free from the terrible chains and fetters that bind.

"Ought not Christ to have suffered these things, and to enter into His glory? And beginning at Moses and all the prophets, he expounded unto them in all the scriptures the things concerning Himself. . . And they said one to another, Did not our hearts burn within us, while He talked with us by the way, and while He opened to us the scriptures?''

And then the altar call. How our hearts burned within us! I can yet see John Davis astride the altar, pressing the battle. I can still see Brother Williams ministering under the anointing, the Hand of God was moving, the crowds coming - rushing to rough wooden altar rails to unburden their souls at Calvary. The Lord really had His hand upon that wonderful man, and yes - upon us all.

# Chapter XXIII

## CENTRAL BIBLE COLLEGE GROWS - THE STREAM MUST FLOW

"Oh, so what . . . Just give it to them."

T he humble facilities in the basement of the Pentecostal Church on Campbell and Calhoun Streets was soon unable to handle the number of students applying to the Bible School for training. While Brother Bert Williams was here, he greatly encouraged the Brethren to step out in this ministry, "By all means, get this training center going."

At this time, there was a group of business men in Springfield called the Commercial Club. They held ten to fifteen acres of land north of Springfield and the brethren thought that they might buy it for a campus for Central Bible College. When they went before the Commercial Club to buy it, Dad, being the Treasurer of our local church, went along. When he came home, he related the following story to us.

After the request was submitted, the Commercial Club debated among themselves what the terms of the sale would be. First, they said the price must be so much. Then someone jumped up and said, "No, this is a religious body and that's too much money." Then they said, "Well, they must put down so much money and then within a certain length of time, they must have at least one hundred thousand dollars worth of buildings on it." We had no money. The Assembly of God was not a wealthy church by any of the world's standards. A hundred thousand dollars? They might as well have said a hundred million!

Then, while the Commercial Club was debating the terms of the agreement among themselves, tempers began to rise,

233

they shook their fists at one another, chairs were knocked over and several of the Commercial Club members began to fight with each other right in the club. The brethren stood there not knowing what to make of all this. Then, lo and behold, someone said, "Oh, so what . . . Just give it to them." They took a vote - and that's what they did. They just turned it over to the Assemblies of God, without any strings attached. And that is how the property was acquired for the campus for Central Bible College. God's plans move slowly, but they are sure.

The first building to go up on the new campus out on Grant Street was built by Arthur Dake, the "yellow jacket" that had thrown an egg back in the wooden tabernacle on Boonville Street, years before. They had teams of horses with slips to dig the basement. Many of the brethren and the church young people came out and assisted. I remember carrying cement to help pour the footings and also the roofing material later on. I have often wondered, over the years, if the roof leaked or the foundations ever shifted. In the March, 1938, Issue of The Central Bible College Fellowship News ( Vol. 3, No. 3), Stanley Frodsham wrote an article called "And It Came To Pass."

"Another Pentecostal saint of those days was Miss Benedict. . . .

Thirty years ago, Miss Benedict, as a school teacher in Springfield, helped to launch a tent-meeting. She spent whole nights praying under the canvas. She prayed for a Pentecostal Assembly in Springfield, and on the very site where she prayed, the Central Assembly now stands. She prayed for a Pentecostal Publishing House, and within a short distance is located today the Gospel Publishing House. She prayed also for a Pentecostal Bible School, and within two miles of that spot is

Central Bible Institute.

> . . . it had been a source of great praise to Sister Benedict, before she died, to see how marvelously God answered her prayer. Surely, He is doing exceeding abundantly above all she asked or thought. May the stream flow on fuller, faster, and farther until Jesus comes."

Over the years, many dedicated, Spirit-filled people have been a part of the Central Bible Institute faculty and student body. Many have laid down their lives on the foreign fields. As L.B. Richardson wrote, "This stream must flow."

# Chapter XXIV

## BITS AND PIECES FROM A PENTECOSTAL SCRAPBOOK

". . . wave after wave of glory."

There are a number of little incidents that we would like to document. They don't really fit into the history at any one particular place, but they do reflect how God deals with the daily affairs of His people. Some are humorous and some are tragic, but they all reveal the wondrous tapestry of God's love. "He doeth all things well." No matter what the situation may be - Jesus is the answer. Though darkness may surround and all appear to be lost - this is the very point in space and time, in your life and mine, where God can come on the scene and reveal His wondrous love and mighty salvation to ordinary people. God has never let His people down.

### The Miracle Chickens

The State of Missouri had a poultry experiment station at Mountain Grove, Missouri, and one year they held a poultry show in part of White City. Dad let me go to see it and this got me interested in White Plymouth Rock chickens. I used to raise them and wash them for the country poultry shows. I'd even keep records of their performance and I was very proud of them. One morning, in the Fall of 1912, I went out to feed them and discovered that forty of them were missing. Someone had stolen them and had taken all of the prize winners that would roost near the front of the chicken coop. My heart was broken, but Mother said, "Don't worry Fred, we will pray that the Lord will lay it on the heart of the thief to return them all." I let it go at that, and Mother prayed for the thieves. The following Sunday, we drove the buggy into the yard on our return from church. The whole front yard was full of white chickens! I got some feed and called to them and they all came running back into the pen. All my prize winners were there, and not a one was missing! I never knew who took them or how they were returned, but God had answered my Mother's prayers. Yes, the Lord who caused an axe head to float one day, even cares about a little boy's chickens. They were truly miracle chickens.

### Tragic Accident - A Miraculous Healing

My brothers, Paul and Artemus, loved to hunt. They would take old Dee Dee, our dog, and hunt all over the outskirts of Springfield. Back in the days before World War I, you could hunt quail and rabbits all over what is now the grounds of Evangel College and up and down Glenstone Avenue. They had been out hunting on French's dairy farm one evening and it was starting to get dark. Artemus said, "Paul, hurry up. Come on, let's go home." Paul had climbed through a fence and as he pulled the shotgun through the fence after him by the barrel, the trigger caught in the bushes, or on the fence and discharged, exploding into his upper left arm and armpit. The shot severed the artery and veins and stripped most of the top flesh of the arm away.

Artemus made a tourniquet and was able to retard the bleeding somehow. We had no regular doctor, as we had just trusted the Lord and we were all healthy. The only doctor Artemus could think of was an osteopath named Dr. King at the square. So he rushed Paul into town and the osteopath called in a surgeon named Dr. Fulbright. Immediately, they got Paul in St. John's Hospital. The main artery and main blood vein had been severed. One of Paul's friends, that helped rush him in, finally got a chance to see what had happened and at the sight of Paul's severed arm, he fainted right in the hospital. Dr. Fulbright brought in his tools to amputate Paul's arm. There was a young nurse present named Grace

Packer, who had gone to Shady Dell School with Paul. They say that she got on her knees and begged Dr. Fulbright not to cut Paul's arm off.

Artemus called home and was able to reach Fred and told him what had transpired. Mother and Father had already gone to church to the Wednesday night prayer meeting. Fred ran to the church as hard as he could go and got Dad aside and told him what had happened. The whole church went to the altar rail for God to undertake. Brother W.T. Gaston was our pastor then, and how he groaned in the Spirit and sought God to restore the arm. The hospital wasn't far away and Father quickly got there and said, "You cannot cut his arm off. I will not give my consent." Dr. Fulbright said, "Well, it will be cold and dead by morning. It will have to come off." Dad said, "You can't do it. I won't allow it." Paul was eighteen at the time. Many of the saints at the church prayed all that night.

The next morning, when Dr. Fulbright came in, he looked at Paul's arm, then looked at my father and said, "A miracle has taken place. The little capillaries, through the night, have taken the place of the big vein and main artery!" Paul was only in the hospital for two weeks and he was never sick. Paul was very athletic and soon could use the arm again. There was a slight trace of shakiness, but otherwise his arm was quite normal. He became a construction engineer, handling as many as a hundred men at a time, building bridges, high schools, and college buildings in Massachusetts, New Hampshire, and New York. Years later, when he had a physical examination, the doctors were thoroughly confused by his x-ray. He had to explain to them that buckshot was all through his back and chest cavity, and this had caused the strange marks which they saw on the x-ray.

"Oh, to lean on Jesus breast, while the
tempests come and go!
Here is blessed peace and rest, where the

238

healing waters flow.''

## The Influenza Strikes

Some of the older readers may remember the terrible influenza epidemic that occurred at the close of World War I. People would be walking down the street, apparently in good health, and they would just drop dead. Thousands and thousands died across the country. In Springfield, the newspaper would come out with a long daily list of those that died the previous day. Smith Wigglesworth said that the cause was all the demons that had been freed up as a result of the many deaths which occurred in World War I.

My brother, Artemus, lay dying with the influenza. He had an extremely high fever and lay unconscious for days. But, in response to the prayer of faith, God came and healed him and made him perfectly whole. He later taught high school and coached basketball in El Paso, Texas.

## A Broken Arm

I must also mention another little girl in our church that fell and broke her arm. They brought her to the preachers. When they laid hands on her and prayed, they heard her arm snap back into place. There are so many more stories like this. It pays to serve Jesus.

## Brother Lamb

There was a drunkard that used to wonder around Springfield. He lived down in the poorer section of town. He came into the meetings one night and got wonderfully saved and tried to straighten out his life. Surprisingly, his wife wouldn't accept Pentecostal people. After Brother Lamb got saved, he went back to his wife and she would torment him. But he lived it straight and tried to get work to support her.

Dad heard that one of the little villages down the railroad tracks at the next junction needed someone to work for the sanitary department of the town. So back in those horse and buggy days, Brother Lamb got the job with a rake and a shovel, cleaning the dusty public streets of the town. One day, we were passing through the town and Mother stopped the buckboard to see how Brother Lamb was getting on. She met him on the street with a rake and a shovel in his hands and after greeting and talking said, "Well, this is sort of a one horse town." Brother Lamb looked back up at her and said, "Sister Corum, if you had my job, you wouldn't call this a one horse town!

Brother Lamb's wife continued to torment him, and she made life miserable for him. He finally lost the victory and backslid. He came home drunk one night and thrashed her to within an inch of her life. Mrs. Lamb rushed to the church the next morning, all black and blue, and begged the brethren to go and straighten him out again. She said she liked him better when he was saved. He later came back to the Lord and his wife got saved and became "one of them holy rollers" too.

### Given up to Die - But Found by a Saint

Sister Hoy was Mother's dearest friend after Sister Benedict went to be with the Lord. She had joined with us about 1911 and she was a great worker and prayer warrior. We described her briefly in Chapter XIV. Not only did she have a sweet singing voice, but also the heart of a true servant. This marvelous woman was greatly used of God. She would go into homes where there was sickness and poverty. She would bring them food and often do their washing on a washboard, while ministering to their spiritual needs. She would go out and walk the streets of Springfield, testifying and *looking for impossible situations for the Lord to work in*.

Once she heard of a boy that had tuberculosis and lay dying. His name was Ira Moses and he had been given up by the State Tuberculosis Sanitarium at Mount Vernon,

Missouri. He was in the last stages of the disease, where not only the lungs were gone, but the bones also. She went and found him and prayed and he was marvelously saved, and the whole family got saved. Their faith sprang alive and they brought him back to Springfield to the church to be prayed for - and God thoroughly and completely healed him.

The family was very poor and when he came to church, his clothes were ragged and worn. After he was healed, he went out and got a job, in construction of houses, to get the money to buy a new suit to wear to church. The first job he got was hauling brick with a wheel barrow. This, after the x-rays had shown his lungs had been eaten out! He said that he thought he was so weak that he couldn't stand to hold up the wheelbarrow, but the more he would push it, the more he would praise the Lord. And the more he praised the Lord, the stronger he felt.

He went back to the doctor (a Dr. Sherman) and the doctor sent him back to the sanitarium where they x-rayed him again. They were incredulous. They could not find a trace of tuberculosis in his body! Dr. Sherman wrote on the discharge, "I know for a fact he was in the last stages of tuberculosis and that he was dismissed from the State Sanitarium because he was going to die and there were others that were not in as bad a condition and could make better use of the facilities. Whereas the second x-ray shows that his lungs are completely healed up, there is no trace of tuberculosis."

Thank God for Sister Hoy and her aggressive faith in our Lord to challenge impossible circumstances and to wrestle the enemy's trophies from him

### Father is Filled

Father gladly accepted the message of Pentecost when Aunt Rachel first came and Mother received the Baptism on June 1, 1907. However, like many others, he saw that it was scriptural, but seemed unable to pray through. In the early 1920's, Mother and Hazel took a trip out to visit Aunt Rachel in Los Angeles. One evening, while he was all alone and praying by himself, at home in Springfield, he received the precious Holy Ghost Baptism. In his words, "I was filled with wave after wave of glory. If I had only know how simple it is to yield into the hands of the Lord, I would have been filled many years sooner. It is a wonder that everybody that is saved doesn't experience Acts 2:4."

Father sent Mother a long telegram describing his wonderful experience. Hazel said that when the Western Union delivery boy brought the telegram to Aunt Rachel's door, Mother let out a shout and started dancing around the parlor. Aunt Rachel talked with the delivery boy and got him down on his knees seeking the Lord. Before he left, he confessed salvation. Back in those days, a telegram had to be retransmitted at many locations along the line before it reached its destination. Consequently, it passed through many hands. When mother showed the telegram to Bert Williams, he said, "What a wonderful witness it must have been, telling the message of full salvation to every telegraph operator from Springfield to Los Angeles

### Ed Atkinson

Back in 1918 or 1919, while we were holding church in the little tabernacle on Central Street across from the Courthouse (or it may have been when we were meeting in the old City Hall), I was the young people's leader and directed the youth meeting on Sunday evenings before church. One Sunday evening, I noticed a young man and woman sitting in the back of the church. They looked like they were going to get up and leave, but I invited them to join us in the young peoples' service. Later that night, we got them to come to the altar and pray through to salvation. I never thought anything more about it after that.

Many years later, while I was visiting Springfield, Hazel told me that this man, Ed Atkinson, had gotten a tent and held a glorious tentmeeting on the South side of Springfield. Over the years, hundreds have been led to Christ by his ministry and he pastored a large assembly, named Calvary Temple, which was built on Grand Street. Hazel told me that Brother Atkinson told her that I was the one that had led him to Christ. He said that when we get to heaven, we would share the stars in our crowns. "Whatsoever thy hand toucheth shall prosper."

### The Powers Of The Air Are Overcome

There were several times on the old farm out on East Division Street when it seemed that all was lost. When Dad went to be with the Lord, Brother J. Roswell Flower preached his funeral at Central Assembly in 1948, and he recalled these several events:

". . . many is the time that Brother Corum slipped into the church for prayer. . that he might pray and seek the face of the Lord, and he testified many times to being lifted spiritually so that the weariness of the day ...[was] completely forgotten as a result of the blessing of the Lord.

Faith in God and a daily walk with Him became so common that the miraculous often was experienced. For instance: the home was encumbered by a mortgage with the danger of a foreclosure and loss of home. It was in the Springtime when a late freeze and blizzard endangered the peach crop. In fact, all the peach crop in the surrounding county was destroyed. But Brother and Sister Corum spent the night in prayer, claiming the promises of God, and God met them. Although

243

the freeze took the neighbor's crop just across the fence, the Corum crop was preserved and they were given a bumper crop of peaches, sufficient to lift the mortgage and preserve their home.

On another occasion, there was a county-wide invasion of the army worm. Again the Corums prayed, seeking the face of the Lord earnestly and again God answered prayer, for the worms were turned aside from their property and the few worms that crawled under the fences died without doing any damage.

Brother and Sister Corum were faithful tithers all through the years, giving the tithe which they felt belonged to God and adding to the tithe offerings which often exceeded a second tithe. And God's blessings promised to the faithful tither were abundantly receiv-ed in return." J. Roswell Flower

The greatest of all blessings, however, was the treasure that we had as a family, growing up together, gathered around our hearth. For there we found that the promises of God are true. We have been blessed to hear many anointed preachers over the years. But given them all, we would rather hear Mother and Father open the Word and tell us of the cross of Calvary and "love's sweetest old story" just one more time.

### Seeking The Lost

When I was a little girl and traveled through the Ozark hills in Southern Missouri and Northern Arkansas, I met many people that testified to the wonderful work that Joseph and Rachel Sizelove did. How they helped the people and brought them hope and the joyful message of salvation. They had served the Free Methodists as evangelistic workers during the 1890's. They went to Los Angeles around 1903 to send my cousins to school at the Free Methodist Colony. (By the way, Rachel A. Sizelove was born Rachel Harper in Marengo, Indiana, September 3, 1864, and passed away May 20, 1941, in Los Angeles.) They had preached holiness and sanctification all around the Mammoth Springs, Arkansas, and Thayer, Missouri, hills, back before the turn of the century. They drove a wagon pulled by two white ponies, Vesta and Emma. Perhaps they laid the foundation for the great meeting in Thayer. Certainly, God used them in a wonderful way.

On one occasion, while they were on their way to a meeting, Aunt Rachel looked across the valley and saw a little log cabin high on the side of one of those Ozark hills. She said, "Josie, turn the horses. The Lord has told me that we must go up to that cabin quickly and pray for somebody." As they pulled into the yard in front of the old log house, an old man lay dying and he said to his wife, "They've come. They've come at last." His wife said, "Who has come?" The old man said, "Why a man and his wife, and they are driving two white ponies. They are coming here to pray for me. Just as in my dream." Uncle Josie and Aunt Rachel went in and they prayed for the old man. He was dying and he was not saved. He had prayed that God would send him someone that could lead him through to salvation. He got wonderfully saved and then he passed into glory - saved. This was back before the turn of the century.

The "Pentecostal Fountain" at Mammoth Springs, Arkansas

During the Summer of 1925, Rachel and Josie Sizelove returned to Mammoth Springs, to hold a tentmeeting back in the Ozark Hills. They held the meeting near the grounds which they had homesteaded while they were Free Methodist evangelists back in the 1890's.

In 1925, there had been a tremendous drought all Spring

and on into the Summer. The creeks, wells, and most of the springs all dried up. The local farmers drove their buggies and old automobiles as much as fifty miles, taking loads of five gallon milk cans, to get water to bring back for their livestock. The crops all dried up and withered away under the scorching sun. Rachel's nieces, Hazel Corum and Virginia Taliaferro, were visiting at the time. Aileen and Vernon Green of Thayer, Missouri, (which was just down the road) remembered it well. While they were conducting the tentmeeting back beyond what is now called the Old Bakewell Homestead, the people remembered how God answered the prayer of Joe Duke, sixteen years earlier, for cool air and rain. And so the people gathered together and sought the face of God for relief from the heat and the drought. While they were yet praying, a spring gushed up out of solid rock just outside their tent. The water continued to flow and formed a small stream that provided water for the farms round about. All the farmers around called it the "Pentecostal Fountain". Today if you go back up in the hills where Josie and Rachel Sizelove held their tentmeeting, you can still find it. We have been there, and the story is true, for the "Pentecostal Fountain" is still bubbling out of the rock and the stream still flowing.

### HAVE FAITH IN GOD
By Birdie H. Hoy

Have faith in God when all the world's against you,
Have faith in God for He will take you through.
Have faith in God though storm clouds gather 'round you,
For all His wondrous promises are true.

Have faith in God, the sun will soon be shining.
Have faith in God, the sky will again be blue;
Amidst the clouds a bow of hope is gleaming

And all His promises are written just for you.

Though sickness come and sorrow's gloom surround you
Have faith in God, dark night will turn to day.
The clouds will only lend a glory to the sunset
God's flowers will bloom again along your way.

And when at last we see Him at the dawning
This Christ who went with us along our way,
We then will understand and know the meaning
Of darkest nights which lead to endless day.

# Chapter XXV

## CLOSING REMARKS

**W**ell, that is the story of how Pentecost came to Springfield, Missouri - or as much of it as we can now recall. We were there when it happened, and we have told it just as we saw it. Surely there is more, but someone else will have to recall those events. Most of the other young people that were in our church from the beginning, back in the days before World War I, are now in glory.

Soon the story will be told in full, not from the preacher's side nor from the congregation's perspective, but around the throne we will hear as the Lord Himself recalls each footstep. . . .In the Spirit now I'm transported back to those early days. . .I see a bullet-riddled battle flag marching by, carried aloft by old and wounded Civil War veterans - yea, I see a torn and shredded old gospel tent go by, carried by a white-robed throng and followed by a multitude of the redeemed - those to whom the SPARKLING FOUNTAIN has flowed - its ragged tatters flap in the heavenly breezes. In the Spirit, I hear a song of glorious triumph arise from that white-robed throng. And like the four and twenty elders, they too fall down before Him that sits on the throne and worship HIM that liveth for ever and ever, casting their crowns before the throne saying, "THOU ART WORTHY, O LORD, TO RECEIVE GLORY AND HONOR AND POWER."

We thank God that He loved us and blessed our little church and baptized us with His Holy Spirit. We thank God that He blessed the work in Springfield. It has gone far beyond what we could have ever dreamed. But let us say, in the most explicit terms possible, nobody can ever take the glory. We have no desire to draw credit to ourselves or to our denomination. I left Springfield in the early 1920's, and I have had no part in bringing these things to pass. But we were there while the foundation stones were hewn and laid. We were just laymen, beholding the hand of God as the fountain began to bubble forth. Mother was the first pastor of Central Assembly. We just called it the Pentecostal Church then. Preachers would come through and stay at our home. As we look back, we believe that at times we have entertained angels unaware. God blessed us with the miraculous. Mother couldn't preach. She was only an exhorter. She would just get up and say, "Glory to God! Hallelujah! I'm so glad I'm saved, sanctified, and full of the Holy Ghost." And then they would have testimonies and sing and sing. We remember what a struggle we had just to buy an old secondhand piano. But God blessed the work in so many ways.

In this book, we hope that we have made clear the women's part in the work at Springfield. But we would like to emphasize that no man and no woman can take the credit or glory for what has happened in Springfield. God used humble men, women, young people, and children to pray and that was how the work prospered. God answered prayer.

It did not blossom over night, but slowly. It slowly and resolutely moved forward, taking ground for God. Many of those old prayer warriors, that pressed the battle on their faces before God, never saw the manifestation of their requests in the physical world. But in the spiritual realm, they clearly saw what was soon to be, and they laid hold on to these things, some of which we can now behold with our physical eyes.

To the worldly mind, many of these people appeared eccentric. But thank God, Pentecost will always have something to keep it humble. Even in the early days of the Pentecostal movement, our Pastor, Bennett Lawrence, wrote,

> "Many things have happened in the move-
> ment which have not truly shown the purpose
> or the Spirit of God. Extremes have crept in,

249

both in doctrine and in practice. Into what movement have they not intruded themselves? But with all this, I believe with all my heart that this is the best thing in the land today: that God is more truly manifest in the lives and ministry of the members of this movement than in any other body of believers: that the power and spirituality of the religion of Jesus are more appreciated by these people than by any other: that, though frequently despised by those who rank higher than they in the estimation of the world, these are true aristocrats of heaven: that their names are written in the Lamb's Book of Life: that in the case of thousands of them, God Himself knows that He can depend on them to go anywhere, bear anything for His glory and in His Will.''[1]

So much sham and nonsense has gone out under the name of "Pentecost" over the years. And, there have always been human failures. As Jesus said in the parable, tares have grown up among the wheat. But a wonderful day of judgment is coming when all the stubble will be burned away before the Master's gaze. That which is real and true will stand. Things done in the flesh only last for time, but spiritual things are eternal and will last forever.

What more shall we say? Surely we are encompassed about with a great cloud of witnesses: these people gave their all for the cause of Christ. Why did they do it? We believe that they were completely motivated by the value of the eternal souls of the people around them.

In the spirit world, there is no distance nor time. Let us also fall on our faces before God for a worldwide move of the Holy Ghost in our generation which brings "love's sweetest old story" into every crisis and into every home on this terrestrial globe. Wise generals are necessary, but inevitably it is the infantry which decides the outcome of a military conflict. God has used humble and despised folk to move mountains before, and to ...subdue kingdoms bring righteousness, obtain promises . . .wax valiant in fight, turn to flight the armies of the aliens. Surely, He will do it again, and once more "take us over the top" in Jesus mighty name. The Lord is working in His Church today. There shall be no Alps! We can only echo the closing paragraphs of Bennett Lawrence's book of 1916.

> "Let the prayers of God's people everywhere ascend to the throne that this great body of God's children may do the thing for which they were raised up: may not be divided and hindered by men of corrupt minds: may not lose sight of the heavenly business of preparing a people for His name, and of bearing witness to all, that the end may come. Great blessings and profits have been ours in these happy days of heaven upon earth: great responsibilities also rest upon us. 'To whom much is given, of him much is required.'"[2]

Dear reader, has God placed it upon your heart to be strong and do some exploit? Then, with all the wisdom that God can give you, carry it through on your knees, for it will prosper.

These are the last days and the Church triumphant is entering into the most glorious period of her ministry. As Frank Bartleman once wrote:

> "Heroes will arise from the dust of obscure and despised circumstances, whose names will be emblazoned on heaven's eternal page of fame. The Spirit is brooding over our land again as at creation's dawn. . ."[3] (*Way of Faith*, Nov. 16, 1905)

The gospel shall be preached in all the world. The glorious message of Calvary shall be heard and seen in full demonstration of the Spirit by every hungry and longing soul. Consider the beautiful bride that so enraptured the heart of Solomon. "Thou are beautiful, O my love . . . comely as Jerusalem, terrible as an army with banners." Nothing can stand before her - "Whether the wrath of the stormtossed sea, or demons, or men, or whatever it may be . . ." For, she has been girded with strength unto the battle. She has been sent forth on His behalf to proclaim liberty to the captives and the opening of the prison to them that are bound. Arise, put on thy strength, O Zion, put on thy beautiful garments, O Jerusalem! Listen as the Bridegroom calls to the daughters of Jerusalem:

"I've sent the Holy Ghost and fire
To gather into one
My virgins fair and the undefiled
And the Father's will be done.
But you must run the race, my dove,
Until the day is done,
Listen, I'm calling to thee."[4]

While we reviewed this manuscript, we were filled with great joy and sensed afresh the glorious presence of our precious Redeemer. No honor and no praise to any man or organization - all glory to the Father, Son, and Holy Ghost. We can only bow and humbly repeat that this has been the Lord's doing: it is marvelous in our eyes.

### What Next?

Again we hear the voice of the Welch evangelist, "Bend us, oh Lord!" Evan Roberts said, "It is useless to pray for the fire of heaven to descend when the altar is unbuilt and the sacrifice unprepared." Let the altar be repaired and the sacrifice be made ready. Lord God of Elijah, let the fire from heaven fall once more. As we look out over Pentecost

The Sparkling Fountain

today, through eyes of faith, in the Spirit we see a floodgate of holiness and righteousness about to pour forth on those that are seeking the face of God. The work is not done, but we sense "a going in the tops of the mulberry trees" and we can only echo the words of Frank Bartleman (published in a tract that was printed less than two weeks before the fire fell in Los Angeles in 1906),

"Some Tremendous Event is About To Transpire!"[5]

****

"When the Church of Jesus tarries, Pentecostal fire will fall.
Sin and wrong will be defeated, Sinners on the Lord will call.
She will march to glorious victory, Over every land and sea,
Lifting high the bloodstained banner, Holiness Her motto be.
Pentecostal fire is falling, Praise the Lord it fell on me,
Pentecostal fire is falling, Brother it will fall on thee."[6]

Benediction

Lord, Let the fire fall!
Lord, bless these readers.
Lord, use them for your glory and make them workers for Thee.
And as you send them forth to work, let the anointing of the Holy Ghost flow out through them to every soul in Adam's race.
And let the blessings of God rest upon their labors until the whole world has had an

opportunity to be washed in the precious fountain that flows from Your riven side.

## REFERENCES

1. **The Apostolic Faith Restored**, by Bennett F. Lawrence, The Gospel Publishing House, St. Louis, Missouri, 1916, PP. 114-115.
2. Reference 1, Pg. 114.
3. **How Pentecost Came To Los Angeles**, by Frank Bartleman, 3rd edition, 1925, Pg. 39. (Reprinted from *Way of Faith*, November 16, 1905.) Reprinted as **Another Wave Rolls In**, Voice Publications, Northridge, Ca., 1962, Pg.44, reprinted as **Another Wave of Revival**, Whitaker House, Springdale, Pa., 1982, Pg. 38.
4. Early Pentecostal Campmeeting song. Author unknown.
5. Reference 3b, Pg. 45.
6. Song by Rev. George Bennard.

## Chapter XXVI

### EPILOGUE

"Is this death? Oh, it is glorious!"- D.L. Moody

One of the authors of this book, Fred T. Corum, went to be with the Lord on Saturday, June 5, 1982, at 1:30 A.M. It was his great burden that this book be written and that the Azusa Street Papers be republished. What we would like to tell briefly in this chapter are the remarkable events which accompanied his passing. He had lived a remarkable life and his life was unique even in its final hours.

#### Into The Jaws of Death - And Back

In the Spring of 1979, Dad began to suffer much with a prostate gland condition and by August, his kidneys had failed. Near the end of August, I received a telephone call from my brother, Kenneth, that Dad had been taken to the hospital and that the doctors said he would only last a few weeks and that his certain death was not far off. My wife, Linda, and I were about to go to Pittsburgh, Pennsylvania for a Saturday afternoon meeting with R. W. Shambach. We decided to continue with our plans, and I would go the following weekend up to Lowell, Massachusetts, to visit Dad in the hospital, if he lasted that long. Needless to say, we were very concerned about Dad and kept praying for him all through the afternoon meeting. Brother Shambach spoke on "How to Reverse a Prophecy". Somehow, faith sprang alive and I received the assurance that Dad would not die but would go home from the hospital and start work on these Pentecostal books.

The following Saturday, on Labor Day weekend, I entered Dad's room in the hospital, and oh, what a terrible sight.

He had been unable to eat anything for almost a week. He had become skin and bones and his flesh had turned a horrible dark color. When I got there, they were trying to feed him, but he threw up what little he could swallow. We prayed briefly and he soon fell off to sleep.

Brother Richard Grimes, Pastor of Calvary Temple Assembly of God in Lynnfield, Massachusetts, where Mother and Dad attended church, stopped by. As we all sat in a circle about Dad's bed, talking about the good things of God, about Jehovah-Rapha, the Lord our Healer, and the precious things of the Word - the doctor's prophecy was reversed. Dad awoke, sat up, and said, "I believe I'd like to have a bite to eat." The nurse brought him some food, his flesh color immediately went back to normal, and the doctors just couldn't believe their eyes. When I saw Dad on Sunday afternoon, he even did several sit-ups in bed! When I left him Sunday evening, he was telling us about the great tentmeeting in Thayer, Missouri, in 1909, and singing some of the old songs:

> "At the feast of Belshazzar and ten thousand
> of his lords,
> As they drank from golden vessels as the Book
> of Truth records.
> See the great captive Daniel as he stood before
> the throng,
> And rebuked the haughty monarch by the
> hand upon the wall
> 'Tis the hand of God upon the wall.
> 'Tis the hand of God upon the wall.
> Shall the record be found wanting
> Or shall it be found trusting
> While the hand is writing on the wall.''

But Dad was still very weak and they didn't let him go

home until Thursday. A few weeks later, I received the following letter from Dad.

October 29, 1979

Dear Jimmy:

I am feeling much better. . . .I only have to visit him (the doctor) once every three months now. Rev. Cunningham, Editor of the Pentecostal Evangel, wrote that he heard I was ill and that Sunday morning, Pastor Wannamaker of Central Assembly prayed for my healing. I also received a letter from the President of Central Bible College that they were praying for me.

I also felt that I should obey the fifth chapter of James and I had them pray for me at Church in Lynnfield.

. . . Last Monday, we went to the doctor's office. He examined my records, looked up at me and said, "Mr. Corum, Someone up there loves you. Your last test shows much improvement and your kidneys are working again."

I have no pain and I feel much stronger and I still believe that the fervent effectual prayer of a righteous man availeth much.

Sincerely,
Dad


An amazing letter from a man who was given less than a week to live. God touched his body. This was in the Fall of 1979. Dad lived another two years and nine months. Just after he got out of the hospital, he went and got the Azusa Street Papers prepared for printing and five thousand copies were finally reprinted in September of 1981. (Remarkably, five thousand copies of the first issue had been published in September of 1906, exactly seventy-five years earlier.)

Dad had written much of the material which appears in this book back in the mid 1930's. But those were depression days and the work on the books which he had in mind got

257

set aside. He spoke of them many times, and as children, he told us these stories over and over. But it wasn't until after he had been within the jaws of death and back again that he began to complete the work.

### Proclaim It Wherever You Go

In mid May, 1982, I spent a week with Dad going over most of the manuscript for the present book. He was especially concerned that the story of Brother E.N. Bell be told for future generations, and he dictated many pages of notes for me to arrange into a chapter. This was the last chapter which he wrote. (The chapter on Bert Williams had actually been written prior to this.)

Dad had also intended separate chapters for Mother Barnes (much could be said about her rescue homes and short-term Bible schools), Brother Welch[1] (who was a business man turned preacher with a heart of gold), Amiee Semple McPhearson (Paul drove her from the Colonial Hotel down to Convention Hall each day when she spoke in Springfield and Dad was later able to get her to come to hold meetings in Boston at the Boston Garden), Smith Wigglesworth (who was a dear friend of Brother Frodsham's and came and held meetings in Springfield in the early 1920's), Brother Ward, and Brother Argue (and their precious families). These chapters will have to be written by someone else. Unfortunately, Dad was able to scratch out only a few pages of notes concerning these people before he passed away.

---

[1]For more information on ''Daddy Welch'', see the articles by Brother Frodsham, Brother Vogler, Brother Flower, and Brother Perkin in the July 29,1939, issue of the Pentecostal Evangel. He had received the Baptism of the Holy Ghost in November of 1911.

I had arranged for a business trip to Boston on Wednesday, June 2, 1982, and was going out of the door of my home in West Virginia when Mother telephoned and said that Dad had been very uncomfortable for the past three days and that she was taking him to the hospital (St. Joseph's Hospital in Lowell, Massachusetts). He had been very weak for the previous four months. I had written up most of the material on Brother Bell, but still felt that Dad must go over the chapter to make sure that it was stated the way he wanted it and that nothing which he thought important was left out. It was near midnight when I got to our old home, and Mother lay exhausted across the bed. Rather than wake her, I slipped off to an upstairs bedroom.

I awoke on Thursday at 7:00 A.M. and went downstairs and got ready for the trip to the hospital. Then the phone rang. It was the doctor and he said, ''Mr. Corum, I'm sorry to inform you that your father, Fred Corum, was pronounced dead by two nurses and the hospital physician about five minutes ago. I'm very sorry.'' This was at 7:30 A.M. Mother began to weep. And then we both said, ''Oh, the Lord has been so good. This is no time for weeping. We must call Kenneth and tell the rest of the children.'' And we did. Joyce caught a plane from Baltimore, Maryland; Esther, from Bear River, Nova Scotia; and Ruth-Ellen, from St. Louis, Missouri. Then Kenneth, Mother and I sat down and began to talk about the riches of God and the great blessing that Dad had been to all of us over the years. Kenneth said, ''You know, when I wheeled Dad into the hospital, he was saying', 'Take me over the top, Lord. Take me over the top''. Oh, if I could have only spent one more evening with Dad. I needed so much for him to go over this chapter on Brother Bell with me. Why didn't we write this book twenty years ago? Our conversation was very peaceful and we all sensed the comforting presence of the Lord there with us. And then, at 9:45 A.M., the phone rang. I answered it. ''Mr.

259

Epilogue

Corum, this is Dr. Maletz again. I have some very shocking news for you. I don't know how to tell you this. It has never happened in the history of the hospital before - but your father is. . . well, he's sitting up talking to the nurses.'' I put the phone down, turned to Mother and Kenneth and said, ''That was Dr. Maletz. Dad is alive.'' The look on Mother's and Kenneth's faces told me that they both felt the same warm wave of heavenly joy that was rolling through my soul. Mother said, ''Surely the Lord is about to do something special. Let's hurry to Dad's bedside.''

When we arrived at the hospital, Dad was in a small amount of pain and as we gathered around his bed this seemed to subside. This was Thursday, June 3, 1982. We were yet to spend two more glorious days with one who, like Lazarus of old, had been resurrected from the dead. They were very peaceful days. His mind was sharp and clear right to the end.

Dear reader, I wish that my words could fully describe the scene which we became part of. Dad was in two worlds. He would speak to us, ''Precious Redeemer. Precious Redeemer. I know my Redeemer liveth. Proclaim it wherever you go.'' And, then he would fade off in heavenly languages. Sometimes he would just stare off into the distance and say, ''Glory to God, Glory to God.'' On one occasion I asked him, ''Dad, do you remember the great Thayer tentmeeting? Can you tell us about those wonderful things?'' He continued to look into the distance and said, ''Not now, no, not right now. All is glory. Mighty God, mighty Shiloh! God is here. My Redeemer liveth. Glory to God and the Lamb forever.'' I believe that we were in the presence of angelic hosts. Then he was back in our world and began to sing, ''Someday we'll drink the King's new wine and then we'll sing the new new song.'' Again he was back in the Spirit and said, ''Oh Mamma, Mamma - The Glory! The Glory! - It's too much, it's too much! I can't take it!''

Thursday evening, Dad fell off to sleep and began to gain

260

ground. The doctors were thoroughly confused and indicated that perhaps he could go home in a few days. Not really knowing what to do, Joyce and Kenneth returned home to get some sleep and Mother and I decided to remain with Dad throughout the night. Dad awoke late Thursday evening and from ll:00 P.M. on into the early morning hours of Friday, he went over the chapter on E. N. Bell with me. He regarded Brother Bell as one of the godliest men that he had ever met. His mind was so clear and precise that he recalled even the minutest details of places and events occurring almost seventy years ago - even how Brother Bell took his handkerchief and wiped the oil lamp in his living room on the night he coached Dad for his winning oration on the Progress of Democracy. Finally, at about 4:30 A.M., he fell asleep. The next day, Joyce was with him most of the time, while Mother and I got some sleep. It was a very peaceful day for Dad. Esther arrived from Nova Scotia on Friday evening and Dad was so glad to see her. There are many more things which we could write,but space does not permit.

In the final hour, in Mother's arms, he cleared his throat, breathed out, and fell asleep in Jesus. It is a privilege to have the veil of eternity drawn back for just a few moments, to have a glimpse of the other side, and to hear the glories of that heavenly city which John beheld. I have often read of D. L. Moody's final hours, ''Earth is receding. Heaven is approaching. Is this death? Oh, it is glorious!'' But, I never dreamed that it could be seen in our day and age. Oh, our mighty Redeemer is alive! Earth's transient joys and sorrows are brief, and Heaven is really there!

A short time later, I received a letter from Mother Flower at Springfield. Dad had always said that when she came to Springfield in May of 1918, she was a wonderful and wise councilor, and such a blessing to the young people in the church, as she has been to many, many young people since then. Sister Flower, now in her nineties, wrote:

June 18, 1982

Dear Brother Corum

". . . You were privileged to have such a father who has left a testimony behind of devotion to God's Word and the spreading of the gospel message. No doubt you know that he published the first book of mine when he was editing *Word and Work*. And you have been privileged to see him enter into his reward as a true soldier of the cross . . . Adele joins me in Christian greetings.

In His gracious keeping,
Alice Reynolds Flower

### Wisdom, Stature and Favor With God and Man

Back in the late 1930's, Dad wrote a message on "Common Sense Christianity", which Mother recently found in a filing cabinet. I have an excerpt here before me.

### Our Problem

"The question for us is not of the future, but of the present. Has Christ triumphed in your life? Is your life fulfilling His purpose? Let us strive for the fourfold development in our own lives, that we may 'increase in Wisdom, and in Stature, and in favor with God and man', that we may grow intellectually, physically, spiritually and socially. That is common sense Christianity and we can then say:

'Build thee more stately mansions, O my soul,
As the swift seasons roll!'

Words of Faith

Hope springs eternal in the breast of every Christian. Faith penetrates the veil. We are born for a higher destiny than that of earth. There is a realm where the rainbow never fades; where the stars will be spread out before us like the islands that slumber on the ocean; and where the beautiful will stay in our presence forever.

Thrice happy he, whose path is that of the just, which beaming brighter and brighter, day by day, is lost at length in the noontide splendors of the Heavenly Glory!

The prophet Isaiah looked down through the corridors of time and saw a perfect man:

'Behold a King shall reign in righteousness and princes rule in judgment. And a man shall be as an hiding place from the wind, and a cover from the tempest; as rivers of water in a dry place, as the shadow of a great rock in a weary land.' (Isaiah 32:1,2)

And who is that rock in a weary land? Who is he? . . It's JESUS.''

My brother, and sisters, and I have been twice blest. Not only have we had Godly parents, but we have also known Grandparents that loved to walk with the Lord. So many times as a family, as we gathered together in our old New England farmhouse, Dad would open some new treasure from the Word, which uniquely revealed our precious Redeemer. The Glory Cloud would descend upon us and, like those disciples on the Emmaus Road, our hearts would burn within us as he, beginning with Moses and all the prophets, would explain the Scriptures to us. This made our home a heaven.

As a teenager, one of Dad's favorite songs was:

"Holy, Holy, Holy is what the angels sing,
And I expect to help them make the courts
of heaven ring
But when we sing redemption's story.
They will fold their wings.
For Angels never knew the Joy
That our salvation brings."

The stories retold in this little book are true. And they can happen to you. Heaven is real! Don't miss it. There are many glad reunions ahead for all of us, and Jesus is coming. We will meet our loved ones at the Marriage Supper of the Lamb.

Our family is united this day, and like David, the sweet singer in Israel, we say:

"Thou, oh Lord, hast given us the rich heritage of those that trust in Thy Name." ( Psalms 61:5)

God bless you all. (J.F.C.)

****

"Take us over the top, O Lord, Take us over the top!"

# Appendix

STATEMENT OF FAITH

The Apostolic Faith Mission
312 Azusa Street
Los Angeles, California
September, 1906 (Vol. 1, No. 1, Pg. 2)

## THE APOSTOLIC FAITH MISSION

Stands for the restoration of the faith once delivered unto the saints - the old time religion, of camp meetings, revivals, missions, street and prison work and Christian Unity everywhere.

**Repentance** - Mark 1:14,15 Godly Sorrow for Sin, Example - Matt. 9:13; 2 Cor. 7:9,11; Acts 3:19; Acts 17:30,31. Confession of Sin - Luke 15:21 and Luke 18:13.

**Forsaking Sinful Ways** - Isa. 55:7; Jonah 3:8; Prov. 28:13. **Restitution** - Ezek. 33:15; Luke 19:8. And Faith in Jesus Christ.

**First Work** - Justification is that act of God's free grace by which we receive remission of sins. Acts 10:42,43; Romans 3:25.

**Second Work** - Sanctification is the second work of grace and the last work of grace. Sanctification is that act of God's free grace by which He makes us holy. John 17:15,17 "Sanctify them through Thy Truth; Thy word is truth." 1 Thess. 4:3; 1 Thess. 5:23; Heb. 13:12; Heb. 2:11; Heb. 12:14.

**Sanctification** is cleansing to make holy. The disciples were sanctified before the Day of Pentecost. By a careful study of Scripture you will find it is so now: "Ye are clean through the word which I have spoken unto you." (John 15:3; 13:10) and Jesus had breathed on them the Holy Ghost (John 20:21,22). You know, that they could not receive the Spirit

265

if they were not clean. Jesus cleansed and got all doubt out of His church before He went back to glory.

**The Baptism with the Holy Ghost** is a gift of power upon the sanctified life; so when we get it we have the same evidence as the Disciples received on the Day of Pentecost (Acts 2:3,4), in speaking in new tongues. See also Acts 10:45,46; Acts 19:6; 1 Cor. 14:21. "For I will work a work in your days which ye will not believe though it be told you." Heb. 1:5.

**Healing** - We must believe that God is able to heal. Exodus 15:26. "I am the Lord that healeth thee." James 5:14; Psalm 103:3; 2 Kings 20:5; Matt. 8:16,17; Mark 16:16,17,18. "Behold I am the Lord, the God of all flesh; is there anything too hard for Me?" Jer. 22:27.

Too many have confused the grace of sanctification with the enduement of Power, or the Baptism with the Holy Ghost; others have taken "the anointing that abideth" for the Baptism, and failed to reach the glory and power of a true Pentecost. The Blood of Jesus will never blot out any sin between man and man they can make right; but if we can't make wrongs right the Blood graciously covers. (Matt. 5:23,24.)

We are not fighting men or churches, but seeking to displace dead forms and creeds and wild fanaticism with living, practical Christianity. "Love, Faith, Unity" are our watchwords, and "Victory through the Atoning Blood" our battle cry. God's promises are true. He said: "Be thou faithful over a few things, and I will make thee ruler over many." From the little handful of Christians who stood by the cross when the testings and discouragements came, God has raised a mighty host.

# BIBLIOGRAPHY

## Books

**A Man Called Mr. Pentecost**, by David Du Plessis, Logos International, Plainfield, New Jersey, 1977.

**A Spiritual Memoir**, by Lewi Pethrus, Logos International, Plainfield, New Jersey, 1973.

**Acts of the Holy Ghost**, by Mrs. M.B. Woodworth-Etter, John F. Worley Printing Co., Dallas, Texas, 1912.

**Adventures in God**, by John G. Lake, Harrison House, Tulsa, Oklahoma, 1981.

**Aimee Semple McPherson: The Story of My Life**, Word, Incorporated, Waco, Texas, 1973.

**All Things Are Possible**, by David Edwin Harrell, Jr., Indiana University Press, Bloomington, Indiana, 1975.

**Anointed to Serve**, by William W. Menzies, Gospel Publishing House, Springfield, Missouri, 1971.

**Antiquities of the Jews**, Josephus, translated by William Whiston, 1737. Reprinted by Kregel Publications, Grand Rapids, Michigan, 1960.

**Around the World by Faith**, by Frank Bartleman, 2nd edition, Los Angeles, California, n.d.

**As At The Beginning**, by Michael Harper, Logos International, Plainfield, New Jersey, 1971.

**Aspects of Pentecostal-Charismatic Origins**, Vinson Synan, Editor, Logos International, Plainfield, New Jersey, 1975.

**Azusa Street and Beyond**, L. Grant McClung, Jr., Editor, Bridge Publishing Inc., South Plainfield, New Jersey, 1986.

**Bridehood Saints**, by George D. Watson, J. Edwin Newby, Noblesville, Indiana, 1972.

**C.T. Studd**, by Norman Grubb, Christian Literature Crusade, Fort Washingto;n, Pennsylvania, 1982.

**Charismatic Experiences in History**, Cecil M. Robeck, Jr., editor, Hendrickson Publishers, Peabody, Mass., 1985.

**Christ the Healer**, by F.F. Bosworth, Fleming H. Revell Co., Old Tappan, New Jersey, 1973.

**Christ, and Christian Experience in the Tabernacle**, Office of God's Revivalist, Cincinnati, Ohio, 1903.

**Coals of Fire**, by G.D. Watson, 1886.

**Contending For The Faith**, by Zelma Argue, Messenger of God Publishing House, Burnaby, B.C., Canada, 2nd revised edition, 1928. (Previously published as **What Meaneth This**, 1923).

**Deeper Experiences of Famous Christians**, by James Gilchrist Lawson, The Warner Press, Anderson, Indiana, 1911.

**Divine Healing Diamonds**, by Lilian B. Yeomans, Gospel Publishing House, Springfield, Missouri, 1933.

**Ever Increasing Faith**, by Smith Wigglesworth, Gospel Publishing House, Springfield, Missouri, 1924.

**Faith That Prevails**, by Smith Wigglesworth, Gospel Publishing House, Springfield, Missouri, 1928.

**From Under The Threshold**, by Alice Reynolds Flower, Christian Workers' Union, Framingham, Mass., 1936.

**Garments of Strength**, by Zelma Argue, Gospel Publishing House, Springfield, Missouri, 1935.

**Give Me That Old Time Religion**, by Martha Childers Humbard, Logos International, Plainfield, New Jersey, 1977.

**God's Eagles**, by G.D. Watson, God's Revivalist Office, Cincinnati, Ohio.

**God's First Words**, by G.D. Watson, J. Edwin Newby, Noblesville, Indiana, 1973.

**Grace for Grace**, by Alice Reynolds Flower, Springfield, Missouri, 1961.

**Great Revivals**, by Colin C. Whittaker, Gospel Publishing House, Springfield, Missouri, 1984.

**Help From the Hills**, by Mrs. A.W. Kortkamp, Full Gospel Temple, Moline, Illinois, 1935.

**How Pentecost Came To Los Angeles**, by Frank Bartleman,

3rd edition, 1925; reprinted as **Another Wave Rolls In**, Voice Publications, Northridge, Ca., 1962; reprinted as **Azusa Street**, Logos International, Plainfield, New Jersey, 1980; reprinted as **Another Wave of Revival**, Whitaker House, Springdale, Pa., 1982.

**In The Latter Days**, by Vinson Synan, Servant Publications, Ann Arbor, Michigan, 1984.

**In Those Days**, by Thomas R. Nickel, Great Commission International, Box 538, Montery Park, Ca., 2nd edition, 1962.

**Ivan Spencer, Willow in the Wind**, by Marion Meloon, Logos International, Plainfield, New Jersey, 1974.

**John G. Lake - Apostle to Africa**, Gordon Lindsay, editor, Christ for the Nations, Dallas, Texas, 1972.

**Lessons from the Life of Elisha**, by Allan A. Swift, Maranatha Park, Green Lane, Pa., n.d.

**Like A Mighty Army**, Charles W. Conn, Church of God Publishing House, Cleveland, Tenn., 1955.

**Like As of Fire**, [a reprint of all 13 issues of *The Apostolic Faith* - as published at Azusa Street (September 1906-May,1908)], collected by Fred T. Corum, 1981.

**Lorenzo Dow: The Bearer of the Word**, by Charles Coleman Setters, Minton, Balch & Co., New York, 1928.

**Lost and Restored**, by Amiee Semple McPherson, Christian Worker's Union, Montwait, Framingham, Massachusetts, n.d.

**Mountain Trail Sermons**, by Paul L. Robbins, Christian Workers' Union, Framingham, Mass., 1937.

**Origin and Structural Development of the Assemblies of God**, by Mario G. Hoover, M.A. Thesis (History), Southwest Missouri State College, August, 1968.

**Power From on High**, by John Greenfield, Warsaw, Indiana, 1928.

**Praying Hyde**, by Francis McGaw, The Sunday School Times Company, Philadelphia, 1923; reprinted by Bethany Fellowship Inc., Minneapolis, 1970.

**Questions and Answers**, by E.N. Bell, (Pulpit and Pew Full Gospel Series), The Gospel Publishing House, Springfield, Missouri, n.d.

**Rees Howells, Intercessor**, by Norman Grubb, Christian Literature Crusade, Fort Washington, Pennsylvania, 2nd edition, 1975.

**Remarkable Incidents and Modern Miracles Through Prayer and Faith**, by G.C. Bevington, God's Bible School and Missionary Training Home, Cincinnati, Ohio, n.d.; reprinted as **Remarkable Miracles**, Logos International, Plainfield, New Jersey, 1973.

**Seven Pentecostal Pioneers**, by Colin C. Whittaker, Gospel Publishing House, Springfield, Missouri, 1985.

**Signs And Wonders**, by Marie Woodworth-Etter, 1916. Reprinted by Harrison House, Tulsa, Oklahoma.

**Smith Wigglesworth Remembered**, by W. Hacking, Harrison House, Tulsa Oklahoma, 1981.

**Smith Wigglesworth: Apostle of Faith**, by Stanley Howard Frodsham, Gospel Publishing House, Springfield, Missouri, 1948.

**Smith Wigglesworth: The Secret Of His Power**, by Albert Gibbert, Harrison House, Tulsa Oklahoma, 1982.

**Soul Food**, by G.D. Watson, God's Bible School Book Room, Cincinnati, Ohio.

**Stanley Frodsham - Prophet with a Pen**, by Faith Campbell, Gospel Publishing House, Springfield, Missouri, 1974

**Suddenly From Heaven**, by Carl Brumback, The Gospel Publishing House, Springfield, Mo., 1961. Part I (PP. 1-150) reprinted as **A Sound From Heaven**, and Part II (PP. 151-380) reprinted as **Like A Mighty River**, GPH, 1977.

**Talmud** (Yoma, f. 21, C. 2)

**The Apostolic Faith Restored**, by Bennett F. Lawrence, The Gospel Publishing House, St. Louis, Missouri, 1916.

**The Apostolic Faith**, compiled, edited and printed by veteran members of the headquarters staff, The Apostolic Faith Publishing House, Portland, Oregan, 1965.

**The Assemblies of God: A Popular History**, by Edith Waldvogel Blumhofer, Gospel Publishing House, Springfield, Missouri, 1985.

**The Assemblies of God: A Popular Survey**, by Irwin Winehouse, Vantage Press, New York, 1959.

**The Beauty of the Cross**, compiled by Zelma Argue, Zondervan Publishing House, Grand Rapids, Michigan, 1937.

**The C.M. Ward Story**, with Douglas Wead, New Leaf Press, Harrison, Arkansas, 1976.

**The Commandments and Promises of Jesus**, by John G. Lake, Harrison House, Tulsa, Oklahoma, 1981.

**The Great Shepherd**, by S.A. Jamieson, Gospel Publishing House, Springfield, Missouri, Pulpit and Pew Full Gospel Series, n.d.

**The Happiest People on Earth**, by Demos Shakarian, Fleming H. Revell, Old Tappan, New Jersey, 1975.

**The Harvester**, (a pictorial history of the Kansas District of the Assemblies of God - 1913 to 1955), Kansas Christ's Ambassador's Department.

**The Heavenly Life**, by G.D. Watson, God's Bible School Book Room, Cincinnati, Ohio.

**The Holiness-Pentecostal Movement**, by Vinson Synan, Eerdmans, Grand Rapids, Mich., 1971.

**The John G. Lake Sermons**, Gordon Lindsay, editor, Christ for the Nations, Dallas, Texas, 1982.

**The Lady Who Came**, by Burton K. Janes, Good Tidings Press, St. John's, Newfoundland, 1982.

**The Latter Rain Covenant and Pentecostal Power**, by D. Wesley Myland, Evangel Publishing House, Chicago, Illinois, 1910; reprinted by A.N. Trotter, Temple Press, P.O. Box 26, Billings, Missouri (65610), 1973.

**The Life and Epistles Of St. Paul**, by W.J. Conybeare and J.S. Howson, Eerdmans Publishing Co., reprinted, 1968, Pg. 409.

**The Life of Smith Wigglesworth**, by Jack Hywel-Davies, Servant Publications, Ann Arbor, Michigan, 1988.

**The New John G. Lake Sermons**, Gordon Lindsay, editor, Christ For The Nations, Dallas, Texas, 1971.

**The Pentecostal Movement**, by Donald Gee, Victory Press, London, 1941.

**The Pentecostals**, by John Thomas Nichol, Logos International, Plainfield, New Jersey, 1966.

**The Pentecostals**, by W.J. Hollenweger, Augsburg Publishing House, Minneapolis, Minnesota, 1972.

**The Promise Fulfilled**, by Klaud E. Kendrick, Gospel Publishing House, Springfield, Missouri, 1961.

**The Rainbow of Hope**, by J.E. Perkins, Gospel Publishing House, Springfield, Missouri, Pulpit and Pew Full Gospel Series, n.d.

**The Real Faith**, by Charles S. Price, C.S. Price Publishing Co., Pasadena, California, 1940; republished by Whitaker Books, Monroeville, Penna.,1968; reprinted by Logos International, Plainfield, New Jersey, 1972.

**The Spirit Bade Me Go**, by David J. Du Plessis, Logos International, Plainfield, New Jersey, 1970.

**The Spirit Within and Upon**, by Allan A. Swift, Maranatha Park, Green Lane, Pa., n.d.

**The Temple**, by Alfred Eidersheim, Eerdmans Publishing Co., Grand rapids, Mich., 1978.

**The Victorious Life**, by Benjamin A. Baur, Glad Tidings Publishing Society, Rochester, New York, n.d.

**The Wellsprings of the Pentecostal Movement**, by David A. Womack, Gospel Publishing House, Springfield, Missouri, 1968.

**The Wind Bloweth Where It Listeth**, by Lewi Pethrus, Bethany Fellowship, Inc., Minneapolis, Minnesota, 1968.

**The Winds Of God**, by Ethel E. Goss, Word Aflame Press, Hazelwood, Missouri, 1958. Revised, updated and reprinted 1986.

**They Saw It Happen**, by Gordon Lindsay, Christ for the

Nations, Dallas, Texas, 1972.

**This Side of Heaven**, by Ira Stanphill, Hymntime Ministries, Inc., Fort Worth, Texas, 1983.

**Touched By The Fire**, Edited by Wayne Warner, Logos International, Plainfield, New Jersey, 1978.

Unpublished Autobiography, by Rachel Sizelove, n.d., (225 pages).

**Unto You Is The Promise**, by Robert W. Cummings, Gospel Publishing House, Springfield, Missouri.

**Visions Beyond the Veil**, by H.A. Baker, Whitaker Books, Monroeville, Pennsylvania, 1973.

**With Signs Following**, by Stanley H. Frodsham, The Gospel Publishing House, Springfield, Missouri, 1926.

## Other Sources

*"An Unforgettable New Year's Prayer Meeting"*, by Robert C. Cunningham, *Pentecostal Evangel*, December 31, 1978, PP. 10-11.

*The Apostolic Faith*, Reprinted in **Like As of Fire**, collected by Fred T. Corum, 1981.

*"A Great Man in Israel"*, by J. Roswell Flower, *Pentecostal Evangel*, July 29, 1939, Pg. 2.

*"A Sparkling Fountain for the Whole Earth"*, by Rachel A. Sizelove, *Word and Work*, 56, No.6, June, 1934, PP. 1,11, 12.

*"A Sparkling Fountain"*, by Rachel Harper Sizelove, *Word and Work*, Vol. 57, No. 3, March, 1935, PP. 1, 2, 12.

*"Azusa's First Campmeeting"*, by Fred T. Corum, *Word and Work*, Vol. 58, No. 1, January, 1936, PP. 1, 4, 5.

*"Great Revival In Wales"*, tract published by the Osterhus Publishing House, Minneapolis, Minnesota, n.d.

*"Harry Bowley (Tribute)"*, by J. Roswell Flower (*Pentecostal Evangel*, Pg. 16).

*"Harry E. Bowley With Christ (Obituary)"*, by U.S. Grant, (*Pentecostal Evangel*, Pg. 16).

"*Harry E. Bowley*", *Word and Work*, Vol. 55, No. l2, December, 1933, Pg. l3.

"*How A Handmaiden of the Lord Kept the Army in Rank*", by Mrs. J.J. Corum, *Word and Work*, July, 1934, PP. 1, 10.

"*My Experience of the Baptism of the Holy Ghost*", by Lillie Harper Corum, Tract published by The Christian Worker's Union, Framingham, Massachusetts.

"*My Personal Experience at the Azusa Mission*", by Earnest S. Williams, printed as Chapter 13 in **Touched By The Fire**, Edited by Wayne Warner, Logos International, Plainfield, New Jersey, 1978, PP. 45-46.

"*Raised From the Dead*", by Joe Duke, *The Latter Rain Evangel*. Reprinted in *Word and Work*, Vol. 52, No. ll, November, l930, PP. 16, 21.

"*Revival in Wales*", by Sherwood E. Wirt, *Decision Magazine*, Part 1 - February, 1964; Part 2 - March, 1964, Pg. 11; Part 3 - April, 1964, Pg. 6; Part 4 - May, 1964.

"*The Great Oneness-Trinitarian Debate*", by Edith Waldvogel Blumhoffer, *Assemblies of God Heritage*, Vol. 5, No. 3, Fall, 1985, PP. 6-8.

"*The Great Ozark Mountain Revival*", by Harry E. Bowley, *Assemblies of God Heritage*, Vol. 2, No. 2, Summer, 1982, PP. 1,3.

"*The Great Revival at Thayer, Mo. - Part 1*", by Harry E. Bowley, *Pentecostal Evangel*, June l2, l948, PP. 3,-.

"*The Great Revival at Thayer, Mo. - Part 2*", by Harry E. Bowley, *Pentecostal Evangel*, June l9, l948, PP. 5, 12-13.

"*The Great Thayer Revival*", **Thayer Assembly of God - 70th Anniversary**, 1979, PP. 2-4.

"The Pentecostal Church of Springfield", typed notes by L.H. Corum, n.d., circa 1921.

"*The Temple*", by Rachel Sizelove, *Word and Work*,Vol. 58, No. 5, May, 1936, PP. 1,2,12.

"*When Geronimo Smiled*", by Frcd T. Corum, *Pentecostal Evangel*, February 27, 1977, PP. 6,7,8. Reprinted December 11,1988, PP. 6,7,22.

276

277